Studies in Social Policy

'Studies in Social Policy' is an important new series of textbooks intended for students of social administration and social welfare at all levels. The books are directly related to the needs of under-graduate and postgraduate students in universities, polytechnics and similar institutions as well as vocational students preparing for careers in a variety of social and other public services. The series includes the following topics:

the roles of different public and private institutions such as social services departments and building societies in meeting social needs;

introductory guides to new technical and theoretical developments relevant to the analysis of social policy such as political theory and the newly emerging specialism of the economics of social care;

contemporary social policy issues such as the use of charges in the delivery of social welfare or the problem of determining priorities in the health and personal social services.

Studies in Social Policy

Editor: Ken Judge

Published

The Building Societies
Martin Boddy

Access to Welfare
Peggy Foster

Health Policy in Britain
Christopher Ham

Policy-making in the National Health Service
Christopher Ham

Pricing the Social Services
Ken Judge (ed.)

Choices for Health Care
Gavin H. Mooney, Elizabeth M. Russell and Roy D. Weir

Power, Authority and Responsibility in Social Services
Malcolm Payne

Political Theory and Social Policy
Albert Weale

Forthcoming

Introducing Social Policy
Ken Judge and Roger Hampson

The Economics of Social Care
Martin Knapp

The Economics of Poverty
Alan Maynard

Health Care in the European Community
Alan Maynard and Anne Ludbrook

Access to Welfare

An Introduction to Welfare Rationing

Peggy Foster

Department of Social Administration
University of Manchester

First published 1983 by
THE MACMILLAN PRESS LTD
London and Basingstoke
Companies and representatives throughout the world

ISBN 0 333 32119 7 (hard cover)
ISBN 0 333 32120 0 (paper cover)

Typeset in Great Britain by Illustrated Arts

Printed in Hong Kong

To my Father

Contents

Acknowledgements

I am grateful to all my colleagues in the Department of Social Administration, University of Manchester, whose support made the writing of this book possible. In particular I would like to thank Ian Gough and Joyce Wolfson for their encouragement. I am especially indebted to Paul Wilding, whose constructive criticism and encouragement were invaluable. I am also indebted to Ken Judge for his incisive comments and excellent editing and to Steve Kennedy of Macmillan for all his help and hard work. No one but the author, however, bears any responsibility for the final text. Last but certainly not least, my thanks go to all those who so efficiently and stoically typed many versions of the manuscript, especially Jean Ashton, Janice Hammond, Hilary Thornber and Elaine Lewis.

Manchester   PEGGY FOSTER
December 1982

Introduction

All advanced industrial societies, whatever their political or economic systems, face the problem of equating the demand for consumer goods and services with their limited supply. In Britain, most goods and services are bought and sold in the private market where supply and demand are kept in equilibrium by the price mechanism. The smaller welfare sector, however, has largely eschewed the use of price as a distributive device. Welfare providers working in the statutory social services have therefore had to devise various forms of administrative rationing to control surplus demand for limited goods and services. This book is primarily concerned with administrative rationing and the effects it has on individuals' access to welfare.

In recent years, critics of the traditional empirical approach to the analysis of social policy have emphasised that a narrow concern with administrative procedures within the social services cannot lead to a full understanding of the distribution of welfare in a capitalist society. They claim that the answers to key questions such as 'How and why do some individuals rather than others gain access to welfare benefits?' and 'How and why do some social classes gain more from certain social services than others?' lie as much outside the social services as within. Issues such as the balance of power between capital and labour, the creation and maintenance of particular ideologies of welfare and the relationship between economic and social goals are now widely recognised as key factors in the distribution of welfare in British society. Nevertheless, a recognition that what happens within the social services is not the sole determinant of individuals' access to welfare does not imply that the process of rationing within the welfare sector is in itself irrelevant or unimportant. Not only does this process play a key role in determining an individual's access to welfare services and benefits, it may also play a significant part in perpetuating class inequalities in the welfare field. This book will therefore concentrate on the process of rationing within the social services, though it will certainly not ignore the broader context in which such rationing takes place.

Chapter 1 discusses the welfare sector's rejection of the price mechanism as a primary rationing device, examines the conflicting aims and objectives of the social services, and enumerates the various types of rationing used within them.

Chapter 2 analyses the concept of need as a key distributive principle in the welfare sector, summarises the debate on the definition and measurement of welfare needs, and discusses critical approaches to the way the concept of need is used in the social services.

Chapter 3 examines client-initiated demand for welfare services and its implications for welfare rationing. In particular it focuses on the role which client demand may play in perpetuating class inequalities in the use of statutory social services.

Chapter 4 begins to analyse the process of welfare rationing itself by examining the reception process in the social services. It focuses in particular on the role played by receptionists in regulating individuals' access to doctors and social workers.

Chapter 5 looks at the way in which professional welfare providers act as gatekeepers to certain social services by controlling clients' initial access to these services.

Chapter 6 continues to focus on the control which welfare professionals exercise over clients' access to welfare services. It examines the ways in which professionals ration both their own time and attention and a range of material benefits over which they exercise control.

Chapter 7 examines welfare rationing from the perspective of welfare rights. It illustrates this issue by focusing on claimants' formal rights to a range of social security benefits and examining the extent to which these rights are undermined by the procedures used in allocating these benefits.

Chapter 8 examines the allocation of council housing. It identifies the various forms of rationing utilised by local authority housing departments and emphasises the external constraints experienced by all those involved in allocating public housing.

Chapter 9 examines the empirical evidence on the effects of charges and means tests on individuals' access to welfare benefits, and relates this evidence to the controversial debate between selectivists and universalists over the use of charges and means tests in the social services.

Chapter 10 discusses the main criticisms levied against existing methods of welfare rationing and evaluates the strategies for reform proposed by administrative reformists, pro-marketeers and Marxists.

1

The Objectives of Welfare Rationing

In order to understand the nature and outcome of welfare rationing in all its forms, we must first understand the aims and objectives of the institutions in which this rationing takes place. This chapter will attempt to explain why the state provides certain welfare benefits without recourse to the price mechanism. There will then be an examination of the conflicting nature of the key aims and objectives of the statutory social services. Finally, the various types of rationing used in the welfare sector will be briefly identified.

Why does the welfare sector reject the price mechanism?

In the private market goods and services are allocated by price. This rationing process offers many advantages to both suppliers and consumers. The seller in the private market is able to distribute his goods without having to take the difficult decision of who should get what. Only the rich can afford the most expensive goods in the private market. Yet fur coat sellers and sports car dealers very rarely suffer any personal attacks on the grounds that they refuse to allocate these commodities to those who would like but cannot afford them. Indeed most consumers in the private market appear to accept with remarkable equanimity the distribution of goods and services on the basis of ability to pay. The price mechanism thus balances supply and demand in the private market smoothly, effectively and with a minimum of fuss. This advantage of the price mechanism can be appreciated by observing what happens when it is tampered with. The bi-annual slashing of prices by major department stores often leads not only to long queues, which may begin several days before the opening of their sales, but also occasionally to quite violent behaviour by bargain hunters scrambling to acquire relatively low priced goods on a first-come, first-served basis.

Most economists in western industrial societies argue that it is extremely difficult to find a device for allocating goods and services as efficient and as trouble free as the price mechanism.

Orthodox economic theory holds that in an ideal market the price mechanism enables consumers to make free and rational choices between alternative goods and services. Moreover prices will reflect consumer demand. Producers will use the knowledge supplied by the price mechanism to respond to changes in demand. In a perfect market system, therefore, consumers are able to maximise their satisfaction.

It is obvious however that the real life situation does not match the theoretical model of the perfect market. There are good grounds for doubting that the consumer is sovereign in the contemporary private market system. Such doubts are expressed by many economists. They argue that the reduction in the number of producers has radically altered the balance of power between producers and consumers; that consumer purchasing decisions are manipulated by advertising and that, in any case, many consumers lack the knowledge to make a rational choice when buying technically complex goods such as television sets and dish washers.[1]

This criticism of the functioning of the private market is not a sufficient argument for replacing the price mechanism by administrative rationing. One would also have to show that administrative rationing gives most consumers more power and freedom of choice than they now enjoy in the private market. However it is generally conceded by supporters of the welfare sector that a major disadvantage of administrative rationing for most welfare consumers is that it rarely allows them as much freedom of choice as they enjoy as paying customers.

The price mechanism is a neutral device. It is not biased in favour of any particular group of consumers. However if goods and services are allocated by price in a society where incomes are unequal, some consumers will have more power and freedom of choice than others. As Reisman has pointed out, 'rationing by price effectively eliminates those least able to pay'.[2] The fact that those with least resources are usually unable to meet all their basic needs in a completely private market system has been regarded as a matter of concern by many different groups. Egalitarians attack the unequal distribution of goods and services as unjust. Their ideological commitment to a more equal society leads them to search for radical alternatives to the unequal distribution inherent in the market system. Many of those who were not supporters of complete equality, nor even of a significantly less unequal society, have nevertheless expressed concern about the existence of hardship and distress amongst the minority of consumers who are unable to meet all their basic needs in the private market. Beveridge, for example, who was certainly not an egalitarian, advocated state intervention in the market in order to abolish 'want', and to ensure that people did not fall below a minimum subsistence standard of living. Those who believe in the private market system may nevertheless support limited state intervention to ensure that the poor are not so alienated from society that they pose a threat to it. Beveridge advocated state action against want, not simply because he believed that the misery want caused was in itself intolerable, but also because he feared that 'misery generates hate'.

The widely accepted argument that if the poor are unable to purchase the minimum essentials for civilised living through the market the state should intervene on their behalf does not in itself justify the state providing certain goods and services free of charge to those in need of them regardless of their income. The simplest and most direct way to help the poor would be to give them some form of financial assistance. Not only would this be cheaper than providing benefits in kind free of charge regardless of the beneficiaries' income, it would also give poor consumers more freedom of choice in their consumption of welfare. Why then does the state provide certain benefits in kind rather than simply giving financial assistance to those too poor to obtain these goods and services in the private market?

In order to answer this question we must draw a distinction between the type of goods and services currently provided in kind by the statutory social services and those distributed through the private market. First, it will be helpful to explain briefly the terms 'public good' and 'private good' so that we can then use them in relation to goods and services distributed by state welfare agencies. A public good is one which, once provided, is open to use by anyone because it is impossible to exclude any individual from its benefits. Clean air, national defence and street lighting are examples of public goods. The benefits of private goods, on the other hand, are confined solely to the individual consumer. If a woman buys a cake and eats it she alone benefits from its consumption. However very few goods are purely public or private. Most are a mixture of the two. Goods that at first sight appear to confer purely private benefits often turn out, on closer inspection, to affect others apart from those who directly consume them. Take the example of a man who buys some paint with which to paint the outside of his house, solely because he hates the existing colour. One might assume that this paint was a private good. However the direct consumer of the paint cannot stop his neighbours, who also hate the existing colour of his house, from receiving a free benefit from his outlay of cash, time and energy.

Even the most extreme anti-collectivists argue that pure public goods must be provided by the state because the benefits from them are indivisible. If one man were to pay for the provision of street lighting, for example, he could not prevent everyone else from benefiting from it without payment. No one would be prepared to pay individually for a good under such circumstances. For this reason it is agreed that the state must provide pure public goods and finance them from taxation.

However, most of the goods and services provided by the statutory social services are not pure public goods. Their consumption produces a mixture of private and public benefits. Some of the benefits from education, health care and social work clearly do accrue to the individuals who consume these services. On the other hand they also provide benefits for society as a whole. For example while those being educated have their intellectual and creative potential enhanced and their career prospects improved, the mass provision of education results in such public benefits as increased productivity of the work force, socialisation of the young and the preservation and development of the national cultural heritage. Although the extent to which state education fulfils these functions is open to debate it is certainly the case that the governments of advanced capitalist countries have *believed* the collective benefits of education to be great enough to justify state provided compulsory education. They have believed that the private provision of education would not produce a level of educational consumption commensurate with the needs of society as a whole. State education can, therefore, be termed a merit good. A merit good is one which, 'reflects the preferences of an elite or ruling group and results in consumption being imposed on individual consumers.'[3] Whenever the government decides to provide a welfare service in kind financed through taxation it is imposing consumption of that service on individuals and can, therefore, be said to be creating a merit good.

There is no general agreement as to the extent to which the consumption of state provided social services benefits society as a whole. Anti-collectivists argue that supporters of the welfare state exaggerate the benefits that accrue to society from individuals' consumption of state-provided welfare goods and services. Some of the services provided by the state do appear to be mainly private goods. A university course in Sanskrit and the treatment of infertility are two examples of services which appear to be of little tangible benefit to anyone apart from the direct consumer and perhaps their immediate family and friends. At the other end of the spectrum we find services which appear to benefit the rest of society more than the individual consumer. For example a man who does not wish to work can be sent, against his will, to a re-establishment centre run by the DHSS. One justification for this type of 'social service' is that society as a whole will benefit if a 'work-shy' person can be persuaded to seek work. Although the argument that society as a whole benefits from individuals' consumption of goods and services provided by state welfare agencies is probably valid as far as some areas of welfare are concerned it cannot be accepted as a blanket justification for the state's provision of welfare benefits in kind.

A second justification for the state's imposition of welfare goods and services on individuals is that they may be too helpless, ignorant, foolish or reckless to make wise choices about their own consumption of such goods and services. Even anti-collectivists usually agree that the state should provide (either directly or through a private or voluntary organisation which it pays) some form of welfare for dependent groups who are incapable of making rational choices for themselves. The mentally handicapped, the severely mentally disturbed and young children fall into this category. Compulsory schooling is sometimes justified on the grounds that the state has a duty to protect children both from feckless parents who might otherwise fail to ensure they were educated and from their own lack of appreciation of the possible long term benefits to be received from schooling.

It is only when the state imposes the consumption of welfare on rational adults that it is open to the charge of paternalism. In answer to this charge it can be argued that state paternalism is justified if individuals are unable or unwilling to calculate their future welfare needs accurately and make adequate provision to meet them. For example no one knows whether or not they are going to need major surgery at some time in their life whereas everyone knows that they must make provision to obtain basic foodstuffs and clothing. Moreover the cost of medical treatment for a serious illness is usually too great to be met on an *ad hoc* basis. Unlike the risk of such illness, the chance of living beyond retirement age is now very high yet many young people might well choose not to save for their retirement unless the state coerced them into so doing. One can, of course, accept the argument that the state needs to coerce individuals to provide for the risk of illness and for an income in old age without accepting that the state itself should provide health care and pensions. The state could simply coerce individuals to insure themselves privately against such contingencies, give cash support to those unable to afford private insurance and merely provide small, state run 'safety net' services for those, such as the severely handicapped, who would be uninsurable.

A non-paternalistic argument in favour of state provision of welfare services is that it is sometimes administratively simpler to provide services directly rather than to attempt to give cash support in relation to people's needs.[4] Even if the government were to substantially diminish inequality of income some individuals would still enjoy lower levels of welfare than others since their welfare needs would still be greater. In order to provide appropriate cash benefits to allow people with special needs such as those suffering from physical disabilities or chronic disease to buy the extra welfare goods and services they would require, the state would have to make a number of complex calculations. It would have to assess each individual's welfare needs, calculate the cost of meeting those needs in the local private market and ensure that the private providers of services did not overcharge. Given these difficulties, those who wish to ensure that all citizens are equally able to satisfy their basic welfare needs can support the statutory provision of welfare benefits in kind as the simplest and most practical way of achieving this goal.

A further practical argument in favour of state provided social services is that they are more cost effective than private services. If the state can procure a monopoly or near monopoly in the provision of certain types of welfare, it should be able to keep down the costs of that welfare by paying less for equipment and staff than smaller, competing private concerns. Defenders of the NHS have certainly argued that it is able to secure the services of doctors and nurses far more cheaply than can private health care systems.[5] On the other hand anti-collectivists argue that the waste and inefficiency inherent in large non-profit making bureaucratic organisations outweigh any cost advantages these services enjoy in theory.

A number of justifications for the state provision of welfare benefits in kind have been put forward. These have included the need to ensure a socially optimum level of consumption of certain goods; the need to protect individuals from their own ignorance or short-sightedness; the practical advantage of providing certain benefits in kind in order to fulfil the objective of redistributing resources according to need; and the high cost effectiveness of state welfare provision. On the other hand the argument has been presented that it is not logical for the state to attempt to tackle the problem of poverty through the distribution of welfare benefits in kind to all when it would be simpler and less paternalistic to give cash benefits to the poor. It should be pointed out, however, that many of those who wish to see a less unequal society strongly support the existing state distribution of welfare in kind on the grounds that although this may not be the most direct way to attack inequalities, it does at least protect the most vulnerable members of society from the rigours of the market place.

The social services' conflicting objectives

Most traditional definitions of the social services emphasise that they aim to meet individual need. According to Muriel Brown, 'collective provision to meet need in the hallmark of a social service',[6] while Marsh states, 'the social services are those provided by the community for no other reason than that of maintaining or improving individual well-being.'[7] If the sole aim of the social services is to meet individual need one would expect that, in theory at least, all welfare rationing would be designed to distribute benefits solely according to the priority of individuals' needs. This view is put forward by many traditional works on welfare rationing. Cooper states, for example, 'The NHS attempts to ration the scarce resources allocated to it by governments not in accordance with the individual's ability and willingness to pay but in accordance with each individual's relative need.'[8] However, as we have already noted, social services are intended not only to benefit the individual but also to meet the needs of society as a whole. It is, therefore, misleading to over emphasise the social services' goal of helping the individual whilst ignoring their other, important objectives.

Although as theoretical models it is possible to discern a dichotomy between the private market system run purely according to the price mechanism and the welfare sector concerned solely with the welfare principle of 'to each according to his need', in practice the edges between the two systems are extremely blurred. The welfare sector does not function in complete opposition to the predominant goals and values of the capitalist society in which it is situated. On the contrary, the statutory social services play a key role in maintaining that society. They do this partly by helping to meet industry's needs for a healthy, competent and conveniently situated work force. Although there is considerable debate over the exact extent to which state education, for example, has improved the productivity of the labour force, the abolition of free education and health care services would probably impair the quality of the labour force. As Sleeman has pointed out, education and other social services are, 'a form of investment in the country's human capital which is just as essential as investment in physical capital.'[9]

The conflict which exists within the social services between meeting the needs of industry and meeting the needs of the individual can be illustrated by examining the 'Great Debate' on education which took place in the late 1970s. A major theme of this debate was the complaint made by employers that secondary schools failed to prepare young people adequately for the world of work, and that industry was consequently suffering from a lack of suitably trained and motivated young workers. In reply to these criticisms teachers argued that they were solely concerned to provide the best possible education for each individual pupil. They were not prepared merely to educate pupils to fit into an existing labour market which offered very few real opportunities to the majority of school leavers. Dr. John Rae argued, for example, that education, 'should be directed to the full development of human personality' and that, 'this aim cannot be reconciled with the sort of measures that government may think necessary to achieve economic viability.'[10]

A second conflict of objectives which may occur within the social services is that between meeting individuals' needs and exercising social control over them. The use of the term social control by sociologists has arisen from their observation that there exist in all societies means by which behaviour is regulated. However, the exact meaning of the term social control is elusive. According to Higgins the meaning of the term social control in relation to theories about social policy has been 'rarely defined, frequently misused and considerably abused.'[11] Berger and Berger have defined social control as, 'any social mechanism by which individuals are compelled to abide by the rules of society or of a particular segment of society.'[12] This definition contains a hint of the main controversy over the use of the term social control in discussions about the welfare state. Is the exercise of social control through welfare providers designed to benefit all members of society equally, or is it solely concerned to bolster the interests of a certain segment of society at the expense of the rest? Marxists, who espouse a conflict model of society, argue that social control works only in the interests of the dominant group in society, whereas those who put forward a consensus model of society argue that the exercise of social control over deviant members is functional for the whole of society and is even in the interests of those who are controlled. The main debate over the exercise of social control by welfare providers has thus centred not on the issue of whether or not social control occurs, but on whose behalf it is exercised, the rich and powerful or the poor and deprived.

According to Bowles and Gintis the main purpose of schooling in advanced capitalist societies is to maintain and uphold the existing social and economic order.[13] They maintain that schools teach the majority of young people to become disciplined, docile workers; that schools do not provide real equality of opportunity but simply sort out young people into the pre-ordained roles which they are to fill in the labour market. Schools are thus agents of negative social control. They repress the majority of their pupils by teaching them to conform to a system which is against their own interests. Many educationalists would reject such a negative view of the effects of schooling on the majority of its pupils. They would accept that one of the key purposes of state schooling is the socialisation of the young and that this involves encouraging young people to conform to the values and norms held by the society in which they live. They would not, however, regard this process of socialisation as social control in its negative sense, i.e. repression of the working class by the dominant class.

Most commentators on this country's social security system agree that it is intended to exercise negative control over certain of its clients. It is generally agreed, for example, that one of the main aims of the social security system is to ensure that no one becomes, or remains, voluntarily unemployed. However, there is a strong disagreement over the ultimate purpose of this control. Radical critics claim that our social security system, 'protects the interests of capital in general and runs against the collective interests of the working class . . .'[14] While supporters of the existing system claim that its control of the work shy is essential for the good of society as a whole.

Whatever the ultimate aim of the control exercised over individual claimants by the social security system, it is clear that its objective of reinforcing the will to work conflicts with the system's other main objective of supporting those, who for one reason or another, are unable to support themselves or their dependents. The social security system makes a clear distinction between deserving and undeserving claimants. Anyone who is deemed to have rejected the work ethic is denied full access to welfare benefits. Only those claimants judged to be deserving, usually because they are unemployed through no fault of their own, are fully entitled to a subsistence level of income from the state. Even the needs of claimants accepted as deserving are sometimes sacrificed to ensure that work incentives are fully maintained. Until it was abolished in 1975 the wage stop rule ensured that no unemployed person received more in benefit than he gained from work. At its peak in 1970 the wage stop affected 35,000 claimants. Thus, through the operation of the wage stop, the social security system officially left many families to live on incomes below the poverty line in order to ensure that no one was better off out of work than in work.

The conflict between meeting individuals' welfare needs and exercising social control over them can also be seen in the personal social services. One of the key debates amongst social workers in recent years has been over their role as agents of social control and the extent to which this role conflicts with their caring functions. According to the British Association of Social Workers' working party report on 'The Social Work Task', social workers do perform a dual function of control and caring but these two aspects of their role are not incompatible since control is exercised on the client's behalf – 'control however is not an end in itself for a social worker. It is a means of enhancing a client's social and personal functioning and will therefore be linked with the meeting of other needs, belongingness and love needs or esteem, respect and status needs.'[15] This view of social work has been challenged by those who regard control and care as conflicting aspects of the social worker's role, and who see social control as acting predominantly in the interests of the 'ruling class' and against the interests of most social work clients. The Case Con Manifesto, for example, totally rejected the traditional view of social workers as 'helping' clients by making them 'accept responsibility'. It held that this approach amounts to little more than an attempt to, 'force individuals to come to terms with basically unacceptable situations.'[16] Radical critics of social workers have not only accused social workers of exercising social control through casework with individual clients. They have also claimed that social workers use their control over the allocation of material benefits to clients as another means of social control and thus deliberately deny material or financial help to some of their most needy clients (see Ch. 6).

If the social services are not solely concerned to meet individuals' welfare needs but are equally, if not more, concerned to meet those of the economy and to impose social control on deviant members of society, we would expect the rationing which takes place within these services to have similarly conflicting objectives. The extent to which welfare rationing performs a variety of functions, not all of which are intended to help individual clients, will be a major concern of this book.

Types of welfare rationing

The rationing of state provided welfare can be divided into two distinct activities. First, resources are allocated to the providers of welfare. Second, the providers of welfare distribute these resources in the forms of benefits and services to individual consumers. Judge has labelled these two distinct but closely related processes 'financial rationing' and 'service rationing'.[17] Financial rationing is a complex and lengthy process, which can be divided into three main stages. First, a decision is taken on the total amount of resources to be devoted to the social services as a whole. Second, resources are distributed between the main social services. Third, resources are allocated to individual programmes within each service. Many groups of decision makers play a part in financial rationing including national and local politicians, civil servants and local government officials, social service staff and, at a very general level, the voting public. Since this book is primarily concerned with service as opposed to financial rationing, the complexities of the latter will not be pursued here.[18]

Not only can financial rationing be distinguished from service rationing, we can also distinguish various types of service rationing. One major distinction is between formal and informal methods of service rationing. Formal methods are normally explicit and overt. The rules governing formal methods of rationing are usually written down and available for public scrutiny. Eligibility rules are an extensively used type of formal rationing. They ration welfare by explicitly excluding all but a strictly delineated group from benefit. Almost all of the cash benefits distributed by the social security system, from child benefit to retirement pensions are allocated according to detailed eligibility rules laid down by statute. Most social security claimants consequently enjoy, at least in theory, clearly delineated rights to benefit. However in practice formal eligibility rules may be modified by the discretionary decisions of those who apply them. In certain cases, the effects of such informal decisions can negate claimants' statutory rights to benefit (see Ch. 7). The rules are also modified by informal decisions regarding eligibility and entitlement made by supplementary benefit officers and insurance officers.

Although the eligibility rules governing social security benefits are uniform throughout the country their application can vary from one local office to another. Other types of welfare benefits may be allocated according to locally determined eligibility rules. Local councils, individual social service institutions and groups of individual welfare providers frequently devise and implement their own formal rules. Many local councils, for example, now allocate council housing according to a published points system (see Ch. 8). Not all eligibility rules are operated overtly. Researchers have discovered that many local housing authorities have at some time or another operated covert systems for grading applicants for council housing in terms of their suitability for different standards of accommodation.

Eligibility rules are by no means the only type of formal rationing used in the welfare sector. Official waiting lists are also widely used to ration a range of services and benefits including council housing, home helps and hospital beds. Such waiting lists rarely operate on a first come first served basis however and applicants are usually assessed according to the priority of their need. Although this may accord with the aim of allocating benefits according to need, it does mean that official waiting lists for welfare services are often very difficult for clients to understand. Charges and means tests, two other widely used types of formal rationing, may also confuse many welfare consumers.

The main advantage of formal overt types of welfare rationing is that they are open to public scrutiny and criticism. They can also help to ensure that clients with like needs receive similar, if not identical, treatment from the services to which they apply for help. However many other factors such as ignorance or misunderstanding of the benefits available may influence formal rationing processes and lead to a less equitable distribution of welfare. Although in theory formal and overt methods of rationing should enable clients to claim their 'rights', in practice many welfare consumers may find the complexities of formal rationing devices such as means tests quite beyond their comprehension (see Ch. 7).

Informal methods of welfare rationing are usually less obvious and less open to scrutiny than formal methods. Most individual welfare providers, but particularly professionals, are free to implement their own personal and informal rationing systems. Delay, dilution, deterrence and withholding of information are all methods of informal welfare rationing. Busy service providers frequently delay providing help to those in need. Social workers sometimes take weeks to respond fully to a request for help, whilst certain GPs may delay patients' access to them by a variety of strategies (see Ch. 4). GPs and social workers may also decide to spend less time with their patients/clients than they judge to be necessary. They will rarely inform consumers that they are receiving a diluted service. Dilution is therefore a particularly difficult method of rationing to detect and scrutinise since clients themselves may be unaware that it is taking place.

Welfare providers can use a variety of strategies to deter excess demand or unpopular clients. They can be deliberately rude to clients in an attempt to deter them from further using their services. In some cases, busy or harassed social service staff may inadvertently deter clients by being short-tempered with them. This occurrence seems particularly common in the supplementary benefit system where overworked and sometimes ill-trained staff have to deal with large numbers of claimants some of whom are themselves rude and aggressive. Not all forms of deterrence which occur within the social services are the fault of individual members of staff. Many of those who write about the welfare system now accept that rather than being accidental, deterrence is an integral part of all welfare services which provide significant benefits to those who are deemed 'undeserving' by large sections of society. Thus services for the homeless and the unemployed have always been provided in ways which are intended to deter the 'undeserving' claimants from seeking help. Individual welfare providers often share society's attitude towards 'undeserving' welfare consumers. In some cases they covertly categorise individuals as deserving or undeserving and then deter those whom they have labelled undeserving from receiving benefits or services. The Chairman of the Supplementary Benefits Commission admitted in 1976, for example, that it was difficult for supplementary benefits officers administering discretionary benefits, 'to discriminate between one needy case and another without resorting to moral judgements of the kind which should be excluded from their decision.'[19]

Withholding of information is the final form of informal rationing which has been identified. If claimants or clients are unaware that certain benefits or services exist, they will not demand them. In some cases ignorance may be deliberately fostered by social service staff who fail to acquaint consumers with their 'rights'. Some supplementary benefit officers have been accused of deliberately withholding information from claimants about a range of extra payments for special needs and circumstances to which they may be entitled. GPs may fail to tell patients about particular forms of expensive or scarce treatment in order to protect consultants from excess demand. Apparently, many GPs simply do not refer elderly patients to renal dialysis and transplant units in order to protect consultants from the painful decision of telling such patients that they have not been chosen for life saving treatment.

All methods of informal rationing create the same kinds of disadvantage. First, they fail to secure uniform treatment for clients with like needs. If individual welfare providers, professional or not, are free to take personal decisions about whether particular clients should receive help, welfare consumers with similar needs will inevitably receive different amounts and types of help. Second, it is very difficult for a dissatisfied client to challenge or appeal against an informal or covert decision. Third, social policy makers cannot ensure that their intentions are being carried out if their policies are at the mercy of uncontrolled individual decision making.

Social policy makers have the power to determine the limits within which welfare providers are free to exercise discretion over the allocation of particular services and benefits. In certain instances policy makers have laid down very clear cut and detailed eligibility rules which determine the allocation of particular benefits and have thus left the staff who administer the allocation of these benefits little room for discretionary decision making. Much welfare provision, however, deals with very complex individual needs and circumstances and it would be impossible for legislation to anticipate every exceptional case. Thus according to Hill, 'In very many cases discretionary freedom is accorded to officials not because of a careful decision by the law-makers that this is the best way to deal with a particular kind of situation but either because that situation has not been fully anticipated or because it has not proved possible to draw up rules to deal with it.'[20] Since individuals' needs for many welfare services, especially those provided by professionals such as health care, social work and education, are so complex and individualised, it is hardly surprising or disturbing that social legislation in these areas allows for a great deal of professional discretion. On the other hand in certain instances social policy makers may deliberately leave difficult rationing decisions to the discretion of individual social service staff in order to avoid making unpopular decisions. Hill illustrates this tendency in his study of discretion within the old national assistance scheme. He claims that the politicians and civil servants who framed the 1948 National Assistance Act deliberately placed the onus of distinguishing between the deserving and undeserving poor on individual national assistance officers. They did so, according to Hill, because while not wishing openly to espouse the notion of the 'undeserving poor', they were unwilling to risk the public criticism which would result from an approach to poverty relief which did not incorporate such a distinction. Similarly it could be argued that politicians and health service administrators have traditionally avoided taking politically controversial decisions on life and death issues such as the development of transplant programmes within the NHS. The medical profession, acting both as a group and as individuals, has largely been left to take a wide range of rationing decisions which are by no means based solely on clinical judgement. Cooper has pointed out that, 'Rationing in the NHS has never been explicitly organised but has hidden behind each doctor's clinical freedom to act solely in the interests of his individual patient.'[21]

Conclusion

Parker has identified three broad groups of rationing strategies: restrictive strategies such as charges or delay; dilutant strategies which reduce the level of service provided to individual clients; and termination, where a service is ended sooner than the provider thinks is desirable.[22] Rees has identified ten principal forms of service rationing. He has also made a useful distinction between overt or obvious and covert or hidden rationing.[23] Both these authors have provided a useful clarification of what, for many years, had been an unexamined issue. They have not, however, explored the wider contexts of welfare rationing. In order to fully understand the role played by welfare rationing in determining the distribution of welfare benefits and services in our society, we must go beyond an administrative analysis of the various types of methods of rationing which have now been identified. We must attempt to understand the aims and objectives – both stated and implicit – of the social services and social service staff who utilise these devices. We must also take our analysis even further and discuss welfare rationing in relation to the economic, political and ideological constraints which are imposed upon the provision of welfare in a capitalist society. Much useful research has now been undertaken into how service rationing operates within the statutory social services. This book attempts to look beyond the issue of *how* rationing operates to the wider issue of *why* it apparently fails in so many ways to distribute welfare in a fair and equitable manner. In order to answer this question, we must study not only the administrative failings of particular rationing methods but also the external pressures and constraints which set limits to the freedom of action enjoyed by welfare providers and determine to a significant degree the outcome of welfare rationing in all its diverse forms.

2

Welfare Needs

The fundamental importance of the concept of need as a distributive principle in social policy is undisputed. According to George and Wilding, 'Need is not only the basic criterion, it is the sole criterion for the allocation of social service benefits.'[1] In fact, social services are not always allocated solely according to need, nor are they universally intended to be so. Nevertheless few would dispute the view that social service benefits ought to be allocated primarily according to need. Welfare providers, particularly welfare professionals, have publicly emphasised their dedication to meeting clients' needs, whilst academics in the field of social administration have undertaken a great deal of research in this area. They have 'discovered' new needs, measured and publicised existing unmet needs and called for increasing provision to meet them. Researchers have also revealed the extent to which certain services have failed to distribute their benefits primarily according to need.

The word 'need' has been over used and sometimes abused by all those involved in the social policy field. Why is this? Primarily perhaps because those who use it believe that it has a strong moral appeal and use it as a call to action. It has generally been taken as self-evident that any need brought to society's attention ought to be met. Yet, unless all those using the term to further their particular cause agree on its meaning, need runs the danger of becoming a mere political slogan as opposed to a meaningful concept.

This chapter will attempt to unravel the concept of need in the context of the provision of welfare services. It will begin by looking at attempts to find a universal definition of need. It will then look at the uses of need in the welfare field and at attempts to measure welfare needs. Finally it will discuss approaches to need which challenge its central position in the theory and practice of welfare provision.

Defining need

Distinguishing needs from wants

Philosophers have attempted to define the concept of need by distinguishing it from the closely related concept of want. Their attempts are of interest to those in the welfare field since it is generally agreed that the statutory social services are intended to meet individuals' needs but not their wants. As Plant has pointed out, 'It would certainly be odd to say that the welfare services exist to satisfy wants – I may desire or want a colour television set or a new car but these are not goods which are available from the social services. On the contrary . . . those who use the concept of need to demarcate the sphere of the social services are willing to concede that at least within western societies it is the economic market which provides the institutional framework within which wants are articulated and satisfied to the extent that they are.'[2]

Some philosophers have claimed that we can distinguish between needs and wants on the grounds that want is a purely subjective state, whereas need is an objective fact about a person. David Miller explains this distinction thus: 'Wanting is a psychological state which is ascribed on the basis of a person's avowals and his behaviour. Needing, on the other hand, is not a psychological state, but rather a condition which is ascribed objectively to the person who is its subject.'[3] Fowler's modern English usage states this case more succinctly. 'Need implies an objective judgement, want a subjective'.[4] According to this view if one wishes to find out what it is an individual wants one must ask him and accept his opinion, whereas to determine a person's needs one must gather together objective facts about that person. In the latter case we cannot rely on the view of the individual himself since he may well be unaware of his own needs. An undiagnosed diabetic might want to eat sweet foods whereas a doctor having assessed his physical state would inform him that he actually needed to cut out sugar altogether from his diet.

If needs can be defined as observable, objective conditions it follows that the judgements of experts or independent observers as to whether or not an individual is in need should take precedence over the opinion of the individual himself. Individuals will have only a limited, subjective view of their condition. Some will be quite unaware that they are in need at all. Others may believe that their needs are far greater than they really are. A third party, on the other hand, particularly an expert on the type of need in question, will be able to ascertain all the facts about their condition and thus determine objectively their actual state of need. This attempt to distinguish needs from wants on the basis of an objective/subjective dichotomy relies on the premise that a third party can accurately determine individual need without recourse to any form of subjective value judgement.

Culyer, attempting to define need in relation to the distribution of statutory welfare benefits, takes an extreme position on the importance of a third party in distinguishing between needs and wants. He argues that need is always defined by reference to some third party's views as to what a particular individual or class of individuals *ought to receive*. According to Culyer's definition of need, even a man dying of thirst in the desert only needs a glass of water if others agree he ought to have it. 'If they do not, he may want it as much as is possible to want anything but he does not, by our definition, need it.'[5] It may be objected that this example is absurd, that the dying man clearly needs water whether or not anyone else thinks he ought to have it. Culyer's example is unhelpful since it is difficult to imagine a third party who would not agree with the dying man that he needed water. However let us suppose that this man had been condemned to death by due legal process for some particularly serious crime, would supporters of capital punishment still feel outraged by Culyer's claim that the man only wanted water? Let us take the less extreme example of an unemployed man who claims he needs more money from 'social security' because he has no money left to buy food. If hard-working citizens knew that this man had drunk and gambled away all of his unemployment benefit, would they define him as being 'in need' of extra state support?

Common usage of the word need is often linked to moral judgements about whether or not an individual deserves a particular form of help. Social policy makers and welfare providers sometimes appear to use the word need as synonymous with the phrase 'deserves to'. 'Young hooligans need a short sharp shock', for example, may really mean 'Young hooligans deserve harsh punishment'. However a clear logical distinction can be made between individuals' welfare needs and the issue of whether or not they deserve any help. It is perfectly logical to argue that smokers who develop lung cancer *need* medical attention regardless of whether or not they should take the blame for bringing ill health upon themselves. Nevertheless it is important to note that the word need serves a number of rather different purposes in the English language and that this sometimes leads to a confusion within the welfare field between the two quite separate issues of welfare needs and welfare deserts. If the issue of deserts is logically distinct from the definition of welfare needs, we cannot distinguish needs from wants simply by defining needs as those wants which a third party judges an individual deserves to have met. In what other ways might we attempt to distinguish between needs and wants?

Several writers argue that we can objectively distinguish wants and needs by examining the consequences for people of not having their needs or wants met. According to Plant, 'If a man is held to need something, he lacks something and will be harmed by his lack of it . . . and getting what he needs will overcome this harm . . . This is not so in the case of a particular want or desire. A man may want something for a particular purpose, but not be harmed or ail by his not getting what he wants and, conversely a man getting what he wants may harm him or cause him to ail.'[6] For example a well fed woman may want some sweets but she will not be harmed by not getting them, whereas an undernourished woman 'needs' food, that is, she will suffer physically if she does not obtain it. The problem with this attempt to make a clear cut distinction between needing and wanting based on the idea of harm is that it merely throws the problem of providing a universal, objective definition one stage further back. In order to be able to define need objectively we have to reach an objective definition of harm. Is such a definition possible? At a very basic level it would appear that physical harm at least is a straightforward objective concept. If a man has an accident and loses an arm or a leg there is surely no doubt that he has been harmed. Yet even at this basic level there is room for doubt since the degree of harm suffered by an individual must depend partly on his or her perception of it. Two people experiencing the same degree of physical harm may perceive that harm in very different ways. Whereas one person's life may be shattered by the amputation of a leg or an arm, another person will adopt such a positive attitude towards overcoming the same disability that the extent of the harm inflicted on them appears to be minimal. Not only is the definition of harm related to people's subjective perceptions, it is also affected by their particular life styles. A manual labourer, for example, will be more likely to suffer a drop in income because of a physical disability than a man who supports himself mainly by using his brain.

If harm can only be assessed in relation to a particular individual's perception of it, it would appear that a universal objective measure of harm and hence of need is impossible. Several writers having acknowledged this problem have tried to find a way around it. Miller attempts to define harm in relation to an individual's 'plan of life'. 'Harm for any given individual', he claims, 'is whatever interferes directly or indirectly with the activities of his plan of life, and correspondingly his needs must be understood to comprise whatever is necessary to allow these activities to be carried out.'[7] Several criticisms can be made of this approach to the definition of need. How are we to decide what is or is not essential to a person's life plan? If a woman's life plan is to be an artist how many easels and paints does she need? A more fundamental criticism is that it does not explain why an individual's life plan is in itself a basic need rather than a want. A young man may claim that his life plan is to be a top class racing driver and that he therefore needs a very expensive racing car. It is doubtful whether the rest of society would accept this kind of claim as the basis for distributive justice.

If we cannot define harm by reference to individuals' life plans, can we reach a universal objective definition of harm in any other way? Plant, having rejected Miller's arguments, attempts to provide us with an alternative universal definition of harm. He identifies two basic goals which he claims all moral codes should and do recognise: physical survival and human autonomy, which he defines as the ability to perform purposive actions. If we accept physical survival and autonomy as basic human goals we have found, according to Plant, a universal and objective method for defining the concepts of harm and need. Anything which prevents an individual from pursuing these basic goals must be defined as harm. All societies must recognise as need the prevention and removal of such harm. For example since physical survival is a basic goal, starvation must be universally recognised as a harm and the provision of food to prevent starvation must consequently be defined as a universal need.[8]

Even if we accept the logic of Plant's reasoning he himself admits that recognising physical survival and autonomy to be basic human needs will not help us greatly in our attempt to specify needs in any particular society at any given time. The problem is that whilst certain needs such as those for food and shelter can be regarded as basic and universal, the satisfaction of those basic needs remains culturally relative. 'Even if we grant something like hunger or shelter are basic needs relating to the fundamental good of survival, it does not follow from citing the need what level of diet or shelter would satisfy it.'[9]

The relativity of needs

At the level of the implementation of social policy, the main concern is with what Dale calls 'intermediate needs'.[10] Intermediate needs are the means which lead to the meeting of an individual's ultimate goals. Most discussions on welfare needs never get beyond considering intermediate needs such as those for education, health care and housing. Such needs are all relative. They are related to the customs and standards of one society or community at a particular time. For example all people need shelter but the type of shelter they need depends on their environment and on the standards and expectations of the society in which they live. A family living in one room in Glasgow a hundred years ago might well have regarded a modern high rise flat on a 'problem' estate as the height of luxury. Today many tenants of such dwellings persuasively claim that they are living in a deprived environment and therefore 'need' to be rehoused. Not only is the satisfaction of basic needs culturally relative, but individuals living in advanced technological societies can actually be said to have more needs than people living in primitive societies. The cultural relativity of need was recognised as long ago as 1776 by Adam Smith who wrote in *The Wealth of Nations*, 'By necessaries I understand not only the commodities which are indispensably necessary for the support of life, but whatever the custom of the country renders it indecent for creditable people, even of the lowest order, to be without.'[11]

The main conclusion we can draw from a brief look at the attempts of philosophers to find a universal and objective definition of need is that they have failed. Needs, at least for all practical purposes, and at least insofar as they are the concern of social policy, are relative. They change over time and vary from place to place. Moreover our definitions of need involve some form of value judgement and are therefore partly subjective. Finally we should note that even basic needs may conflict with one another. According to Gough all people do have basic human needs and these include not only physical requirements but emotional and intellectual needs. But these basic needs inevitably conflict with each other, 'they do not constitute a single harmonious system of needs.'[12] Gough refers to the Freudian view that man seeks two irreconcilable types of happiness – intense pleasure and contentment. Because basic human needs conflict, Gough argues, it is necessary for all human societies to choose between needs according to a system of values. Such a choice inevitably leads to conflict.

Given the lack of concensus over the definition of need as a concept; given the possibility that even the basic needs of human beings are irreconcilable, and given the relative and value laden nature of secondary or intermediate needs, debate and arguments over the meaning of needs are inevitable. However much experts ponder over the basic meaning of the concept they are highly unlikely to produce a consensus view. Yet despite continuing disagreement and uncertainty over the meaning of need in its general sense those involved in the welfare field have made great use of the concept in a variety of contexts.

Determining welfare needs

Welfare providers' use of need

The power and status of professional welfare providers such as doctors and teachers rest partly on their claim to be the only group in society capable of defining and evaluating the needs of individuals with respect to certain types of welfare. They also claim that they are best qualified to distinguish between unnecessary demand and genuine need for a particular service. The distinction between wants and needs in the field of health care, for example, has traditionally rested on the claim that whereas wants are subjective states felt by individual patients, medical need is an objective state which can be scientifically determined only by a medical expert. According to this view untrained patients are not only incapable of defining their own health care needs, they may not even be aware that they are ill. A man with high blood pressure may be quite unaware of his need for any type of medical attention. Even if he suspects that he has high blood pressure he is extremely unlikely to have any idea as to what type of medical treatment he may need. Patients can thus want or demand medical attention but only doctors can define patients as being in medical need. Cooper states that, ' 'Needs' are those demands which in the opinion of the doctor require medical attention. That is they are the expert's view of our health state.'[13]

Teachers and social workers as well as doctors now claim that only qualified professionals have the knowledge and expertise to define the needs of clients in their particular field, and that neither the clients themselves, nor other groups in society such as politicians or rate payers have sufficient expertise to participate in the definition of welfare needs. Teachers argue that they must control the curriculum because they alone have the expertise to assess accurately the educational needs of each individual pupil. Professional social workers argue that they are uniquely qualified to distinguish their clients' real needs from the problems they say they have. According to many social workers what the client says he needs is not to be taken as a satisfactory definition of his problem. Smith, having studied the way in which social workers in one Scottish social service department defined clients' needs, concluded, 'The predominant ideology about the assessor of social needs, embodied operationally in the allocation procedures of this department, is that professional social workers are seen as the most appropriate assessors of need. It is felt that the client himself is not capable of assessing his own real needs since this is a skilled task best performed by the welfare professional.'[14]

At the heart of most rationing systems operated by the providers of welfare lies the belief that social service staff can ration welfare by using their expertise to distinguish objectively those in real need from a much larger group of potential clients who merely demand or want help. In recent years, however, the belief that the definition of welfare needs is the prerogative of welfare providers has come under increasingly strong attack. Critics of the traditional emphasis on the experts' view of need claim that so called experts are hardly more objective in their definitions of need than clients themselves. According to this argument it is impossible to reach a purely objective definition based on scientific facts, of even the most basic of individuals' needs. It is now widely acknowledged that even the practice of medicine is as much an art as a science. Whether or not a patient needs a particular type of medical treatment is usually determined more by medical opinion than by scientific fact. As the Radical Statistics Health Group pointed out, 'contrary to the popular image of a scientifically based medical profession, the reality is that few of the techniques used by doctors have been evaluated in a scientific manner, before becoming generally used . . . conflicting views exist with the result that doctors use treatments to a varying extent and in varying circumstances.'[15] Operation rates for tonsillectomy, for example, vary widely not only between countries but also between regions within countries. Since there is no evidence to suggest that tonsil related complaints vary from place to place, we can only conclude that a doctor's decision to perform tonsillectomies is partly based on subjective, non-scientific factors.

It is now becoming more widely accepted that medical need, as defined by doctors, is an amalgam of scientific opinion, professional ideology and particular factors which influence individual doctors, rather than an objective, unchanging concept. Other welfare professionals have always found it more difficult to convince the rest of society that they alone are capable of defining welfare needs objectively. Teachers have always had to face a challenge from certain parents who believe that they know best the particular educational needs of their own children, while social workers have never achieved anything approaching an unchallenged position as expert definers of need in their particular field. Critics of welfare providers have also claimed that they sometimes allocate benefits according to the perceived merits of clients rather than their needs (see chs. 6 & 8). One solution suggested to this problem is that far more account should be taken of clients' own perception of their needs in the process of allocating welfare benefits.

The client's perspective of welfare needs

The traditional, rather dismissive view of welfare clients' own view of their needs is well expressed by Bradshaw (1972, p. 64). 'Felt need' (i.e. need as defined by the client) he argues, 'is by itself an inadequate measure of "real need". It is limited by the perceptions of the individual – whether they know there is a service available, as well as a reluctance in many situations to confess to a loss of independence. On the other hand, it is thought to be inflated by those who ask for help without really needing it.'[16] Today, however, many critics of the traditional systems of welfare distribution argue that far too little attention has been paid to the client's view of welfare need. As individuals, clients are inevitably limited by their lack of knowledge of available services and their own subjectivity, yet they can still usually distinguish between their own wants and needs. A person may say, for example, 'I want a new coat but I don't really need one', or 'I know I need to cut down on my drinking but I don't want to'. Although individual clients may be quite capable of distinguishing between their own wants and needs, traditionally they have not been trusted to do so by welfare providers. Clients have usually been regarded as having demands or wants which may or may not be legitimate. Only welfare providers have been credited with the expertise to distinguish wants from genuine need. According to Piven and Cloward the major premise of all welfare interviewing is that, 'mere unsubstantiated assertions of need are never sufficient to establish eligibility'.[17]

In recent years many client based groups have begun to challenge official definitions of their needs. Gough has labelled the rise of client pressure groups and self-help groups as 'the new politics of need'.[18] Patient pressure groups, particularly women's health groups, have begun to challenge the medical profession's monopoly over the definition and evaluation of women's health care needs. Groups such as the National Childbirth Trust have not only brought to the forefront a discussion of the non-medical needs of pregnant women, they have also challenged obstetricians' definitions of purely medical needs. They have suggested that procedures such as induction and episiotomy may not be beneficial to most pregnant women and have called for much more careful monitoring and evaluation of a wide range of well established medical procedures in relation to childbirth.

Pregnant women are by no means the only client group which has begun to put forward client based definitions of welfare needs. Tenant action groups have emphasised that people's housing needs are far more complex than their basic physical requirements. They have collectively challenged the expert view of planners and architects that families would enjoy living in the sky in modern well equipped tower block flats. In education, the late 1960s saw a challenge by students and even some school children to traditional expert-based definitions of educational needs and institutional responses. Of course, many client based pressure groups still simply demand more resources to meet their particular needs. But alternative approaches to defining welfare needs which emphasise the client's perspective have begun to influence welfare planners and researchers, many of whom now accept that at least some account should be taken of client's subjective needs within the social services.

Measuring welfare needs

In order to plan social services in response to social needs and in order to distribute welfare benefits rationally and fairly, welfare providers must attempt to measure those needs which they endeavour to meet. In order to do this they require universally applicable measurements of need. One of the key aims of traditional research into welfare needs has been to establish such measurements which would be objective and independent of either the supply or demand for social services.

In recent years researchers attempting to establish objective measurements of social needs have made increasing use of need indicators. Because concepts such as ill health and good health, deprivation, and slum housing are in themselves unquantifiable and unmeasurable, planners and researchers have developed indicators which act as measurable surrogates for these unmeasurable concepts. Life expectancy, for example, can be used as a need indicator in the sense that it is a measurement which relates to the unmeasurable concepts of good health and ill health.[19] Two major British studies of welfare needs which use need indicators are the Resource Allocation Working Party's study of relative health care needs in Regional Health Authorities and Townsend's study of poverty.[20] A critical examination of these attempts to measure welfare needs objectively will reveal some of the problems involved in this approach.

The Resource Allocation Working Party (RAWP) had as its main objective 'to secure through resource allocation, that there would eventually be equal opportunity of access to health care for people at equal risk'.[21] In order to achieve this objective the working party sought to find an estimate of relative need for health care which would be 'free of the distorting influences of supply and demand.' In other words the working party sought a measurement of need which would be quite independent from the existing supply of health care services. This independent measurement of need would then be used to 'establish and quantify in a relative way the differentials of need between geographical locations.'[22] It is generally accepted that one of the best, though far from perfect, indicators of need for hospital services is morbidity statistics. RAWP decided, however, that existing morbidity statistics were not accurate enough to permit their use as need indicators. Instead RAWP used mortality statistics to measure relative needs for acute hospital services.

RAWP concluded their report by stating that 'we think it unlikely that (further study and research) would call into question, in a fundamental way, the principles on which our recommendations are based or the methodology proposed for their implementation'.[23] In fact the publication of the RAWP report was followed by a great deal of detailed criticism of RAWP's methodology. In particular their chosen need indicators were far from being universally regarded as objective or even useful. According to the Radical Statistics Health Group the gulf between mortality and morbidity was far too wide to allow the former to be used as a proxy measure for the latter.[24] This group also pointed out that RAWP had not established a completely independent measurement of health care needs. When calculating the overall needs of each region RAWP took into account the existing proportion of national revenue spent on each type of health care service. A more radical, and it could be argued, more independent approach would have been to calculate how much should ideally be allocated to different categories of patients. A more fundamental criticism of RAWP's methodology was that it was a superficial approach to the problem of measuring need. According to the Radical Statistics Health Group RAWP's failure to define or even attempt to define health care needs was a fundamental flaw in their methodology. The Group also argued that 'need is not an objective measure susceptible to arithmetic and statistical analysis.'[25] This criticism of RAWPs methodology illustrates a key problem associated with all attempts to produce quantifiable, independent and objective measurements of particular types of social need. If need cannot be defined objectively, so called objective measurements of need may be built upon false premises.

According to Bosanquet the argument that the need indicators used by RAWP were so poor as to negate the redistributive programme which followed RAWP's report was an exaggeration. He argued that 'more accurate data would have altered the degree of redistribution but not its general direction.'[26] Certainly if the implementation of social policy were to await the discovery of perfect research data no policies would ever be implemented. Nevertheless, judged according to its own stated objectives RAWP's methodology was a failure because it clearly failed to produce universally acceptable objective and independent measurements of health care needs.

Professor Peter Townsend attempted to produce an objective measurement of relative poverty within a particular society. First, he tried to determine the basic 'style of living which is generally shared or approved' by our society, by discovering 'the set of customs and activities' in which individuals or families are expected to share. He then drew up a 'rough and ready' index which he claimed provided an objective list of those customs and activities which comprise a generally shared style of living.[27] His list of sixty indicators of style of living included such factors as diet, clothing, housing, welfare benefits at work, education, health and social relations. Second, Townsend compiled a 'provisional' objective deprivation index comprising twelve characteristics including 'Has not had a week's holiday away from home in last 12 months', 'Does not have fresh meat (including meals out) as many as four days a week', 'Has not had a cooked breakfast most days of the week' and 'Household does not have a refrigerator'.[28] Having produced this index of deprivation, Townsend's third step was to measure the extent to which individuals or families deviate from the normal shared style of living. Those who lack resources to reach a certain level of participation in these shared customs, commodities and activities were defined as relatively deprived. Finally, Townsend established 'cut-off' income levels below which, so he claimed, the extent to which families fail to participate in the generally accepted style of life, increases dramatically.[29] These 'cut-off' income levels form the basis for Townsend's 'objectively' measured poverty line.

Townsend claimed to have produced an objective measurement of relative deprivation in our society, but, his methodology has been criticised for containing a number of weaknesses which undermine its usefulness. Townsend himself admitted the difficulty of establishing a common life-style in a society as heterogeneous as Britain. Those who deviate from the general 'style of living' may do so by choice and cannot automatically be labelled as deprived. It would be absurd to define a vegetarian monk, for example, as deprived because he did not participate in such customs as eating a Sunday joint, taking an annual holiday and buying new clothes.

According to Piachaud there is no prior reason why many of the components of Townsend's deprivation index should bear any relationship to poverty. He claims that:

> Townsend's index offers no solution to the intractable problem of disentangling the effects of differences in taste from those of differences in income . . . A large part of the variation in deprivation scores is merely due to diversity in styles of living wholly unrelated to poverty. There can be no doubt that Townsend's provisional deprivation index is of no practical value whatsoever as an indicator of deprivation.[30]

Another major criticism of Townsend's approach to the measurement of deprivation is that he inevitably uses a form of value judgement to determine the cut-off point between inequality and deprivation below which families suffer a 'dramatic' decrease in their ability to participate in the custom and activities sanctioned by society. Townsend's claim that the cut-off point between inequality and deprivation can be determined objectively is not convincing. Exactly how many foregone customs and activities constitute deprivation? The distinction between inequality and deprivation is as much a matter of value judgement as of fact. An individual who places a high value on the benefits of an unequal society will be unlikely to accept the same cut-off point between acceptable inequality and unacceptable deprivation as that drawn by an egalitarian. As Piachaud points out, 'The definition by an individual, or by a society collectively, of what level represents "poverty" will always be a value-judgement.'[31]

At first sight the need indicator movement looked as though it might solve the problem of measuring such vague and all embracing concepts as deprivation, and ill health. However, in practice, most attempts to use need indicators have been criticised for lacking any theoretical base. According to Catherine Hakim, 'Studies which state explicitly the criteria used in selecting social indicators are as yet in the minority. Probably the majority select indicators on an *ad hoc* basis with little consideration of alternatives or theoretical considerations of what each indicator is supposed to be a measure.'[32]

Bebbington and Davies have recently argued that need indicators can provide useful information for social policy makers but only if they are theoretically based and are specifically tied to the argument about the cost effectiveness of different types of welfare intervention. They clearly believe that welfare needs are susceptible to reasonably accurate measurement and that the concept of need should continue to play a central role in the distribution of welfare services. Their confidence in the future use of need in the welfare field is not shared by a variety of writers on welfare who argue, albeit from very different premises, that welfare providers are misguided and naive in their reliance on need as a guiding principle for welfare distribution.

Challenges to the prevailing view of welfare needs

The predominant view of the concept of need in relation to statutory welfare provision is that while it may be difficult to define need precisely, it nevertheless remains, and should remain, a key concept in social policy. However, we can identify three approaches to the concept of need, each of which challenges in a different way the prevailing view that meeting need is a meaningful welfare objective. First, an ethnomethodological approach to the definition of social need has challenged the widely held belief that welfare needs are objective phenomena. Second, certain economists have argued that welfare needs cannot and should not be distinguished from welfare demands. Third, radical critiques of the creation of needs under capitalism suggest that all attempts by social service providers to meet such needs are ultimately fruitless.

The ethnomethodological approach to need

Gilbert Smith attempts to change our assumptions about the concept of need through the use of ethnomethodological theory and research. Before setting out his view of need, he identifies and describes a notion of need which, he claims, typifies the dominant tradition of research into the statutory provision of welfare. 'The hallmarks of this tradition is that it has undertaken the search for universal criteria of need, criteria to be used commonly by professional practitioners, administrators, clients and researchers alike.'[34]

Smith challenges this traditional notion of social need and attempts to set in its place a new approach to the study of welfare needs. He claims that all traditional attempts to find an unambiguous and objective definition of social need have failed because no such thing exists. Far from being an independent objective phenomenon social need, 'may be viewed as consisting in substantial part of the concepts and percepts of professional practitioners and others who are concerned with the process of "meeting need".'[35] In simpler terms, welfare needs are mainly whatever those meeting them decide them to be. There is therefore no such thing as a universal concept of need. 'The notion of social need is employed in different ways, in different situations and by different personnel to different effect.'[36] Rather than being an 'objective and unambiguous' phenomenon need is, in fact, a 'highly ambiguous' concept, closely dependent on the beliefs and practices of those who use it. Need is not simply a characteristic of a potential client, but rather is created during the process of client/welfare provider interaction. Smith undertook an empirical study of client reception, intake and allocation in a Scottish social work department in order to illustrate the way in which routine administrative procedures combined with social workers' ideologies of need to create certain categories of need into which clients were slotted. For example, the view held by the majority of social workers that the individual client was the basic unit of need, was reinforced by their department's filing system in which details of each member of a family were filed separately. This combination of social work ideology and routine administrative procedure made it difficult for the minority of social workers, who regarded 'the family' or 'the community' as the key unit of need, to put their views into practice. This is just one of many examples given by Smith in order to prove his argument that 'social need' when considered within the framework of welfare services should, 'be viewed as a professional accomplishment, as a social process in itself and as situated within a particular organisational environment.'[37] Even within one particular organisation, Smith argues, definitions of need vary at different stages of the task of meeting clients' needs. He concludes that any notion of social need which does not take into account the ideas and practices of welfare providers and the procedures of the organisations within which they work is of very limited value.

If we accept Smith's view that the traditional notion of welfare need as an objective phenomenon is incorrect we must re-examine the belief that the concept of need can act as a guiding light to welfare providers in distributing welfare resources. If social need is substantially a creation of the beliefs and activities of welfare providers working within the constraints imposed by administrative procedures, it makes little sense to talk about the meeting of social need as a universal goal towards which welfare providers' activities should be aimed. Smith himself believes that 'the concept of social need has been made to work too hard in policy practice and research.'[38] On the other hand he is not denying that clients themselves perceive welfare needs independently of welfare organisations. 'Undoubtedly' he states, 'the notion of social need is employed by clients and other lay publics in situations quite outside the context of the formally organised provision of social services.'[39] Nor is Smith attempting to make a case for the abolition of statutory social services. He is simply calling for a better understanding of their activities. By studying the ways in which welfare providers and organisations define and categorise need, researchers could identify beliefs, activities and procedures which determine whether an individual is accepted as being in need of a particular benefit. They could then suggest ways of changing welfare providers' views and activities in order to change the outcome of their behaviour. In this way researchers might be far more effective in their attempts to bring welfare providers' behaviour more in line with their own perceived views of the ideal distribution of welfare.

Economists' critique of social administrators' use of need

Certain economists have accused social administrators of being sentimental and romantic about the welfare state. They have criticised traditional welfare texts for failing to produce any rigorous analysis or justification of the provision of free and statutory welfare services.[40]

Nevitt takes an economist's view of needs for government provided services. She does not accept that there is any fundamental or theoretical distinction which can be made between luxuries and so called 'needs'. She claims that social needs are simply those demands which society has decided are important enough to be met by government intervention. She criticises the 'needology school' of social welfare for making 'heavily value-laden statements on the "need" for more and better public services' without considering the cost of meeting this need. Since demand is inevitably linked to the cost of supply, Nevitt argues that demand is an immensely more useful concept than 'need'. To talk about a need for a particular good or service without taking into account the cost of meeting that need is, according to Nevitt, no more than useless 'wishful thinking.'[41]

Nevitt suggests that the view that all welfare needs 'ought to be met' regardless of the cost is irrational. It is a trap to imagine, she insists, 'that some government goods have an absolute priority and must be supplied at any cost. So long as prices and quantities are omitted from estimations of need the concept can have neither theoretical nor empirical value and it properly belongs not to the social services but to the vocabulary of political rhetoric.'[42] Certainly some social researchers and welfare providers have been guilty of insisting that absolute priority must be given to the need they have discovered because, by definition, needs ought to be met. Certain doctors, for example, insist that society has a moral duty to provide life-saving operations or machines to all those in need of them regardless of the cost. Nevitt is right to point out that society must consider the cost of meeting alternative needs or demands. It may well be more rational for society to agree to meet lower level, but easily satisfied, needs rather than to spend high sums on meeting the urgent needs of a very few people.

Nevitt's argument against using the concept of need without reference to the cost of meeting needs is a strong one. Her claim that in any case there is no fundamental distinction between needs and luxuries is more contentious. It was pointed out earlier that it is possible to distinguish between needs and wants by reference to the harm principle, but an objective, universal definition of harm could not be found, and it had to be concluded that even within a particular society at a given time the distinction between needs and wants rested partly on the subjective value judgements of individuals. Nevertheless supporters of the welfare state might wish to argue that the limited intrusion of value judgements into the definition of need does not invalidate its use as a distributory principle in the welfare field.

A Marxist view of need

Neoclassical economists are centrally concerned with the dual concepts of supply and demand. Marxist economists, on the other hand, base their critical theory of society around the concept of need, and the failure of capitalism to satisfy human needs.[43] Marxists have criticised traditional social administration studies for their limited view of welfare needs. Taylor Gooby argues that social administration has, in the past, reduced the discussion on need to 'an empirical study of the rationing procedures used by the present day state.' He goes on to say that if the issue of need is seen solely in the context of administrative rationing, 'the concept is robbed of all subversive content – the possibility that human needs may be such that this form of society cannot meet them becomes unthinkable, as does the possibility that values dominant under democratic welfare capitalism may produce unsatisfiable needs'.[44]

Marxists argue that in order to understand the nature of needs under capitalism we must first understand the way in which those needs are created. They claim that the driving force of capitalism is the profit motive and that in order to continue making ever increasing profits, producers of goods must delude consumers into needing an ever expanding range of new commodities. Some critics of capitalism argue that consumers do not really need many products at all. Under a different political and economic system, they claim, citizens would be content with a more basic style of life and with far fewer useless gadgets and gimmicks.[45]

Not only is the capitalist system accused of creating 'false needs' it is also condemned for not being able to meet the very needs it creates. Most consumers living under capitalism spend most of their lives hankering after scarce goods and services which they cannot afford. The creation of excess demand for very limited goods and services is not just a problem of the private market. The same process occurs regarding the provision of statutory social services. Children are encouraged to desire education mainly because parents believe that educational success will guarantee them good employment opportunities. Yet if all children succeeded in obtaining high educational qualifications none of them would secure an edge in the jobs market. Our society has thus created a need (or want?) for a type of educational success which it cannot possibly meet.[46]

Finally, some Marxists argue that the capitalist system not only creates new false needs which it cannot satisfy but it also throws up a constant stream of new forms of deprivation which in turn lead to the creation of new welfare needs. According to Gough, 'The unplanned relentless drive of capitalist development continually generates new needs. Numerous "social problems" from the middle-aged redundant to the victims of urban redevelopment to the thalidomide children can be interpreted as the social costs associated with rapid economic and technological progress.'[47] In the face of this constant flow of new needs the social services have to run just to stand still. They can never hope to reduce substantially the total amount of welfare needs experienced under capitalism. In any case, Marxists argue, the social services are themselves an integral part of modern capitalism. As such they are as much concerned with bolstering up the existing economic system as with meeting the individual needs which that system creates. Consequently they make very slow progress in coping with the diswelfares of the system.

The Marxist critique of capitalist society and of the role played by the statutory social services within it thus challenges the traditional view of welfare needs on two main grounds. First, it criticises those who take a narrow view of welfare needs which excludes any analysis of the relationship between capitalism and the creation of needs and diswelfares. Second, it challenges the traditional approach to the social services which ignores their role within the capitalist state and emphasises that their primary objective is to distribute benefits according to need. Marxists suggest that the failure of welfare providers to meet need is as much the result of deliberate policy as of any inadvertant confusion over the meaning, definition of measurement of welfare needs.

Conclusion

Traditionally social administrators and welfare providers have tended to take the concept of need for granted. In recent years, however, the meaning of need has begun to be questioned and analysed. Evidence that need is a relative concept and that the definition of relative need rests partly on value judgements has begun to undermine traditional confidence in the universality and objectivity of human needs. Supporters of the view that welfare services are primarily based on the meeting of individual need have had their optimism dented from all sides. Critics of the right have suggested that need is a meaningless criterion on which to base the distribution of welfare goods and services. They argue that only the concepts of demand and supply have any real value in relation to the rationing of scarce resources. This claim is itself open to criticism.[48] Nevertheless, these critics have performed a useful service in pointing out the vague and sometimes emotional way in which the concept of need has been used by many supporters of the welfare state. Meanwhile, critics on the left have emphasised that welfare needs cannot be usefully studied in isolation from the capitalist system which creates them, and that the social services are not solely designed to meet individuals' needs. The left has also collected a great deal of empirical evidence which highlights the failure of the social services to meet the needs of the most deprived groups in society.

By the late 1970s, the simple belief that the social services met individuals' needs had been severely shaken. This does not mean, however, that the concept of welfare need is either defunct, devoid of meaning or useless. The debate over the meaning of need has highlighted previously hidden problems in the use of need as the key distributive principle for welfare benefits. But this debate has by no means completely ousted need from its central position within welfare theory and practice. First, it is still generally accepted that a logical distinction can be made between the closely related concepts of demand, want and need, even though such a distinction may involve value judgements. Second, although it is now recognised that intermediate needs in any given society are relative, this does not negate the view that all men share certain universal basic needs which are both physiological and psychological. Third, the fact that social services are not solely intended to meet individuals' needs and that they fail to meet many people's needs does not undermine the argument that social services ought to be based on the principle of meeting need.

3
Client Demand and Welfare Rationing

The precise role which clients play in the process of welfare rationing has yet to be clearly delineated, but it is clear that clients' initial demands on the social services do play some part in determining the final distribution of welfare benefits. We can identify three separate areas of debate over the impact of client initiated demand on the rationing of welfare. First, writers on welfare issues have attempted to assess the impact of client demand on overall levels of social expenditure. The significance of client initiated demand as opposed to other factors such as the demands of industry in relation to overall social expenditure is extremely difficult to calculate. Since we are mainly concerned with the allocation of welfare benefits to clients rather than with the process of resource allocation to the social services, the relationship between client demand and levels of social expenditure will not be explored in this book. A second, controversial, aspect of client demand is the question whether or not clients over use or abuse the statutory social services. A third important question is whether clients themselves play a part in perpetuating social class inequalities in the distribution of certain welfare goods and services. Before exploring these issues further we should note the difficulties involved in any attempt to isolate, measure or evaluate client initiated demand for social services.

Individual clients' decisions on whether or not to seek help from a social service for a particular need or problem have been found to be influenced by a wide range of factors. These include individuals' perceptions of the extent and urgency of their needs; the availability of other means of support such as family and friends, and their knowledge of the service provided. Potential clients of social services will attempt to weigh up the costs and benefits involved in seeking help. This assessment will usually include judgements about the quality and accessibility of the services available, their perception of any stigma attached to the use of such services and their view of any other costs involved in seeking help such as the time and effort involved in filling in a form, making an appointment, or travelling to the required service provider.

Several of the factors which are known to influence client demand are closely related to the nature of the services supplied. A well advertised service is likely to attract more potential clients than a service of which many individuals are unaware. Similarly, doctors who are known to provide a quick, friendly service may attract more potential patients than those who gain a reputation for being curt or inaccessible. Throughout this chapter, therefore, the important influence which supply can exert over client initiated demand will be borne in mind.

Client abuse of 'free' services

Welfare clients are sometimes portrayed as abusers or misusers of 'free' social services. NHS patients are accused of wasting doctors' valuable time by consulting them about trivial complaints or problems. Families who place handicapped or elderly relatives in state institutions are labelled as uncaring. Homeless families are treated as deliberate and undeserving queue jumpers. Most notoriously, social security claimants are branded as 'scroungers' by the popular press. Yet while politicians, the popular press and sections of the public have been concerned with alleged abuses of the social services, researchers have tended to stress clients' under use of the same services. These two views would appear to be incompatible, but it is perfectly possible that those most in need of help under demand it, whilst those least in need over demand and over use the social services.

A great deal has been written in attempt to prove or disprove the view that the social services are misused. In particular the 'scroungers' controversy and the extent to which social security benefits affect work incentives have attracted a great deal of attention. Full justice to this debate cannot be given here.[1] The general controversy about abuse will be illustrated by looking briefly at the accusation against NHS patients and clients of the personal social services.

It is very difficult to gather objective evidence about the extent of abuse in the social services. Bare statistics, such as consultation rates, neither prove nor disprove the claim that NHS patients over use or abuse the GP service. Rising consultation rates can either represent an increase in real medical need or an increase in demand from those with trivial complaints. In any case the experts do not even seem to be able to calculate consultation trends for a given period. Cartwright and Anderson found that the data collected on consultation rates during the 1970s was contradictory and concluded 'on balance the direction of change seems doubtful'.[2] A more useful measure of whether or not patients misuse GP services might be the proportion of consultations defined as trivial. Unfortunately we do not have a universally acceptable definition of a trivial consultation. When GPs were asked by Cartwright and Anderson what they found most frustrating about their work, 40 per cent answered by criticising patients for excessive demands, abuse, consulting with minor or inappropriate conditions, lack of self-reliance and calling the doctor out unnecessarily.[3] The problem with such a response is that it is highly subjective. Five per cent of the doctors maintained that they did not regard any consultation as trivial.

The majority of complaints presented to GPs are self-limiting and certainly not serious in a purely medical sense. The combined results of eight studies on the severity of conditions presented to GPs in the 1970s revealed that almost two-thirds of complaints were minor in the sense that they were self-limiting with no risk to life or permanent disability.[4] But evidence that patients consult doctors over very minor medical matters does not prove that they deliberately bother the doctor over trivia. Surveys of patients have revealed a strong concern about bothering the doctor unnecessarily. Stimson and Webb found that one of the most frequently mentioned problems by patients going to see their doctor was worry about consulting inappropriately.[5] A third of those interviewed spontaneously made comments such as 'They have got enough to do, they don't want me going along on a trivial matter' and 'I have to have something really wrong with me before I come to the doctor'. Complaints that are judged to be minor by doctors are not necessarily perceived as minor by patients. A minor medical complaint may have a very serious effect on an individual's everyday life.

Moreover, patients do not have the medical knowledge to judge whether or not their symptoms are 'nothing to worry about'. A severe headache which the patient fears to be a brain tumour may be diagnosed as trivial by the doctor. A study of two general practices in Manchester revealed a significant discrepancy between the doctors' view of the complaints presented to them and their patients' view.[6] Whereas the doctors judged 68 per cent of the complaints seen as 'not medically serious' only 39 per cent of patients thought that their problem was 'not medically serious', and whereas the doctors judged that 47 per cent of the complaints would not have a serious effect on their patients' everyday lives, only 28 per cent of patients judged their problems to be not serious in this way. One of the doctors in this study explained why he very rarely regarded patients as consulting over trivia. 'Patients come with problems. The problem may be trivial in a medical sense but the patient cannot assess this without seeing a doctor. Some patients do come to see a doctor for reasons which they themselves know to be trivial. This is the only time when one can say the service is being abused.'[7]

Researchers have found that variations in the number of consultations defined as trivial by doctors are due more to variations in the doctors' working conditions than to variations in patients' consulting habits. According to Mechanic, GPs who coped with high demand by practising in a hurried way, and thus had less time to deal with their patients' problems, tended to define far more of them as trivial than did their less busy colleagues.[8]

If it is difficult to determine whether or not patients make inappropriate demands on doctors it is even more difficult to judge whether clients make inappropriate demands on the personal social services. Since the reorganisation of the personal social services the aims of social services departments have been vague and virtually unlimited. Social workers in these departments appear to be expected to deal with any sort of problem presented to them. According to Buckle, the Seebohm reorganisation 'resulted in a blurred image of social work. If social workers are now unsure of their exact role, it would hardly be right to blame clients for asking them for inappropriate types of help.'[9] Research has shown that many people now approach social services departments for information and advice on a wide range of problems, particularly those concerning their dealings with other social service agencies such as the DHSS and local authority housing departments. Although some social workers have suggested that other agencies, such as citizens advice bureaux, might more appropriately provide this type of advice service, there has not been any concerted attempt by social services departments to stop clients using them as general advice centres. In any case it must be emphasised that only a minority of social workers' clients refer themselves for help. Most clients are referred to social services departments by other agencies.

Apart from anecdotal evidence there is little data on the extent to which families make unreasonable demands for institutional care. Individuals' opinions as to the level of care families should be expected to provide for their dependent members vary significantly. Whereas some people believe that the children of elderly parents have a duty to care for them regardless of the sacrifices involved, others argue that society should not expect individuals to give up all hope of an independent life for many years. Apart from value differences, individuals' views on the standard of residential care provided may also influence their opinion of families who seek institutional care for their dependents. Rising standards of institutional care may convince families that their severely handicapped dependents would actually benefit from being placed in an institution. A rise in demand for institutional care cannot therefore be taken as conclusive evidence that families are becoming increasingly irresponsible.

Individuals' values not only influence the debate over families' use of institutional care for their dependent members, they also intrude into the more general issue of the extent to which clients make unreasonable demands on the social services as a whole. Detailed empirical investigations into the extent of client abuse of the social services is unlikely to settle the argument over this issue. Those who strongly believe that the state should provide welfare benefits to all its citizens will tend to define abuse in a much narrower way than those who believe that the provision of generous state benefits undermines self-determination and initiative.

Under-use of welfare services

A great deal of evidence has been collected on the existence of needs in the community which do not give rise to demands for help by individuals. Only a small proportion of ill-health is treated by the medical profession. One general practitioner has calculated that only one symptom of ill health in 38 is reported to a doctor and that if all such symptoms were treated by GPs, the consultation rate would be a staggering 144 visits per patient per year instead of the existing rate of just over five.[10] Of course most of these symptoms would be very mild and would require no form of treatment whatsoever. However a number of studies have revealed the existence of a significant amount of serious illness in the population which is never treated. Cooper has reported several studies which show that for every case of diabetes, rheumatism or epilepsy known to a GP, there appears to be another case undiagnosed, while for psychiatric problems, bronchitis, blood pressure, glaucoma and urinary tract infections, there are likely to be five undiscovered cases for each one treated.[11] One study summarised by Cooper reached the rather disturbing conclusion that there was little obvious medical difference between patients who never consulted a doctor and those who consulted several times a year.[12]

Whilst a great deal of research has been carried out into unexpressed need for medical treatment, little evidence has been produced on the extent of unexpressed need for social work assistance. One study of a social services department in a Scottish city suggested that the general public may be very confused about the role of such departments. It found that the majority of clients, who had been referred by other agencies to the social services department, had not previously known that social work was based there. They had simply thought that the office was somewhere to go to get information. Many of those interviewed confused social work with social security. The study concluded that relative ignorance of social work affected the access of potential clients to these and related services. 'A system which was not known to exist did not exist.'[13]

Apart from ignorance, potential social work clients may be deterred from seeking help by the stigma attached to 'the welfare'. Rees found that most people, faced with the prospect of seeking help from an unknown agency felt a sense of confusion and shame.[14] Mayer and Timms found in their study of clients of a voluntary social work agency that nearly all those who approached the agency for help were extremely distressed and felt themselves to be in serious difficulties.[15] One client described a social work agency as 'the last place anybody wants to go unless they are really desperate.'[16] Mayer and Timms concluded that the stigma still attached to seeking help from such agencies ensured that 'clients do not go to social work agencies unless they are sorely troubled'.[17]

It appears that families only turn to social work agencies for help when they are desperate but does this also apply to those seeking institutional care for their dependent relatives? The statistics show that a very large number of elderly and handicapped people are being cared for by their families. In Great Britain in 1971, an estimated 261,000 handicapped elderly, of whom 132,000 were severely handicapped, were living with their children, while 30,000 severely mentally handicapped children, 70 per cent of the total, were living with their parents. The proportion of elderly people living in institutions during the 1960s and early 1970s was only half that at the turn of the century.[18] These statistics by themselves do not prove that families willingly continue to care for the elderly and the handicapped. They may simply reflect the unavailability of reasonable institutional accommodation. On the other hand, several studies have emphasised that many families appear to shoulder willingly the very heavy burden of caring unaided for severely disturbed and handicapped dependents. Having studied the care of the highly dependent elderly in a seaside community, Cresswell and Parker concluded that the state was 'exploiting the heroism and willingness to put up with hardship' of a large number of people.[19]

Welfare rights campaigners argue that the main problem with our social security system is not abuse but under use. They counter the charge that millions of pounds of benefits are fiddled each year with the accusation that far more money is left unclaimed. The Child Poverty Action Group (CPAG) argues that whereas in 1977–8 the total amount of irrecoverable fraud for all social security benefits was £3.9 million, £340 million in supplementary benefit alone was not claimed by those who were entitled to it.[20] Welfare rights campaigners also complain that the continuing and, in their view, erroneous emphasis on detecting fraud by social security officials contributes to the problem of non-take-up of benefits. Laurence reported from a local DHSS office that 'concern to prevent abuse was probably the single most significant influence on staff's attitudes to and dealings with claimants.'[21] According to the CPAG such an anti-scrounging philosophy frightens off many genuine claimants and brands many innocent people as 'scroungers' or 'fiddlers'.[22]

The argument that the main problem facing the statutory social services is under use rather than over-demand is supported by an impressive array of data demonstrating the existence of significant amounts of unmet needs in the community. However such data is open to different interpretations. An individual who is suffering from symptoms of ill-health may deliberately choose, for a variety of reasons, not to consult a doctor. Similarly, some of those who fail to claim those social security benefits to which they are entitled may freely choose to do without them. Do these examples suggest that the social services are being under used and that welfare providers need to do far more to persuade those 'in need' to seek help, or should the views of individuals who choose not to use state services be respected? There is probably no straightforward, value-free, answer to this question.

Social class and demand for welfare services

One of the key themes in studies of the statutory social services since the Second World War has been the failure of these services to eliminate inequalities in the consumption of welfare benefits. Inequalities take several forms. They can be class based, geographical, racial or sexual but the main concern of social policy analysis has been the persistence of social class inequalities. It is generally assumed that one of the main aims of the post-war welfare legislation was to eliminate class barriers to the use of social services. The 1944 Education Act, for example, was heralded as providing equality of educational opportunity for all children regardless of their social class background. Similarly, the aim of the NHS was taken to be 'to ensure that everybody in the country irrespective of means, age, occupation, should have equal opportunity to benefit from the best and most up-to-date medical and allied services available.'[23]

Yet by 1965 Titmuss was arguing that 'the major beneficiaries of the high cost sectors of social welfare are the middle and upper classes'.[24] In 1982 Le Grand concluded from a major review of statistical evidence on the redistributive effects of the main social services that 'equality, in any sense of the term, has not been achieved . . . there persist substantial inequalities in public expenditure, in use, in opportunity, in access and in outcomes. Moreover, in some areas (though by no means all), there is evidence to suggest that the policies concerned have failed even to reduce inequality significantly.'[25]

Before examining the influence that social class may exert on individuals' demands for statutory education and health care, we must emphasise that demand for and use of the statutory social services forms only a part, and probably not a major part, in determining class inequalities of outcomes in the fields of education and health. Other key factors include the use made of private welfare services, inequalities in the provision of statutory services and above all original inequalities of welfare needs which are not compensated for by positive discrimination within the social services.

It is very difficult to determine the precise relationship between social class and use by individuals of the health care services. Some writers claim that differences in the consumption of medical care by social class have almost disappeared since the creation of the NHS. According to Cochrane, for example, there are now far more important health inequalities to worry about such as regional and functional inequalities in the distribution of health care services.[26]

Support for the view that the NHS has eradicated social class inequalities in the use of health care services can be found in an analysis of consultation rates by social class which show that working class men visit the doctor more frequently than professional and managerial workers. However, in order to make a fair comparison between social classes frequency of use must be related to medical need. It appears that in relation to their high rates of morbidity people categorized as being in the working class do not make as much use of the primary health care service as do people in the middle and upper classes. The Black Committee on 'Inequalities in Health' tentatively concluded, 'The level of consultation among partly skilled and unskilled manual workers does not match their need for health care . . . It is hard not to conclude that poorer groups make relatively less use of GP services, irrespective of the separate question of the adequacy of the services to which they typically have access.'[27] There is very little evidence on the relationship between social class and use of hospital services, but in any case most demand for hospital services is generated by GPs rather than by patients themselves. The most well established and clear cut evidence on the relationship between social class and demand for health care is to be found in the field of preventive health care. A range of studies has found a strong bias in favour of the middle and upper classes in the use of family planning services, ante-natal and post-natal care, immunisation, dental services and screening for cervical cancer.[28] Although the Black Committee pointed out that some of these studies were rather old they nevertheless concluded, 'taken together and in the absence of later evidence to the contrary, a clear relationship between social class and use of preventive services seems to have been demonstrated.'[29]

What explanations have been put forward to account for the apparent social class bias in the use of certain health care services? One group of explanations lays the blame for the under use of health care services on certain characteristics of the poor. For example it has been suggested that less educated working class women will be less aware of the need for ante-natal care or cervical screening than middle and upper-class women. It has also been suggested that the life-style of the poor 'inhibits any attempt at rational action in the interests of future well being.'[30] Presumably the poor have so many immediate problems to face that they have no time to spare for possible future health problems. According to Titmuss the poor are less skilled at using and manipulating a 'free' but complex system. 'Middle income groups make more and better use of all services; they are more articulate and more demanding. They have learnt better in all countries how to find their way around a complicated welfare world.'[31] These explanations may sound like common sense but they should not be accepted as valid unless they have been empirically verified.

A second set of explanations relates differential class use of health care services to the various costs and benefits involved in seeking and using health care. Although the NHS imposes few direct financial costs on patients, this does not mean that use of the NHS is cost-free in a wider sense. Taking time off work to see a doctor may involve loss of pay whilst travel to and from the surgery may be perceived as very costly by those with low incomes. Apart from being more concerned about the financial costs involved in using the health service, manual workers may have less time to spend on health care than managerial and professional workers. MacDonald suggested that working class patients may have far less control over their working hours than managerial and professional staff who very rarely have to clock in and out of work.[32] It may, therefore, be much easier for a professional person to visit his GP than a manual worker particularly now that less and less GPs hold surgeries outside conventional office hours. The fact that until very recently working pregnant women did not have a right to take paid time off work to visit an ante-natal clinic may partly explain 'late' ante-natal bookings by working class women.

Not only may the costs of seeking health care be greater for the poor but the benefits they actually receive may be less. Both Cartwright and O'Brien and Buchan and Richardson found from studies of GP consultations that middle class patients tended to have longer consultations than did working class patients, and they discussed more problems with their doctors.[33] Neither study could establish whether it was the doctor's behaviour or that of his patients which caused this apparent class bias. Do working class patients find it more difficult to talk to doctors, or do doctors feel less at ease with working class patients? Are working class patients less demanding in their interactions with doctors? As yet we do not know the answers to these questions.

Concern has recently been shown over the standard of primary health care services provided in inner-city areas. According to the Royal Commission on the NHS, 'in some declining urban areas and in parts of London in particular, the NHS is failing dismally to provide an adequate primary care service to its patients.'[34] It may well be that low standards of care and difficulties of access to care in inner city areas, such as very long waits for appointments, may reduce demand for GP services in those areas. According to the Black Report the costs to working class people of seeking medical care 'are actually increased by lower levels and perhaps poorer quality of provision to which many have access.'[35] According to Le Grand, 'individuals from lower social groups can find the Health Service – staffed as it is with largely middle class personnel – as at best unhelpful and at worst actually hostile to their interests.' He concludes, 'Costs greater, benefits lower: it is not surprising that the lower social groups demand less medical care than the higher ones, even when there is no charge.'[36]

Whilst seeking to measure and understand social class differences in client-initiated demand for health care services, we must note that decision making by patients in the NHS is usually limited to the initial decision to consult a GP. Once that decision has been taken the medical profession normally takes over. Direct demand on consultant and other hospital services is thus initiated by GPs rather than patients themselves. There is some evidence that upper class patients are referred to hospital by their GPs more frequently than lower class patients.[37] Le Grand holds that although the evidence is far from comprehensive, 'differences in supplier-induced demand cannot be ruled out as an essential part of the explanation of social class inequalities in the use of health care services.'[38]

Unlike health care services where with few exceptions clients are free to decide whether or not to seek help, a great deal of statutory education is compulsory. It is less a question of parents and children demanding schooling than the state demanding that children attend school. Nevertheless, many educationalists believe that differences in demand for education between social classes do play some part in perpetuating class inequalities. It is argued, for example, that middle class parents are more likely to demand that their children are allocated to a 'good' comprehensive school than working class parents, who may accept their children's allocation to the local school, even though it may not have a good academic reputation. This imbalance in demand may reinforce inequalities within the comprehensive school system. Dudley Fiske, Chief Education Officer of Manchester, has argued, 'It is clear that [in Manchester] there is a considerable distortion in the nature of intakes to individual schools and a system based on parental choice tends to reinforce that lack of balance. Parents who are less aspirant, less articulate or less competent in handling an appeal, allow their children to attend less popular schools.'[39] According to the Society of Education Officers, 'The effect of giving 20 per cent of parents the choice (of comprehensive school) may be to depress educational opportunity for 80 per cent of the pupils.'[40]

A second way in which social class is related to demand for education is seen in the data regarding continuance at school or college after the age of 16. Research has shown that holding ability constant, far more bright working class pupils than upper and middle class pupils leave school at the earliest opportunity. In 1978 the Secretary of State for Education told the House of Commons, 'Nearly four in five of the children of professional and managerial families stay on at school past the age of 16 and under one in five of the children of skilled, semi-skilled and unskilled mothers and fathers.'[41] The Secretary of State claimed that many of our most able young leave school at 16 'because they cannot afford to stay on.'[42] Sociologists have suggested that the relationship between social class and demand for post-compulsory education is rather more complicated than a simple equation between low income and parental reluctance to keep a child during extra years of schooling. Boudon, for example, hypothesises that the perceived costs of educational courses are related not only to a family's income but also to its social and occupational position.[43] Upper class children are more likely to choose courses which will allow them to achieve the same high occupational and social status as their parents, even though such courses may be costly both in terms of money and effort. Working class children, on the other hand, will be less likely to choose a course leading to a high status occupation, not only because of the financial costs involved but also because they will be under less social pressure to do so. Moreover, the psychological costs of moving away from the social milieu of their families and friends could be considerable. Boudon's hypothesis suggests that the social class factors which influence demand for post-compulsory education may themselves be extremely complex regardless of all the other factors which determine educational achievement. A simple policy change such as the introduction of maintenance grants for sixth formers would therefore be unlikely to lead to any dramatic change in the social class composition of the higher levels of our education system.

In any case, as Le Grand has pointed out, even if demand for continued education were the same for all classes, it is extremely unlikely that this would ensure equality of use of post-school educational facilities.[44] Most further and higher educational institutions require potential entrants to have passed certain examinations (see Ch. 5). Since examination results are so unevenly distributed between social classes such a system of rationing post-school education inevitably means that the proportion of working class children obtaining such education is smaller than that of children in higher socio-economic groups.

Conclusion

Client demand for welfare services is a complex phenomenon. An individual's decision as to whether or not to demand a particular service or benefit has been found to be influenced by many interacting factors including some which are very personal and subjective. Those who suggest simple answers to the perceived problems of client abuse or under use of social services may well underestimate the complexity of these issues. We should also be aware of the role that ideology plays in such debates. Those who believe that the state has gone too far in its provision of welfare services and has consequently undermined individual freedom and responsibility may argue that much demand for state provided welfare is unnecessary, inappropriate or even irresponsible. Such critics of the welfare state would probably not accept evidence of unmet welfare needs as a justification for the further expansion of the social services. On the contrary they would argue that a contraction of statutory welfare provision, or at the very least, a partial restoration of the price mechanism within the social services, would encourage individuals to be more self-reliant or to meet their welfare needs more appropriately – through voluntary or private networks. Given the lack of evidence to support the view that client abuse of free social services is a significant problem this book will not pursue suggestions for curbing such abuse (but, see Chs. 9 and 10).

Supporters of universal social services believe that far from abusing their provision, many individuals in need either under use the social services or fail to use them at all. It is often suggested that welfare providers should make a much greater effort to ensure that their services reach all those in need who fail to make any demand on the social services. However, given the inevitable shortage of resources within the social services and the almost limitless possibilities for stimulating yet more demand for them, there may be little point in urging welfare providers to raise potential clients' expectations. For example, an advertising campaign designed to encourage families living in poor accommodation to apply for council housing would achieve very little if such families stood no realistic chance of being rehoused in the foreseeable future. On the other hand, policy makers and welfare providers cannot totally ignore the inaccurate picture of need which may be created by relying on individuals in need to initiate contact with a social service.

Those concerned with the differential social class use of certain services have suggested a number of possible reforms. The Black Committee for example, drew health care workers' attention to research which found that services with an 'outreach' capacity such as health visiting, were better able to discriminate in favour of cases of social disadvantage than those services which relied solely on individuals exercising their own initiative to obtain a service.[45]

Le Grand evaluates several methods for reducing social class inequalities in demand for social services.[46] These methods can be divided into three main strategies: policies designed to alter perceptions of working class people of the benefits from social services;

policies designed to raise the costs of middle class people relative to the costs of working class people; and policies designed to change welfare providers' behaviour. Health education programmes are an example of the first type of strategy but those which have been tried are noted for their ineffectiveness. In theory means-tested charges could be used to pursue the second strategy of altering the relative costs of using certain services. However the practical disadvantages of means tests may outweigh their theoretical advantage to the poor (see ch. 9). Reallocating services away from middle class areas into deprived inner city areas might, in theory, both reduce the cost and increase the benefits to the poor of using such services but it is highly unlikely that such policies could have more than a marginal impact. The third strategy could be pursued by giving welfare providers more training to make them more aware of the need to encourage working class clients to use their services but again it would be extremely difficult to secure significant change by such means.

Le Grand considers the possibility of widening compulsory consumption of certain education and health services. Compulsion would effectively eliminate social class differences in initial demand for services but such a strategy might not only be potentially expensive, socially divisive and authoritarian, it would also be unlikely to reduce significantly inequalities in these areas. In both education and medicine, as Le Grand points out, the providers of services play a major role in determining how much help clients receive once they have made initial contact with the services and these providers tend to allocate welfare benefits in ways which perpetuate and reinforce social class inequalities. In the final analysis, therefore, Le Grand is pessimistic about the effects of any form of incremental change within the social services and claims that the only way to alter significantly social class inequalities in a range of welfare contexts is to reduce inequalities in individuals' incomes.[47]

This chapter has focused on client initiated demand and its role in the process of welfare rationing. Although the many factors influencing it should not be ignored by social policy makers, client initiated demand is by no means the major determinant of the distribution of welfare benefits. Much initial demand for help is rejected by welfare providers. Not only do welfare providers closely control would-be clients' initial access to services, they subsequently determine the quantity, quality and nature of the benefits provided through those services. Unlike the private market, where consumers are able to choose between a variety of goods within the limits of their purchasing power, consumers in the statutory social services have little say over the type of welfare they receive. Once they have asked for help their fate is, to a great extent, taken out of their hands.

4
The Reception Process

According to the American psychologist Kurt Lewin, most organ-isations contain gate sections through which individuals wishing to enter or use them must pass. These gate sections, he suggests, are governed either by impartial rules or by gatekeepers. In the latter case an individual or group has the power to make the decision whether an individual is allowed in or not.[1] Lewin's brief introduc-tion to the idea of organisational gatekeeping has been elaborated by Irwin Deutscher who states that gatekeepers in large-scale bureaucratic organisations determine 'just how far [a client] will get and how long it will take him.' He argues:

> In any society, primitive or modern, urban or rural, individuals encounter a series of gates as they move through the life cycle. And at each encounter the decision between in and out is made by the gatekeeper. It may be a foregone conclusion – a ritualistic decision; it may be one that is determined by tradition; it may be the whimsical result of a powerful and capricious individual. It is also possible for such decisions to be made according to formal rules and criteria – or for that matter according to informal rules and criteria. The fact remains that because of his ignorance of such specialised bureaucracies, the common man often finds himself at the mercy of the ubiquitous gatekeeper.[2]

Gatekeeping occurs in the private market as well as in the statu-tory social services. Private welfare providers may enjoy a range of gatekeeping techniques to protect themselves from the demands of their clients. They will usually have at least a receptionist and an appointment system. Top professionals in fields such as law and medicine may tell potential private clients that they are fully booked for the foreseeable future regardless of how much the client is prepared to pay for immediate attention. Professionals who can afford to do so may also choose their private clients according to whether or not their cases interest them rather than according to the fees they are prepared to pay. Despite the existence of such forms of gatekeeping in the private market, private clients usually face little difficulty in gaining initial access to the services of their choice provided they are prepared to pay for them. Potential clients of the statutory social services on the other hand are not able to buy their way into them. Even if clients wished to do so, the rules of the game do not allow access to the statutory social services on these grounds. Lacking the power of the purse, clients in the statutory welfare field must rely either on rules and regulations or on individual staff to open the gates and let them through to the particular service they require. The absence of the price mechanism as an automatic gatekeeping device greatly enhances the gatekeeping role of front line staff in the statutory social services.

A variety of gatekeeping systems can be found within the statutory social services. Some are impersonal, others highly personal. Some are governed by detailed clear cut rules, others are based on personal decision making or discretion by social service staff. Some services involve no personal contact between service seeker and service provider. A number of financial benefits such as family income supplement can be applied for and received by post. The reception process in such cases basically consists of form filling. In the majority of social services however the reception process is a personal one, and in order to obtain help an individual must come into personal contact with a welfare provider or a series of welfare providers who act as personal gatekeepers to their particular services. Social service gatekeepers can be roughly divided into three main groups. Those with the most power to make individual decisions as to whether or not would be beneficiaries should be allowed initial access to help are professional welfare providers such as doctors and social workers. Their role as gatekeepers will be fully discussed in the following chapter.

A second group of gatekeepers is made up of a variety of non-professional social service staff such as social security officers, housing officers, home help organisers and untrained social workers, or social work assistants. Their role will be illustrated in Chapters 7 and 8. The third group of gatekeepers comprises secretaries, telephonists and other clerical staff. These staff have not generally been credited with exercising any significant influence over clients' access to social services. Nor do they usually see themselves as important decision makers in the gatekeeping process. Yet a growing body of evidence suggests that in practice the decisions such employees make do have an impact on the progress made by clients through welfare agencies.

The significance of the reception process

Commercial enterprises, usually keen to attract the business of potential customers, devote considerable resources to ensuring that their reception facilities are both attractive and efficient. In contrast, the statutory social services have generally shown little concern over the reception of clients. Personal reception processes often involve applicants waiting, sometimes for several hours, in reception areas or waiting rooms. Critics have complained that the poor standard of reception facilities and furnishings found in many welfare agencies, especially local DHSS offices, stigmatises and even occasionally deters potential beneficiaries. In response to such criticisms some services have made a considerable effort to brighten up and hence decrease the stigmatising effect of their reception facilities. One notable, nationwide example was the creation, in the 1970s, of purpose built self-service Job Centres. These centres were designed to be as attractive as possible to job seekers and to incorporate modern furnishings, fitted carpets and attractive open plan lay outs. They were generally regarded as a great improvement on the old poorly furnished employment offices.

Some attempts to improve reception facilities have also been taken at a local level. The reception facilities of one social work area office in Northampton were transformed in 1981 from a 'dark dingy' waiting room with plastic chairs to a social work 'shop' with 'soft furnishings, low coffee tables, hessian covered walls, carpets and a large play area divided from the waiting area by a raised indoor garden.' According to Sweet the old reception facilities were 'a breeding ground for frustration, anger, depression and conflict' which 'humiliated' clients. 'The overall effect was to lower professional standards, damage relationships and militate against any image of caring.'[3] Despite these examples of reform many reception areas in hospitals, social services departments and social security offices are still very unattractive and uncomfortable.

Prottas suggests that slow, uncomfortable or difficult reception processes in public welfare agencies are not simply the result of neglect, lack of concern or lack of money. He claims that the long discouraging experience of applying for public welfare benefits or services is a cost deliberately imposed on welfare applicants in order to make access to a 'free' service more difficult.[4]

The traditional lack of interest in the reception process in public welfare agencies cannot be explained by its intrinsic lack of importance. The way in which a social service initially receives a potential client can often determine the outcome of the whole welfare process. In an impersonal system an incomprehensible form may prevent a potential claimant from even applying for help. Where individuals have to make personal contact with a service provider they are often nervous or confused. Most clients will be in a very weak position *vis-à-vis* a service gatekeeper. It is consequently all too easy for an unhelpful gatekeeper to deter – wittingly or unwittingly – a potential client from continuing to seek help. According to Sweet 'the first time a client touches an organisation determines the framework in which that client will view the organisation. It will confirm or alter any preconceived image and decide the tone of the relationship between the public and the service.'[5] Buckle has argued in relation to social work services that whereas 'reception tends to be viewed as a passive role, having little effect on the work of the agency . . . the reverse would seem to be the case . . . once the individual has decided to approach the social services department the attitude of the receptionist and the nature of the intake process are crucial in determining whether or not the contact with the department is maintained.'[6] In 1971 Bessell actually suggested that:

> Possibly the most important single factor which determines the public image [of a social work agency] is the way in which the agency receives its prospective clients and it is no exaggeration to say that, in many cases what happens before the client sees the social worker will not only determine the outcome of the interview, but whether the client will even be admitted to see a social worker and if he does, whether he will return.[7]

Although these statements refer to social work agencies the arguments probably apply equally well to the reception of patients in hospitals, health centres and general practices; the reception of social security claimants in DHSS offices and the reception of would be council tenants in local housing departments. Unfortunately, there is very little written evidence about the impact of reception of clients in the fields of housing and social security. Manchester's senior welfare rights officer has recounted the tale of a claimant who rang her local DHSS office to enquire about a clothing grant and was told by the telephonist that the office no longer gave such grants.[8] In fact this woman's circumstances did entitle her to a single payment under the 1980 regulations. Armed with the requisite information she eventually received payment of £77. Although this tale suggests that DHSS telephonists and other clerical staff may have some impact on claimants' access to benefits we have no information on the extent to which such rationing may take place. The rest of this chapter will illustrate the gatekeeping role played by receptionists in the social services by drawing on empirical evidence taken from studies of general practice and various social work agencies. Receptionists in other services may well play a very similar role but no general conclusion on this issue can be reached until some research has been undertaken into these neglected areas.

The role of receptionists in general practice and social work agencies

In theory non-professional staff who work in bureaucracies such as the social services are strictly controlled by rules and regulations which are enforced by a formal hierarchy of authority. One would therefore expect staff such as receptionists, telephonists and clerical workers to have little freedom of action in their dealings with social service clients. In practice, however, as any one who has crossed swords with a GP's receptionist knows, even low level non-professional social service staff can and do exercise considerable power over clients. They are able to do so mainly because their dealings with clients are not directly supervised by their employers or superiors. Another reason, in some cases, is that they are given specific duties to act as gatekeepers. GPs, for example, may delegate to their receptionists the task of keeping 'awkward' or 'over-demanding' patients at bay. In other cases, front line staff whose actions are supposedly controlled by rules and regulations may ignore or bend the rules in order to enhance their own power and thus gain greater job satisfaction. Blau found that receptionists in an American public employment agency modified the rules governing the giving of interview dates to clients in order to give themselves some discretion over when clients would be interviewed. According to Blau they thus 'transformed a routine mechanical duty into an interesting social experience.'[9] These receptionists enjoyed the feeling of power they derived from being able to 'sneak somebody through' to be interviewed who should not really get through and thus help him to get a job, or from being able to determine whether a client might return within a few days or must wait many weeks. Prottas's more recent research into the power exercised by low level bureaucrats in a variety of American public welfare organisations has confirmed Blau's finding that even the lowliest of staff in public welfare agencies tend to exert some element of power or control over clients' access to those agencies.[10]

Researchers in Britain have shown that one of the powers exercised by receptionists in both general practice and social work agencies is their control over the length of time clients have to wait before seeing a welfare provider. Hall found in his study of receptionists in four pre-Seebohm children's departments that the most common form of power exercised by receptionists was deciding whether to speed up or delay a client's access to a social worker. If a client was not seen quickly by a social worker, the receptionist would often contact the worker and stress the urgency of the case in order to speed up the reception process. On the other hand, a receptionist could cause clients considerable delay by understating their problem. Hall found that various factors influenced whether a receptionist would help a particular client.[11] Firstly, the receptionist's assessment of the client's need influenced her actions. Secondly, a belief that a client was being treated inappropriately or unfairly by a child care officer would spur the receptionist to make great efforts on the client's behalf. Finally, a receptionist's actions could be determined simply by whether or not she liked a particular client. One receptionist's reply to the question 'Do you treat clients differently for any reason?' was:

> No. It doesn't make any difference to me – well – there are those who you feel particularly sorry for, who you think are getting a rough deal. Very often it depends on how hard you push the child care officer or the duty officer as to what gets done. On the other

hand you don't put yourself out for someone who annoys you. Like that woman just now . . . she'd only been in here five minutes before she asked how long she'd have to wait. I don't like that.[12]

Hall concluded that 'The advocacy/suppression activities of receptionists had the effect of promoting or inhibiting the chances of a visiting client making contact with a social worker in the agency. At best a client suppressed by a receptionist would only result in a temporary delay in being seen; at worst a client might be prevented from seeing a social worker at all on that visit.'[13] Since Hall's study the personal social services have undergone a major reorganisation. The role of receptionists in social services departments may now well differ, but no one has yet undertaken a detailed survey of their work since reorganisation. However in 1981 Buckle commented that most applicants approaching social services departments are still seen first by a receptionist who 'can act as an advocate or as a suppressor *vis-à-vis* an applicant being seen.'[14]

In general practice, one of the main powers of receptionists lies in their control over doctors' appointment systems which, in turn, partly determine how long a patient will have to wait before seeing a doctor. Some doctors may lay down rules governing the allocation of appointments but since doctors do not directly supervise their receptionists' activities they cannot, even if they wished to do so, completely restrict their receptionists' freedom of action. In one health centre observed by the author there was a set of written guidelines for receptionists on booking appointments entitled 'Routine Arrangements for Appointments' but the receptionists admitted that they never referred to it. The senior receptionist commented, 'I'm not sure anyone takes much notice of it. It's only a very broad guideline.'[15] Even if the receptionists had tried to follow the written guidelines they would still have had to use their own discretion over how long patients should wait for an appointment, since the guidelines did not lay down any rule on this crucial point. Those rules that were spelt out in the guidelines were not necessarily followed by the receptionists. The guidelines stated that appointments were to be made at ten minute intervals but that once all these spaces had been filled the receptionists should book patients in at five minute intervals. In practice receptionists always told patients that the surgery was fully booked after all the ten minute appointments had been filled. They only fitted patients in to the five minute gaps if they decided that they were a genuinely urgent case or if a patient was particularly adamant about seeing the doctor urgently. Some patients questioned the time they had to wait for an appointment or the unavailability of their own doctor but in reply receptionists would simply emphasise that no other time was available and patients would usually accept this.

Patients who claimed that their problem was urgent and asked to see the doctor immediately posed more of a problem for the receptionists than patients making a routine request for an appointment. The written guidelines did lay down a procedure to be followed in dealing with patients who attended without an appointment and asked to be seen urgently. This procedure was that 'If a patient claims urgency always leave the doctor to make the decision as to whether or not he can be seen.' However receptionists frequently decided for themselves whether a patient's claim of urgent need was valid and whether to allocate that patient an urgent appointment or to reject their request. In doubtful cases the receptionist would ring the doctor and ask for advice but this was certainly not routine procedure. One patient, for example, arrived at the practice at four o'clock in the afternoon and asked to see the doctor that same day, volunteering the information that he had been having dizzy spells and was sweating profusely. Before making a decision on whether to fit this patient into a fully-booked surgery, the receptionist attempted to make her own assessment of the urgency of his need by asking, 'How long have you been having these dizzy spells?'. The patient replied, 'Four days now.' The receptionist, who had only recently joined the practice, then went to ask the advice of a more experienced receptionist before fitting the patient into a gap in that evening's surgery. In order to make a decision as to whether or not to give an immediate appointment to a patient who asked for one, the receptionists frequently questioned the patients closely about the nature of their complaints. They also drew on their knowledge of a patients' past behaviour and illnesses in order to assess the validity of their demand for an immediate appointment. For example, one patient came into the practice at 9.30 a.m. and asked if he could see the doctor that morning about his ankle. The receptionist told him 'You can't see him this morning, he's booked up.' Despite the patient reiterating that he needed to see the doctor that morning, the receptionist refused to fit him in and would only offer him an appointment for four o'clock that afternoon. After the patient had gone the receptionist told her colleague. 'He's a known nuisance. He's tried this on before.' (That is he had previously come to the surgery without having an appointment and had asked to see the doctor immediately.)[16]

Certain categories of patients appeared to be given priority by the receptionists. The senior receptionist told the author that small children were always fitted into a full surgery if their parents claimed their condition was urgent. Patients whom the receptionists knew to be suffering from serious diseases were also given urgent appointments more readily than patients whom the receptionists categorised as normally fit and healthy. This evidence suggests that receptionists in general practice not only influence the length of time which patients have to wait before seeing a doctor but they may also base their decisions on judgements about the nature of patients' complaints.

Several studies have found that many patients dislike medically untrained receptionists questioning them about the nature of their complaint before allowing them access to their doctor. Kaim-Caudle and Marsh found in 1975 that 30 per cent of the patients they interviewed objected to having to tell the receptionist why they wanted to see the doctor.[17] In 1977 Cartwright and Anderson found that 19 per cent of patients in their study were always asked by the receptionists why they wanted to see the doctor, 18 per cent were sometimes asked and 57 per cent were never asked.[18] One in five of those patients who had been asked why they wanted to see the doctor were critical of this practice. One patient commented, 'It's between your doctor and yourself. Someone asking you why you want to see the doctor leads you at times not to make an appointment. It's intimidating and shouldn't happen.'[19] Cartwright and Anderson concluded that 'when receptionists asked patients why they wanted to see the doctor, this created a barrier between patients and doctors and discouraged some people from consulting the doctor.'[20] On the other hand, their finding that 72 per cent of all patients felt that receptionists helped them to get to the doctor, suggests that we should not exaggerate patients' dislike of 'busy-body' receptionists.

Given the shortage of appointment spaces and the duty of receptionists to allocate them in some way, it may be quite reasonable for receptionists to attempt to give priority to those in greatest need, but since receptionists are medically untrained, the system is not only irritating to many patients, it may also carry an element of risk. Klein reports a case where a doctor was held responsible for the actions of his receptionist who had turned away a patient not realising that it was an emergency.[21]

Doctors' receptionists may not be alone in making what many would perceive as decisions regarding clients' needs which should only be made by professionals. Hall found that receptionists in some of the social work agencies he observed exercised their judgement as to what type of service a client really needed.[22] For example, one receptionist decided that a woman asking for a residential placement for her child actually needed a day-nursery place and directed her accordingly. Hall suggested that this type of work which involves an assessment of clients' needs would normally be regarded as a task for a trained social worker. Studies conducted since 'Seebohm' have also discovered receptionists undertaking tasks which might be regarded as professional. In the early 1970s Younghusband found that it was common practice in social services departments for an initial interview to be undertaken by clerical staff before the client had any contact with a social worker.[23] Buckle claims that since reorganisation heavy bombardment of area offices has led to *ad hoc* decisions being taken by receptionists who first process clients' requests for help and decide whether they should be seen by a social worker and whether their problem is an appropriate one for a social services department to handle. Yet social workers usually claim that such decisions are essentially 'professional' tasks which require an expert assessment of the clients' needs. According to Buckle, 'premature filtering without a fairly full discussion of the relevant matters can deprive applicants of the service they require.'[24] If receptionists in social work agencies are widely employed as initial filterers or gatekeepers, as the small amount of evidence so far collected would suggest, it is certainly a practice which needs to be further investigated.

Apart from their role as suppressors or advocates of clients and their role as initial filterers of clients' demands, receptionists can also act as the protectors of professional welfare providers. In general practice some receptionists appear to act as a buffer between doctors and their patients. According to the 'Medical Secretary's Handbook' 'The secretary [receptionist] should never be a barrier to a patient but a bridge by which he can approach the doctor.[25] Its author advises 'It is never the place of the receptionist to act as filter or disuader.'[26] Yet even this guide to perfection admits, 'It may be necessary to protect the doctor when his time is already occupied but this must always be done in such a way that the patient does not see he is being brushed off.'[27]

Another textbook, this time written for medical students, takes what may be a more realistic view of a receptionist's activities. It states, 'the receptionist's role is to tailor the demands for care to the resources of the practice.'[28] A 'good' receptionist can protect a doctor from patients in many different ways. Several GPs have claimed that a well trained receptionist can convert many requests for home visits into surgery attendances. In May 1973, *The Times* reported a paper given at a medical conference which claimed 'The employment of responsible level-headed nurses and well trained receptionists to give advice by telephone frequently converted requests for a visit to attendance at the surgery . . . patients were expected to justify to the receptionist or nurse their request for a visit.'[29] Receptionists may also take the brunt of any criticisms patients have of the services offered by their doctor. Some patients appear to blame their doctor's receptionist if they cannot get an immediate appointment when the fault may lie with the doctor. Comments such as, 'she always makes you wait for an appointment' imply that receptionists are wholly responsible for any delays patients experience in gaining access to their doctor.[30] Although they usually have considerable discretion, many receptionists work within a system which will inevitably cause delay to some patients. It is doctors who set the parameters of their own appointment systems. They decide how many hours a week they will hold surgeries and whether or not they will see late comers. Medical receptionists are employed by doctors. They will usually be very aware of their employer's likes and dislikes. The receptionists at the health centre observed by the author knew which doctors would and would not complain about a fully booked surgery; which doctors disliked receptionists fitting in last minute urgent cases and which doctors were in general 'soft' with their patients. Receptionists acted towards patients according to their knowledge of what would please or displease particular doctors. Whereas awkward patients are only at the practice for short periods of time, doctors are constantly in close contact with their staff and may be quick to express their annoyance if inconvenienced by the actions of their receptionists.

It appears that receptionists in social services departments may play a similar role in protecting social workers from clients' demands. When one area office tried to establish direct contact between new clients and a social worker there was some initial resistance among social workers who felt apprehensive about losing the protective barrier of receptionists.[31] Hall's study reported that receptionists complained that some social workers 'took liberties' and asked receptionists to refer clients to other agencies without allowing them a social work interview.[32] In one office it was not uncommon for social workers to tell a receptionist that they did not want to see a particular client that day. The receptionist then had to tell clients that their social worker was not in or unavailable. Hall concluded that, 'for at least some social workers, the existence of reception permitted the delegation of certain responsibilities which they themselves, for a variety of reasons were unable or unwilling to fulfil.'[33] Although there is very little evidence on receptionists' role in post-Seebohm social services departments it appears that duty social workers may still be using receptionists to protect them from the demands of new referrals. Buckle refers to the job of receptionists being made increasingly difficult when, 'as was, and *often still is* the case no social worker is committed to seeing new applicants . . . An increased burden is thus placed on the receptionist to deal with or redirect the applicant and thus free the duty social worker from the duty of interviewing new applicants.'[34]

One of the consequences of professionals' use of receptionists to protect themselves from their clients' demands is that the power and discretion of receptionists is increased. How do clients respond to this power? There is virtually no evidence on social work clients' views of the reception process in social services departments but some research has been carried out into patients' reactions to reception in general practice.

According to Stimson and Webb some patients have learnt to respond to receptionists' delay and deterring tactics with counter strategies. One woman said, 'The receptionist always asks me what is wrong with the child. But I've got so used to her now that I've got a bit catty and I say, "Well if I knew that well I wouldn't be calling the doctor out would I?" '.[35] Stimson and Webb found that other counter strategies included insisting on speaking to the doctor or exaggerating the symptoms and the discomfort. But they commented:

When access to the doctor is limited, patients are competing with one another so the advantage gained by exaggerating may be lost if the tactic comes into widespread use. It may also be devalued for the individual patient if it is overdone, done too often or if subsequent events reveal to staff that it was exaggeration. Once the patient has gained a reputation among surgery staff for being 'difficult' or the 'worrying kind' then this will tend to stick and credibility will subsequently be reduced.[36]

Despite some attempts to use counter strategies most patients have very little bargaining power to counter the power of receptionists. They are generally not in any position to know whether the receptionist is telling the truth about the availability of the doctor. Nor do they know whether she is acting on the doctor's instructions or using her own initiative. Receptionists at the health centre studied by the author frequently conveyed the impression to patients that they were powerless when faced with a fully booked surgery. They implied that they themselves would like to help the patient but that there was nothing they could do. They did this by using such phrases as, 'I can't make it this afternoon, he's completely booked up' or, 'Well, I'm sorry but there's nothing I can do about it.'[37] In fact there were very few occasions when the receptionists at the practice studied could not have given the patient priority if they had wished to do so.

It appears that patients' complaints about doctors' receptionists are rising. In the mid 1970s the Patients' Association reported that 17 per cent of the complaints they received about general practices were concerned with the role of receptionists and the association commented that such complaints were on the increase.[38] On the other hand a number of studies have found that the great majority of patients are reasonably happy with the service provided by receptionists. Half the patients interviewed by Cartwright and Anderson in 1977 described their doctor's receptionists as 'very helpful', 40 per cent as 'helpful', 3 per cent as 'unhelpful' and only 1 per cent as 'very unhelpful'.[39] It is interesting to note, however, that Cartwright and Anderson found that patients under 35 seemed to have the poorest relationship with doctors' receptionists. Only 30 per cent of them thought the receptionists were very helpful compared with 57 per cent of older people.[40] Nevertheless they concluded that, 'The stereo-type of the dragon protecting the doctor from importunate patients would appear to be a reality for only an unfortunate few.'[41] Unfortunately, we simply do not know clients' views of receptionists in other social services.

Conclusion

With the growth of the role and power of receptionists within the statutory social services calls have been made for them to be better trained. At present receptionists usually receive very little formal training for their role as initial filterers and gatekeepers to certain services. Hall found that none of the receptionists he studied had received any formal training for their work. What they should do was simply passed on by word of mouth to new receptionists. The decisions they made were based not on formal rules and regulations, since there were none, but on informal codes of practice.[42] Receptionists, on the whole, simply used their own judgement and common sense to decide what to do in any given situation. They were free to exercise so much discretion partly because the importance of their role was consistently underestimated by their professional colleagues. A similar situation appears to exist in general practice. In the one health centre observed by the author new receptionists were not given any formal training before starting work. They were simply instructed on the job by more experienced receptionists. The doctors took no interest in this process.[43] Like the social workers in Hall's study they did not appear to regard the reception process as particularly important or worthy of their personal supervision.

Hall has objected to the suggestion that in social services departments receptionists should be trained on the grounds that such training would simply increase their involvement with clients and their power to make decisions about the type of service they receive. A similar problem could occur in general practice. Already many elderly patients rarely actually see the doctor, they simply collect a repeat prescription which has been written out by the receptionist and signed by the doctor. Training receptionists could make the problem of gaining access to professional welfare providers worse rather than better. An alternative solution to uncontrolled receptionists is to attempt to make professional welfare providers more aware of the importance of their receptionists' actions. Although some welfare providers may be quite unaware of the important role played by their receptionists in regulating clients' access to them, others deliberately use receptionists to keep their clients at bay. Nevertheless, if welfare professionals took a closer look at the way in which their receptionists controlled clients' access to them they might tighten up or implement rules governing this process. One of the doctors in the health centre observed by the author told her that patients at his practice were allowed to see any of the doctors regardless of with whom they were registered, yet the receptionists insisted to the researchers and also to the patients that they could only see the doctor with whom they were registered unless he were not available.[44] If this doctor had been more aware of the importance of the reception process he might have taken steps to ensure that his receptionists actually followed the procedures he assumed to be in operation. However, if welfare providers were to tighten the rules governing their receptionists' work it seems likely, on the evidence of Blau and other researchers, that unsupervised receptionists would simply bend those rules in order to continue to exercise a considerable degree of discretion in their work.

We must be careful to locate this issue in its proper place. Receptionists in the social services are able to delay, speed up, or occasionally even prevent clients' access to professional welfare providers primarily because those providers are either unwilling or unable to expose themselves directly to those seeking their help. Professional welfare providers argue that they must protect themselves against potential abuse and exploitation by placing certain barriers between themselves and their clients. According to Stimson and Webb, 'Patients generally perceive themselves to be relatively powerless, yet in some ways the profession perceives the lay world as threatening. To protect themselves against potential abuse and exploitation the profession needs ways of controlling the demands of those desiring their services and the way in which those demands are met.'[45] Receptionists form just one part of the defence systems which professionals build up to protect themselves from their clients. The argument about whether barriers to access in the social services are primarily a result of over-demanding clients or over-protected providers is not easily resolved but whatever the cause of such barriers, there is little doubt that they are unlikely to be removed in the foreseeable future. Under the present system welfare professionals, particularly doctors, cannot simply be ordered to provide easier access to themselves and their services. Indeed, given increasing shortages of resources in the welfare field, all the signs are that as demand further outstrips a reduced supply of services, barriers to those services will increase or grow stronger. Anyone wishing to curb or reform the decision making powers of social service receptionists will discover that fundamentally their quarrel lies not with the receptionists themselves but with the organisations in which they work and with those who control the way in which those organisations operate.

Of course, individual receptionists will exercise their own discretion in different ways. Some will try to be as helpful as possible to all clients, while others will enjoy exercising negative power over those clients whom they dislike or regard as too demanding. Much will depend on the personality of the individuals concerned. A few receptionists may occasionally side with a client against a welfare provider. In the long run, however, most receptionists are bound to comply with the wishes of those who employ or supervise them.

Finally, it should be emphasised that receptionists and the reception process in general play only a limited role in the overall selection of social service clients. Even in those services where receptionists do play an initial role in filtering out or delaying client demand, most clients do eventually gain access to welfare providers and it is they who make the key decisions which determine clients' access to benefits and services.

5

Professional Gatekeepers

Traditionally personal contact between client and service provider has been hailed as one of the great strengths of the social services. According to this tradition personal attention from a service provider ensures that individual clients' needs are met as effectively and as appropriately as possible.[1] This view of personal care as positive and client centred is rather one sided. Even if those working in the social services wished to assist all those asking for help they would not have nearly enough resources to do so. Social service staff inevitably limit as well as facilitate clients' access to statutory welfare. They may provide a personal service to some welfare seekers but may also deny help to others. They do so in some cases because of a straightforward lack of resources but in others denial can be used as a form of social control. As Pinker has pointed out:

> Social services in complex industrial societies are strongly orientated towards meeting individual need on a personal basis. Yet there is another recurring feature in the structure and function of social services – they always allow for the possibility of an expert having access to a layman. This access ensures that a social service can fulfill both therapeutic and sanctioning functions and there is no other easy way of ensuring that both functions can be discharged.[2]

In other words, personal contact with a service provider is not always intended to be wholly beneficial to the potential client. According to the London Edinburgh Weekend Return Group most welfare clients' experience of the social services is contradictory. On the one hand most people, especially those in the working class, need things from the state. On the other hand, the group argues, 'State provision leaves a bad taste in our mouths. State institutions are often authoritarian, they put us down, they tie us up with regulations.'[3] Of course many of those working in the social services would deny that they deliberately 'put clients down'. In recent years, radical welfare providers have claimed that they attempt, albeit not always successfully, to help their clients combat the more negative and controlling aspects of the statutory social services. Nevertheless, critics of welfare providers have accused those working in the social services of organising such services primarily for their own benefit at the expense of their clients.

Clients may feel that all social service staff whether professionals or non professionals are all equally powerful and unapproachable, but different types of social service staff enjoy varying degrees of power and autonomy over their sphere of work and concomitantly over their dealings with clients. As fully fledged professionals, doctors and university lecturers enjoy a particularly high level of autonomy and control over their sphere of work[4] and are thus free to exercise considerable control over their patients and students unhampered by many of the rules and regulations which often restrict the autonomy of less powerful workers in the welfare field.

Welfare providers such as teachers, social workers and nurses do not enjoy complete autonomy over their sphere of work. Sociologists sometimes refer to this group of welfare providers as semi-professionals or aspiring professionals. Etzioni suggests that teachers and social workers are only semi-professional because, 'their training is shorter, their status is less legitimated . . . theirs is less of a specialised body of knowledge and they have less autonomy from supervision or societal control than "the professions".'[5] Social workers have certainly complained that the insensitive bureaucratic rules and regulations of local authority social services departments often hamper their efforts to provide a flexible individual and positive service to their clients. Radical teachers have complained that although individual teachers are relatively autonomous in their classroom, 'the rules and regulations and the expectations of the staff higher up the hierarchy . . . are never far away from the classroom teacher.'[6] Despite their complaints, individual teachers and social workers are usually free to make a wide range of decisions which have significant effects on their clients. They owe this power not only to their semi-professional status but also to the nature of their work. Once teachers are in their classrooms or social workers are out on visits, they are very rarely observed or monitored in any way. Their front line position thus enhances their freedom of action in dealing with clients.

Prottas refers to all front line staff working in public welfare organisations as 'street-level bureaucrats' and makes little distinction regarding their professional status.[7] Certainly non-professional front line social service staff do take individual decisions which affect clients' access to services and benefits. However, in general, it can be assumed that non-professional welfare providers work within a more restricting framework of rules and supervision than welfare professionals and thus have less overall power over clients' access to welfare services. Although non-professional staff can exercise power by interpreting, bending or ignoring the rules governing access to services, the very existence of such rules does provide some protection to clients. Clients of professional welfare providers are far less protected against the vagaries of individual decision making.

GPs as NHS gatekeepers

General practitioners act as gatekeepers to the NHS in two distinct ways. First, they control patients' access to their own time, attention and expertise. Second, they largely control patients' access to a range of health care resources including prescribed drugs and medicines and most hospital and consultant services. This section will concentrate on GPs' control over patients' access to themselves. Since the majority of complaints presented to the NHS are dealt with completely at general practice level, this form of control is clearly of importance to patients. Under the NHS, there are few formal rules or regulations to protect GPs from patient demand. The only formal protection GPs enjoy is the right to cross a particularly trying patient off their list.

Recent evidence suggests, however, that in practice some GPs refuse to accept patients deemed to be awkward or demanding on their lists in the first place. Cyril Taylor reported in 1981 that in inner city Liverpool several residential hostels for ex-mental patients and a NACRO hostel for the single homeless were having difficulty in securing registration for their residents: one practice just outside the area had a 'rule' not to accept patients living in postal district 8 (the 'rough' area) and some very old people and tenants of certain tower blocks were excluded from their nearest practice.[8] Some GPs have also been known to refuse to take patients who wished to exercise their 'right' to change their doctor. According to the Patients' Association doctors in certain areas exercise 'a gentleman's agreement that they won't take on each other's patients.'[9]

Apart from refusing to accept 'awkward' patients, most GPs use a range of informal gatekeeping devices to control patients' access to them. These devices include the use of telephone answering and deputising services to protect themselves from out of hours calls and demands for home visits, the use of ancillary staff, including receptionists and nurses to regulate demand and to deal completely with certain minor problems, and the use of appointment systems.

Empirical evidence suggests that the use of such devices has increased in recent years. A report on changes in general practice which had occurred between 1964 and 1977 found that the proportion of GPs who sometimes used a deputising service had risen from 9 per cent to 44 per cent.[10] In 1964, 15 per cent of the patients interviewed said their doctor had an appointment system; by 1977, this proportion had risen to 75 per cent. In 1977, 99 per cent of doctors had a secretary or receptionist compared to 75 per cent in 1964. Finally, this study found that 74 per cent of the doctors interviewed in 1977 thought that the proportion of their home visits to surgery consultations had fallen in the previous ten years.[11]

These figures by themselves do not show that GPs have tightened their control over patients' access to their services. A decline in home visiting, for example, might be due to an increase in car ownership and consequent easier access of patients to doctors' surgeries. However Cartwright and Anderson found that the percentage of patients who were critical of their GP for not visiting them when asked to do so, rose from 3 per cent in 1964 to 13 per cent in 1977.[12] Similarly, GPs might claim that full appointment systems actually improve patients' access to them by reducing waiting time at the surgery. A number of surveys of patients' opinions of appointment systems have indeed found that most patients are quite satisfied with them. However some research undertaken in recent years suggests that the use of full appointment systems has imposed increasing delay on some patients. The Patients' Association reported in 1974 that it had received many complaints throughout the country about three-day waits for appointments and some complaints of delays of a week or longer.[13] A 1977 study of patients registered with two GPs in Greater Manchester found that 40 per cent of patients had at some time wanted to see a doctor before the earliest appointment offered to them and that this had happened frequently to 19 per cent of respondents. One patient commented, 'You often have to wait nearly a whole week. That's stupid. You can't tell in advance when you're going to be ill.' Another said, 'You can be better by the time you get an appointment', while a third exclaimed, 'By the time you get an appointment you could be dead'.[14]

In recent years more and more GPs have offered an office hours consultation service only. One doctor who supported this change asked the author, 'Can you give me a reason why doctors should work late in the evening in order that patients may consult them out of working hours?' If doctors are to work office hours, they must certainly impose some control over patients' access to them. Given that there are no regulations restricting the type of problems which patients can refer to a GP and given the lack of a price barrier between NHS doctors and their patients, some system of informal gatekeeping is probably inevitable. People cannot expect GPs to work exceptionally long hours if they wish them to maintain a high quality of service. GPs can argue that by controlling patients' access by a variety of informal devices, they are better able to provide a good service to those patients who genuinely need their help. In some cases the claim that informal gatekeeping systems actually benefit most patients may be justified. The use of trained nurses, for example, to treat very minor complaints and thus protect doctors from 'trivial' consultations appears to have widespread support among patients themselves and is very unlikely to lead to any lowering of the standards of treatment.

There is a danger, however, that some types of informal barriers set up by GPs may impose onerous disadvantages on some patients. Even the Royal College of General Practitioners recently admitted that 'care by some doctors is mediocre and by a minority is of an unacceptably low standard.'[15] The college singled out badly run appointment systems as a major fault in general practice. Most patients consult their GP over minor complaints which do not require immediate medical attention. Indeed some GPs argue that many of the complaints presented to them are so trivial as to require no medical attention whatsoever. In such cases appointment systems which impose a waiting time of two or three days on patients may cause them annoyance or inconvenience but will do them no harm. However, there may be a danger that as well as deterring patients with very minor problems, an appointment system which imposes long delays on patients may deter some patients from consulting who are in genuine need of medical advice or treatment. In the study of two general practices in Greater Manchester, one patient who had had pain in her chest but who had not visited her doctor, illustrated this danger. She complained, 'I tried on Monday to get an appointment and not one was available until Thursday although I told the receptionist I had bad pains in my chest. I was very upset about it and would have accepted any doctor but they said none was available. I was very frightened but what can you do? I did feel better by Thursday but things might have been serious.'[16]

Another kind of informal rationing which may occasionally be harmful is the widespread practice of allowing some patients to obtain repeat prescriptions from doctors' receptionists. This practice clearly saves the doctor time and, according to a senior lecturer in general practice, there are many occasions when a doctor is perfectly justified in allowing a patient to receive a repeat prescription without consulting him.[17] Nevertheless, critics of this growing practice have argued that some doctors fail to keep a careful check on the issuing of repeat prescriptions by non-medical staff and that this not only leads to a waste of drugs but is also potentially dangerous.

The growth of appointment systems in general practice has taken place with virtually no patient involvement in the decision making process. In a handful of general practices doctors have sought the views of their patients on the running of appointment systems and have even introduced modifications at their patients' request. In one practice, for example, the system was modified so that patients could choose to sit and wait in the surgery rather than taking an appointment for several days hence. In general, however, the imbalance of power between doctors as professional welfare providers and their NHS patients is so great that doctors can impose unpopular gatekeeping devices on their patients with little fear of any adverse criticisms or consequences.

Intake workers in social services departments

If general practitioners are gatekeepers to the health service, social workers on intake duty can be described as gatekeepers to the personal social services. Like GPs, social workers have to deal with clients' requests for help and must directly deal with the problems of heavy demand unmatched by resources to meet it. Both GPs and social workers deal with a wide spectrum of problems ranging from the trivial to cases of the utmost gravity. Since there are few formal guidelines to determine eligibility for either health care or personal social services, GPs and social workers usually have to use their own judgement to decide whom to help and whom to turn away. Finally, both GPs and 'intake' social workers must decide whether or not to refer a client to a more specialised worker in their field or whether to refer them to another welfare agency. The initial judgements made by individual GPs and social workers frequently determine their service's total response to a particular request for help. They are both in many ways the key determinants of the quality and quantity of welfare supplied by their services to individual service seekers. There are, however, some significant differences between the gatekeeping roles played by GPs and social workers. First, whereas most patients refer themselves to their GP, over half of social service clients are referred by other agencies such as doctors, the police and the courts. Second, while most GPs work entirely as autonomous individuals, most social workers belong to social work teams which are led by a senior social worker. In recent years many social work teams have begun to make collective decisions about which applicants should receive priority and how requests for help should be categorised. The freedom of an individual front line social worker is also restricted by statutory and bureaucratic regulations. Nevertheless front line social workers are free to use their own initiative to make 'no' decisions. According to Buckle individual social workers are 'constantly performing their gatekeeping function and turning down requests for services or referring them elsewhere with relatively little support from their senior colleagues.'[18] The evidence as to how individual social workers perform this gatekeeping function will now be examined.

One of the main hopes of the Seebohm Committee whose recommendations laid the foundation for the reorganisation of the personal social services in 1970–71 was that this reorganisation would make such services more accessible to those wishing to contact them. The Seebohm report stated, somewhat naively perhaps, 'one single department concerned with most aspects of "welfare" as the public generally understand the term is an essential first step in making services more easily accessible.' It continued,

'The organisational structure of these services should not deter those in need and they should be available to all. We believe that a unified comprehensive social service department will be an important step in the right direction.'[19]

The report went on to pay little attention to the process by which clients would gain access to the new service. It said virtually nothing about the role social workers were likely to play in facilitating or obstructing clients' access nor did it discuss the optimum length of time social workers should take to respond to an applicant's request for help. Yet as Perlman has pointed out, someone who seeks help from a social work agency 'feels that his problem is a crisis' and insists that 'something must be done'.[20] If such an applicant does not receive a quick response from the service, his need, at least in the short term, is simply not being met.

Since reorganisation, social work and social workers are based in area teams. In these front line organisations, those working face to face with clients are the ones who initiate work for the service, despite the fact that they are at the bottom of its hierarchy. Decision making in area teams is to a great extent decentralised and front line workers in those teams usually enjoy considerable discretion over their dealings with clients. They are the ones who have to decide whether or not the problems with which they are bombarded are appropriate for their service to deal with. In only a minority of cases does the service have a statutory duty to deal with the problems presented to it. After reorganisation the usual arrangement made to deal with initial applications for help and referrals from other agencies was for all social workers in a particular office to take turns at being duty officers for the day or the week during which time they would deal with all new referrals, whether by telephone or visits. One writer has described the resultant intake system as 'chaos'.[21] Many social workers strongly disliked doing duty. They felt inadequate to deal with the range of problems presented to them and believed that in any case their main responsibility lay with helping their long-term clients.

By the mid-1970s pressure was growing in many area offices for a new intake system. The one most commonly adopted was that of an intake team manned by a permanent group of social workers. These workers were to be responsible for all initial contact with, and assessment of, new clients and were to provide, in most systems, a short term social work service to those clients whom they assessed as being only in need of short term help. By 1980 nearly half of all area offices had set up intake teams but this still left many areas operating a duty rota system. Research into the gatekeeping role played by duty social workers and intake teams suggests that the two systems tend to throw up rather different forms of decision making. The system of social workers undertaking one day a week intake duty has been found to impose considerable delays on new clients seeking help. One survey found that clients had to wait between six and eight weeks before their problem was dealt with.[22] It appears that many duty social workers merely take down a few details about a new referral and promise that 'someone will be in touch'. Several studies of intake teams have found that new requests for help are dealt with more quickly. According to Loewenstein one new intake team provided help much more quickly than the old system of intake although some delays still occurred.[23] Jones studying another newly set up intake team found that whereas under the old system applicants usually had to wait several weeks before anything was done about their problem, intake teams dealt with the problem immediately or followed it up within one or two days.[24]

Rationing by delay is commonly used within the statutory social services. It is sometimes assumed that this type of rationing will inevitably occur unless more resources are made available to meet excess demands. The above evidence suggests that changes in organisational structure can lead to a significant improvement in the speed at which a service responds to clients' requests for help without any new financial costs being incurred.

A second significant difference found between gatekeeping by individual duty social workers and gatekeeping by intake teams lies in the way clients' initial requests for help are either accepted or rejected. Under the duty rota system the decision whether a clients' request for help should be accepted is usually taken by an individual social worker relying solely on his or her own judgement and discretion. According to Buckle duty officers usually make *ad hoc* decisions about whom to help 'often with little sharing or consistency between different workers'[25] with the result that clients with similar types of problems meet a wide variety of responses from the individual social workers dealing with their requests. One duty social worker has commented, 'There are twenty people or however many doing duty and there are twenty different approaches to it',[26] whilst another has stated, 'We've got a great deal of autonomy [on duty] and I think that social workers generally ought to have that responsibility to know what's rightly ours to do and ours not to do and to be able to tell a client right from the start.'[27]

Research into the processing of requests for help by intake teams suggests that social workers in such teams have begun to adopt a more standardised and consistent response, at least at area office level, to client demand. Goldberg and Warburton, for example, refer to one intake team's internal policy of dealing with the financial and material difficulties of young families by advice and referral to the appropriate agencies such as the DHSS and the Housing Department.[28] This suggests that workers in some intake teams at least may be taking a single line in response to similar types of requests for help, and that the importance of individual discretionary decision making by members of such teams may be concomitantly decreased. This view is supported by evidence from Jones who found that the one intake team he observed discussed referrals as a group and collectively decided what response to need would be made in the light of available resources.[29]

A number of criticisms have been made about both types of intake system in social services departments. Social workers in both intake teams and duty rota arrangements have been accused of working in a defensive or self-protective way. One receptionist complained to a researcher that social workers doing 'duty' would often, 'use delaying tactics before seeing a client and would expect the receptionists to have asked clients intimate details of their problem in public so that they could arm themselves with some information before actually seeing them.'[30] Some duty social workers appear to give priority to their long term clients and consequently to avoid as much as possible having to deal with a bombardment of new referrals. Research has found, for example, that some duty officers arrange office interviews with their long-term clients on 'duty days' leaving receptionists to deal with callers who either had a very long wait before seeing the duty social worker or did not get seen at all.[31] One of the theoretical advantages of intake teams is that social workers in them will see new referrals as their primary concern and therefore give them full attention. In practice, however, intake teams have been accused of seeing their primary goal as the protection of long-term social workers from increased demand rather than the meeting of clients' needs. Jones suggests that faced with high levels of demand some intake teams have become agency orientated rather than client centred. The intake team Jones studied began to get job satisfaction from the number of cases handled and closed rather than from the meeting of need *per se*. Administrative efficiency became more important to them than good social work practice. Jones concluded, 'so long as demand continued considerably to exceed resources, the intake group paradoxically assumed the function of protecting the agency from demands rather than of helping to meet community needs.'[32]

Ivory-tower gatekeepers

Whereas almost all people in Britain are free in principle to approach a GP or social worker for help, only a minority have traditionally been regarded as eligible to apply for a place at a British university. Access to higher education is partly governed by a clear set of published rules. Each university publishes the minimum qualifications it requires from those wishing to take a first degree course. Simplifying these regulations, one can say that any student with two passes at 'A' level and three at 'O' level in additional subjects will be recognised as formally eligible to undertake a degree course by any British university. Unfortunately, demand from eligible students outstrips the supply of places on most university courses. Universities, or rather individual faculties or departments, must therefore reject many formally eligible applicants in order to balance supply and demand.

Each university is completely free to make this further selection as it sees fit. According to the Robbins Report, 'It would obviously be an infringement of freedom were academic institutions forced to accept or reject any particular student.'[33] In most British universities the selection of entrants is regarded as an academic task to be carried out by members of staff of individual departments. Where demand for places is high professional judgements made by individual academics can exert a significant influence over candidates' chances of gaining access to the course of their choice.

University selection is not based solely on 'A' level results. Demand for places on some courses is so high that the staff who teach them are forced to use their own judgement to make a selection between candidates all of whom are likely to get good 'A' level results. The influence of individual selectors over the selection process is also increased by the strange system under which most applicants apply for a university course before their 'A' level results are known. Individual selectors consequently have to use their personal judgement and 'hunches' based on the limited evidence available to them to predict which students are going to do well in their 'A' levels and then continue to perform well at university.

Despite a general concern among university staff about the quality of entrants they receive, responsibility for admissions in many departments is delegated to one or two members of staff who are then completely free, within the confines of university regulations, administrative procedures and departmental rules or conventions to work out their own selection process. The admissions tutor for Law at a university where demand far outstripped supply, told the author, 'I'm basically left to my own devices. I am solely responsible for reading the 2,000 UCCA forms in my spare time and as I read each form I make a decision whether to reject or accept it.'[34] The History admissions tutor at the same university enjoyed a similar freedom of action. 'I've been running admissions for four years now', he explained, 'and I've never been asked any questions about my decisions from the rest of the staff although my colleagues did once express some concern over the lack of Northerners in our intake.'[35] None of the selectors interviewed at this university had received any training in the art of selection although some of them had worked alongside an experienced selector before taking over responsibility for admissions. Yet their decisions were rarely, if ever, questioned by their colleagues. As Reid has pointed out:

> The ability to assess and select suitable entrants to a department is felt to be at least latent in anyone who has been a member of a department long enough to have absorbed its mores and, at the same time, anyone who is put into a position to exercise this ability assumes and is accorded the same 'academic freedom' which he would claim for his teaching or his research.[36]

Although individual selectors do have considerable freedom studies have found that they all use evidence of past academic performance and indicators of future academic promise as the main criteria on which to base their decisions. Since all selectors are working in the first instance from standard UCCA forms, initial decisions on applicants will be based on the information provided by these forms. Selectors interviewed by the author agreed that 'O' level results, 'A' level predictions and headteachers' opinions of an applicant's potential were the main determining factors. However the weight which individual selectors gave to these various items of information varied considerably. For example the attitude of the selectors interviewed by the author to headteachers' reports varied from, 'If our view of the candidate differed strongly from a head's report we would be inclined to take the view that the school knew him best' to 'Often schools are not as good judges of university candidates as we are, they tend to overrate them.'[37] One selector would 'interview a candidate whose UCCA form looked good apart from a bad head's report' whereas another would 'probably reject a candidate whose head says he is of low quality.'[38]

Whatever the real value of headteachers' reports as evidence of academic promise, it appears that the differing attitudes of individual selectors to these reports introduces an element of arbitrariness into the selection process. Use of interviewing may well increase the influence of personal judgement over the selection of university entrants. In some cases departments use interviews to try and help certain candidates who do not look very strong on paper. One selector explained, 'We do interview in marginal cases in order to try and find something in their favour.[39] Other departments interview all candidates who look good on paper with the main objective of ensuring that these candidates 'really would be an asset to the department'. The freedom individual university lecturers enjoy to include or exclude particular applicants to their departments is a very clear example of the extent to which individual professionals, working within the statutory social services, are able to make important decisions which will determine whether or not individuals gain access to those services.

Apart from illustrating the power which professionals can exercise over clients, or rather potential clients, a study of the objectives which lay behind university selectors' decisions regarding applicants also throws some light on the extent to which welfare professionals give priority to their clients' interests, as opposed to pursuing their own interests. Given the restrictions on numbers in higher education laid down by government policy and the universities, most departments have no choice but to use some sort of criteria to select applicants. However the need for some sort of selection does not explain why university selectors choose the applicants they do out of a large field of formally eligible candidates. It appears that a major objective of some university selectors is to choose those candidates who would prove to be the greatest asset to the course or the department. They rarely seem to consider the issue from the other side by asking which candidates would benefit most from the course they have to offer.

Reid concluded from his study of the selection process in a sample of English university departments in the early 1970s that the basic objectives of university selectors were 'collegiocentric'.[40] In other words, the selectors were mainly concerned to benefit their departments and their colleagues. Interviewers seldom judged applicants by criteria such as whether they could profit from the teaching resources which could be deployed on their behalf: whether they might benefit other than through the acquisition of a degree; whether a candidate's weaknesses are of a kind which could be put right by suitable tuition. This view is supported by comments made by selectors interviewed by the author. One selector openly admitted, 'I try to pick the candidates who will be the easiest to teach. I should hate to inflict a problem student on my colleagues.' Another commented, 'when selecting candidates we think in terms of "what will they contribute to the course".'[41] Some selectors openly aimed to obtain for their departments students who were of higher academic ability than those taken by other universities. One selector explained smugly, 'we just sit back and cream off the top.'[42] Reid concludes his discussion of the admission process by stressing that university selectors are mainly concerned with pleasing or impressing other members of their own departments or to some extent other departments of similar interests; 'Inevitably most decisions are made not in the interests of an external public, or of a professional clientele, but in favour of the perceived interests of the institution.'[43]

In most social services, clients who were deemed officially eligible for a particular benefit but who were not chosen to receive it by those personally allocating it, might well regard their rejection as grossly unfair. University applicants appear to accept as 'fair' a rationing system which favours those with the highest 'A' level grades. Selection based on merit is a well established principle in British education. The emphasis on high 'A' level grades is, however, open to criticism. According to Horrobin, for example, medical schools now select:

Those with the best academic records without for one moment asking whether in doing this they may be cheating not the candidates but the patients who will be treated by these super intelligent doctors. It is at least arguable that medicine might in the long run be better served by deliberately and objectively selecting those with moderate academic records rather than those with the best.[44]

There is certainly little evidence to show that the emphasis of medical schools on academic success as the main criterion for admission is based either on the aim of meeting the educational needs of the individual candidate or on meeting the needs of society for the best possible type of doctors. Horrobin suggests that medical schools select candidates according to their academic grades because, 'they are obsessed with a desire to be fair to the candidates and therefore opt for the only route which offers any hope of any objectivity.'[45]

Any move away from the current emphasis on scholastic attainment in the allocation of university places would probably increase the influence of individual judgement in the selection process. It could also be argued that the present gatekeeping system is the result of allowing consumer choice in higher education. Students who decide to take the most popular subjects at the most prestigious universities pay the highest price in terms of the 'A' level grades required of them. It is difficult to see how an element of consumer choice could be maintained under a restricted entry system which did not vary the 'price' of courses according to their popularity.

Whilst acknowledging certain advantages to applicants of the existing system of rationing of university places, the impression remains that a ubiquitous emphasis on high 'A' level grades is particularly advantageous to academics themselves.

Another criticism of the current selection process is that it takes virtually no account of the statistical relationship between school achievement and social class. According to Perkin, 'It is important to notice that the causes of bias in favour of middle class students do not lie in the university which merely chooses those best qualified to enter.'[46] The idea that university selectors should in any way discriminate in favour of applicants from 'poor' backgrounds, whether in terms of their home environment or the type of school they attended, was greeted with shock by some of the selectors interviewed by the author. One selector retorted, 'that would not happen in a proper academic department such as Physics, what we are *not* interested in is sex [sic], geography or social background.'[47]

The admissions tutor for Law admitted that the selection procedure in that faculty might appear to be biased against working class candidates but added that selectors did not intentionally choose students on social grounds. 'It just happens', he insisted, 'that the 100 best candidates academically are 95 per cent middle and upper class.'[48] Other selectors at this university did explain that in borderline cases they would tend to look favourably on someone with a 'grim' background but out of the six departments studied, only the selectors for Sociology placed considerable emphasis on an applicant's background in all cases. One Sociology selector stated:

> We do exercise a general bias in favour of those from a poorer background. We expect applicants from public schools to have very good 'O' and 'A' level results whereas if a candidate with three C's has been to a rotten comprehensive we will still seriously consider him. After all, if you are going to place an emphasis on examination results, you've got to put them in context.[49]

University selectors have a strong case when they argue that the social class composition of the list of successful applicants is not wholly or even mainly their responsibility. Selection of those who actually apply to university, forms only a minor part of a much longer and perhaps more significant selection process. Most of the relevant age group has already been progressively eliminated by a competitive educational system. It is in this system that most working class children are eliminated from the race to university. The undoubted importance of home background and type of schooling received in determining a child's chances of reaching university, led Perkin to conclude: 'The universities can have little influence, short of distorting their whole selection procedure, on their proportions of middle class and working class students. The same is true of the proportion of students from different regions and of women students.'[50] Not all critics of our educational system would fully agree with this statement. Those wishing radically to restructure our educational system in order to eliminate some of the biases against certain classes and types of children, have argued that one of the main barriers to radical change is the elitist nature of British universities.

The extent to which universities and their academic staff should be held responsible for the continuance of educational inequalities in this country is a highly contentious issue which this book will not attempt to pursue. The conclusion will simply be drawn that individual university lecturers do have a considerable degree of discretion over the selection of entrants to their departments and that the evidence which we have presented suggests that they may be as much, if not more, concerned to benefit themselves and their colleagues as they are to ensure a fair or just selection procedure for all applicants.

Conclusion

In this chapter, we have studied the actions and motives of three groups of professional, social service gatekeepers. At times, all three groups appeared to be more concerned to protect those working behind the gates than to facilitate the entry of those waiting outside. This tendency should not be regarded as peculiar to professionals. All social service staff, indeed staff in all organisations, naturally wish to make their work as congenial as possible and to please their colleagues and superiors. Such self-centred motives may sometimes override any social service provider's commitment to the welfare of his or her clients and potential clients. Prottas claims, for example, that welfare providers routinely exclude abnormal clients from use of their services in order to decrease the average time needed to deal with a client.[51] This strategy, Prottas argues, has the additional advantage of increasing welfare providers' apparent success rate.

Self-centred or protective gatekeeping is likely to be particularly common where demand reaches such high levels that social service staff feel personally threatened or overwhelmed by it. Most professional gatekeepers are probably concerned to be as fair as possible to all those seeking entry to the services they guard. Yet, they would be inhuman if they succeeded in eliminating all personal bias or motives from their activities. Most gatekeepers will at some time turn away someone in genuine need as a consequence of their desire to protect themselves and their colleagues from unnecessary, irrelevant or unpleasant work. The problem for those seeking access to welfare is that fallible professional gatekeepers have so much power to determine who will be 'in' and who will be 'out'. No individual gatekeeper can be expected always to exercise his power wisely or fairly. Herein lies one of the key problems of today's social services. At its best an allocative system based on individual gatekeeping ensures that each client receives personal individualised attention. At its worst, a system of personal gatekeeping is arbitrary and even, in exceptional cases, dangerous. Yet bad gatekeeping has attracted relatively little attention in the social services. Little check is kept on the activities of individual gatekeepers and clients have few means of redress if they are seriously wronged by an unfair or unsound gatekeeping decision. Given the power exercised by professional gatekeepers in the social services, it is surprising and perhaps disturbing that so much of their activity remains a relatively unexamined aspect of welfare rationing.

6

Professional Rationing of Welfare Benefits

Professional welfare providers determine the allocation of welfare benefits in two distinct ways. First, they are able in varying degrees to determine the allocation of their own time and attention. Second, they exercise various forms of control over the allocation of material benefits such as prescribed drugs and medicines, NHS operations, school books and equipment and certain types of financial aid. The freedom of professionals to make their own decisions in response to their clients' needs or demands, lies at the very heart of the concept of professionalism. This professional freedom and power is of key importance to those seeking welfare services. As Titmuss pointed out in 1968, 'In the modern world the professions are increasingly becoming the arbiters of our welfare state: they are the key holders to equality of outcome: they help to determine the pattern of redistribution in social policy.'[1]

Traditionally society has allowed professionals to exercise their power without being subject to any detailed public accountability or scrutiny. Moreover clients have generally placed complete faith in welfare professionals and have not challenged their decisions. The traditional patient, for example, has played a passive role within the NHS gratefully accepting whatever help or attention the doctor has given him. Most consumer surveys reveal a remarkably high level of consumer satisfaction with professionally provided welfare services.[2] Despite this apparently widespread consumer satisfaction with the professions, criticism of professionals has grown apace in recent years. Critics have begun to question the view that society is best served by leaving welfare professionals with as much freedom and power as they now enjoy. Some of their criticisms relate to issues such as the overall planning of welfare services and are, therefore, not directly our concern.[3] A number of criticisms, however, relate directly to the issue of the power of professionals over individuals' access to welfare. Critics have challenged on a number of grounds the claims that professionals ration welfare benefits in an expert or professional way and thus always serve the best interests of their clients. It has been suggested that some professionals allocate their time and attention to suit their own interests rather than those of their clients. Professionals have also been criticised for using subjective judgements rather than objective 'professional' criteria to determine how much help clients should receive.

A final strand of the growing criticism of welfare professionals is that they protect themselves too well against dissatisfied clients. The distribution of power between professional welfare providers and welfare consumers is said to be so skewed that most clients have very little effective redress against professional incompetence or bias.

The allocation of professionals' time and attention

There are two main reasons for treating the allocation of professionals' time and attention as an important issue. First, welfare professionals are relatively well paid. One of the major costs of providing social services in this country is the cost of employing trained welfare personnel. If a professional's time is being wasted or inappropriately allocated a significant amount of money is being misused. The second reason for the importance of the allocation of professionals' time and attention is its impact on individual welfare seekers. For many social service users, the amount of time and attention they receive from a welfare provider will be a key determinant of a successful outcome to their request for help. Patients visit their GP not simply in order to obtain specific treatment for a complaint but also to receive reassurance and advice. Some patients visit their doctor solely in order to be able to tell their troubles to a sympathetic but impartial listener. Similarly, some social work clients appear to be helped simply by having found someone to talk to about their problems. Rees recalls a number of 'successful' cases where clients felt much happier because they had established a relationship with a social worker. He commented that, 'Some sense of relationship with a social worker contrasted with feelings of isolation from other people . . . meetings with each worker [sic] often made people feel better about themselves.'[4] It is very difficult to separate the effect of teachers' time and attention on a child's education from the influence of other educational factors such as peer groups, books and parental interest. Nevertheless it is generally assumed that attention from a skilled teacher plays a key role in the educational process. On what criteria do professionals allocate this important welfare benefit, their own time and attention? And what effects do their decisions have on clients' access to welfare?

Doctors

Doctors, social workers and teachers exercise varying degrees of control over the allocation of their own time and attention. All three professional groups are constrained by a variety of working norms and practices. As the most fully fledged and powerful group, doctors have the most freedom to determine their own working patterns. In general practice five minute consultations are widely regarded as the norm. However individual GPs can and do work faster or slower than average. One doctor who refused to ration his services by operating a strict appointment system admitted that as a consequence he worked at a faster rate than average and that this involved 'taking chances and relying on experience and knack to allow him to cut corners'.[5]

Doctors are not only free to determine the average length of their consultations, they can also vary considerably the amount of time they devote to different types of patients and problems. One GP studying his own consultations found that he spent on average 10.5 minutes on each new consultation for a psychiatric problem compared with only 2.1 minutes on new consultations for eye disorders.[6] In the Manchester study the length of the 160 consultations studied varied from well over 20 minutes to an amazingly short 40 seconds.[7] One might suppose, given that every consultation is an interaction between doctor and patient, that the patient would exercise some control over the length of that consultation. In fact several studies have demonstrated that in virtually all cases it is the doctor who controls both the total length of the consultation and the length of time spent in dealing with a particular aspect of a patient's problems. Byrne and Long found in their study of nearly 2,500 recorded consultations that 75 per cent of what took place was 'doctor caused'.[8] In only 10 per cent of those consultations did the patient appear to initiate their termination and even in those cases there was usually some sort of signal from the doctor, such as the handing over of a prescription, which seemed to cue the patient to bring the consultation to a close. Stimson and Webb confirm that time in the consultation is mainly controlled by the doctor who 'signals when the patients may enter his room and, with less predictability, determines the ending of the consultation.'[9]

Buchan and Richardson have suggested that doctors may spend more time dealing with complaints which they find clinically interesting or amenable to successful treatment, or both.[10] They tentatively concluded, for example, that some of the doctors they studied had more or less given up their attempts to help obese patients lose weight on the grounds that their previous efforts very rarely led to a successful outcome. They also concluded that under the existing conditions of general practice the doctors they studied felt unable or unwilling, despite the availability of flexible appointment systems, to afford much time to the 'common and distressing' conditions of anxiety and depression.

Social workers

Social workers have less control over the allocation of their services than that enjoyed by GPs. Since 1971 social services departments have tended to regulate much of the work undertaken by social workers and increasingly subject them to bureaucratic controls, such as supervision by managers, monitoring and record keeping. These controls are intended to standardise their response to individual need.[11] Social workers are also constrained by legislation. Most social workers regard statutory social work, such as compulsory supervision of delinquents, as their first priority and they see it as allowing little freedom of action. Stevenson and Parsloe found that social workers dealing with families with children at risk of non-accidental injury were often requested by their superiors to visit weekly or more often over a considerable period.[12]

Individual social workers are also sometimes constrained by informal decisions on caseload management made by the social work team as a whole or by the team leader. Stevenson and Parsloe found that although most social workers in their study were free to determine their own priorities, a sizeable number discussed such decisions with their team leader.[13] Despite all these constraints and increasing attempts by management to allocate personal social services in a more uniform and planned way, individual local authority social workers still possess a great deal of 'de facto' autonomy, partly because much that they do is not easily open to scrutiny. Stevenson and Parsloe found that apart from some statutory duties, most social workers felt able to allocate their time and skill according to their own assessment of their individual caseloads.[14] Social workers explained to them how they decided whom to visit most frequently. These explanations varied widely. One social worker commented: 'Visiting is often determined for you really by the way clients respond when you see them.' Another stated, 'Children obviously take first priority and after that you work it out for yourself and you think well I wonder which one needs me most?.' A third social worker suggested that her ordering of priorities was more or less subconscious. 'Priority with me is not a conscious thing . . . it just happens, you get involved with a particular situation . . . and you get a series of these situations and so you find yourself visiting maybe half a dozen clients regularly and the rest seem to get pushed aside for a time anyway, and it is not really a conscious thing at all.'[15]

Teachers

Teachers have less control over the allocation of their own time than either doctors or social workers. Most teachers are told how many hours a week they will teach and are also allocated groups of pupils to be taught. Nevertheless once teachers have shut the classroom door behind them they do enjoy considerable freedom to determine the nature of their work and to allocate their time and attention between individual members of their class. The increasing prevalence of mixed ability teaching in schools, which often calls for individualised learning programmes, has probably increased the time which teachers spend with individual pupils as opposed to teaching a class as a whole. Teachers no doubt believe that as professionals they allocate their time and attention solely according to the needs of their individual pupils regardless of other factors such as their social class or sex. Several research studies, however, have suggested that this is not the case. A longitudinal study of one teacher's interaction with her class in an American urban ghetto school found that the teacher allocated the majority of her attention to a group of children whom she perceived to be 'fast learners'. Those whom she judged to be 'slow learners' were taught infrequently. The researcher observed that this teacher's selection of potential fast learners for special attention was based primarily on factors related to the children's home background. Those from 'better' homes were consistently favoured by the teacher. She placed them closer to her and regularly called on one of them to perform a variety of tasks such as reading the weather calendar, leading the class in the pledge of allegiance and taking messages to the office.[16] The hypothesis that teachers do not divide their time and attention equally between all their pupils but favour those whom they regard as more able is supported by Good's study of data on teacher-pupil interaction in the classroom. Good concluded:

> Much research evidence suggests that the wheel of opportunity does not operate randomly in the classroom. Teachers treat pupils differently. Pupils do not get equal classroom opportunities, nor do they get equal amounts of praise from the teacher. Teachers consistently gave high achievers significantly more chances to speak in the classroom than low achievers.[17]

Effects of professionals' rationing of their own time and attention

The esoteric nature of the benefits conferred on welfare clients by the skills and attention of welfare professionals makes it extremely difficult to judge accurately the effect of the individual allocation of these benefits. Take, for example, the criticism that doctors devote too little time to patients with psycho/social problems including depression and anxiety. Critics should ask themselves how effective GPs would be if they did spend a great deal more time dealing with such problems. As one GP has pointed out, doctors can do very little by purely medical means to change intractable social problems. They cannot 'clear slums, provide supportive communities for the isolated or work for the unemployed'.[18] It may be rational and indeed desirable for welfare professionals not to waste their time on intractable or untreatable cases. On the other hand, if doctors spend most time with patients whose problems appear to them to be interesting, important, or treatable, some patients may get little satisfaction from their visit to the doctor. Many patients go to see their doctor about complaints or problems which are not at all serious in the medical sense but which, nevertheless, cause the patient anxiety or distress. The Manchester study found that although there were few overt complaints from patients about the overall length of consultation, some patients were unhappy about their doctor's dismissal of their symptoms. One patient, for example, was very worried about an 'unbearable' pain in his head. After the consultation he still wanted to know what was causing the pain but explained that he had not pressed the doctor for an explanation because the doctor had 'dismissed it as nothing' and 'had not shown any interest in it'.[19]

We do not know the extent to which patients in general suffer fears or worries about complaints which their doctors dismiss as unworthy of attention. We do know that in Cartwright and Anderson's major study of patients and their doctors, 25 per cent of patients stated that their doctor did not explain things to them fully enough and that by 1977 the proportion of patients who felt critical about their doctor for not listening or explaining or taking time had increased markedly.[20] Cartwright suggested that some doctors failed to give their patients adequate information because they were pressed for time, and one doctor has commented that given the short time allowed for an average consultation, 'it is hardly surprising that doctors often cut short their consultations with a prescription. The alternative would be to risk spending twenty minutes explaining to the patient why no treatment was necessary.'[21] Many patients in the Manchester study also excused their doctor for not giving them enough information on the grounds that, 'He is a very busy man.'[22] Nevertheless we should be wary of assuming that doctors just do not have the time to give their patients full explanations. There is some evidence that doctors actually prefer short consultations.[23] Some may also, quite naturally, dislike having to explain repeatedly the benign course of most common complaints. Many GPs do work hard but they can still choose, if they wish, to devote a few extra minutes to each patient to ensure that their fears and worries have been allayed. Most patients, on the other hand, do not appear to have either the confidence or the skill to elicit the information they require from their doctor. They are, therefore, dependent on the medical profession to give them that information unprompted. Until all patients possess much greater medical knowledge they will continue to turn to their doctor to reassure them and inform them about their ill health. Although doctors may gain little satisfaction from dealing with minor self-limiting complaints they might be less bothered with them and thus be able to spend more time with serious and more interesting cases if they were to spend more time explaining the nature of such minor complaints to their patients. Some GPs have found that they can actually reduce overall demand for their services by spending more time educating their patients on the inappropriateness of consulting over very minor complaints. This is one strategy to reduce demand which could perhaps benefit both doctors and patients.

If it is difficult to judge the exact effects of doctors' individual rationing of their own time and attention, it is probably even more difficult to evaluate the effects of social workers' interaction with their clients. However moves by some social work teams to introduce standardised controls over casework have led social workers themselves to compare standardised methods of allocating their time and attention with individual rationing methods. It has been suggested that if individual social workers are left completely free to determine their own priorities there is a danger that informal, almost unconscious, rationing devices will develop in a personal *ad hoc* way to the detriment of overall planning equity and efficiency and perhaps to the disadvantage of those clients whom social workers find least rewarding. Stevenson and Parsloe concluded from their research, which found most social workers making individual rationing decisions, that, 'On the whole, it seemed that in the face of increasing demands and in the absence of a structure or formula, rational or sensible decisions were not always made to ensure that each of the many and varied claims of a caseload received the appropriate measures of priority.'[24] Glastonbury and Cooper suggest that formalised allocation procedures could ensure that the right clients would get the maximum service provided that the correct criteria were used to establish priority.[25] Such formal allocation procedures, however, clash with professional social work values which stress the uniqueness of individual clients and the importance of assessing clients' needs on an individual basis informed by professional knowledge and skills.

Brewer and Lait suggest that professional social work values may be based more on social workers' own interests than on ensuring the most effective service for each individual client. They criticise social workers' apparent attachment to psychotherapeutic casework on the grounds that:

> Choosing a particular treatment merely because one enjoys doing it is surely a rather strange approach to securing maximum effectiveness, and we would suggest that it is an inherently unprofessional approach. If the concept of professional integrity means anything at all, it surely means that the interests of the client should generally take precedence over the interests of the practitioner. It certainly seems that social workers not only favour psychotherapy as opposed to other and possibly more mundane and unexciting aspects of their work, but also favour methods of psychotherapy which do not give the best chance of success.[26]

Naturally most social workers have rejected Brewer and Lait's attack upon their professional integrity as ill-informed and unjustified. Social workers have yet to prove, however, that their preferred forms of intervention are also the most effective and beneficial to their clients.

Those who have carried out research into teachers' allocation of their time and attention in the classroom have criticised teachers, either implicitly or explicitly, for restricting the educational opportunities of some of their pupils. Good, for example, suggested that teachers who encouraged high achievers to answer their questions separated 'low achievers from classroom life and militated against their educational progress.'[27] It may be inevitable and perhaps even desirable that teachers concerned to 'give a good lesson' will interact most frequently with those pupils who are thought most likely to give right, helpful or at least interesting answers to their questions. Nevertheless teachers who allocate their time and attention in ways which favour 'good' pupils may play a part in perpetuating social class or racial inequalities within the school system.

Our present limited knowledge of the effectiveness of professional welfare providers' interventions does not allow us to draw any firm conclusions about the objective effects on clients of the informal individual rationing of professionals' time and attention. GPs and social workers both frequently complain that they are over worked and pressed for time. No doubt professional welfare pro-

viders could spend more time with their clients if they were prepared to work much longer hours. But should society expect welfare
professionals, well paid as they are, to work significantly longer
hours than other workers?

Some professional welfare providers may give more time and
attention to those clients whom they find most rewarding or
interesting. According to Prottas professionals working in public
welfare organisations single out for special attention 'clients who
represent a professional opportunity' in order to enhance their 'self-
image as professionals (as opposed to the inferior image of a
bureaucrat).' 'In addition', Prottas argues, 'success in a professional
case confers more status than does the rapid processing of routine
bureaucratic cases. It is therefore natural that, when time permits,
street level bureaucrats should reward clients who provide such
opportunities. So clients who want psychological counselling
receive a better reception from welfare workers than those seeking
refrigerators.'[28]

Not only is it natural for welfare professionals to favour those
clients who give them most satisfaction, but it may also be more cost
effective for them to devote most time to those type of cases with
which they have most success. Whether all clients share professionals' definition of success however is debatable. Certainly clients who
feel disadvantaged by welfare professionals' allocation of their own
time and attention have virtually no power to counteract or challenge this informal type of welfare rationing.

Professional rationing of material benefits

Professional welfare providers may regard themselves as providing
a highly skilled personal service but to some of their clients they will
appear to be primarily controllers of material benefits. Some
patients do not want any advice or attention from their general
practitioner. They consult a doctor solely in order to gain access to a
particular drug or medicine which can only be obtained through a
doctor's prescription. Some social work clients' sole aim may be to
get financial help. They may resent any attempt by social workers to
turn a request for financial assistance into a 'need' for professional
counselling and support. In this section, we will examine the role
which professional welfare providers play in the distribution of

welfare benefits. But first we need to distinguish between the different contexts in which the professional rationing of such benefits takes place. Some benefits are in such short supply that individual welfare professionals must select only a few from a large pool of potential beneficiaries. Selection of patients for kidney transplants is a dramatic example of this type of rationing. On the other hand, some benefits are, for all practical purposes, unlimited, and professionals are free to allocate them to all those whom they judge to be in genuine need. Most prescribed drugs and medicines fall into this category. Another distinction to be made between different contexts of rationing is between those professionals who face very few hierarchical or managerial constraints and those who are subject to much tighter bureaucratic controls. General practitioners have a virtually unlimited budget for prescribed drugs and medicines and face only very weak attempts by the NHS hierarchy to exercise any control over their prescribing habits. On the other hand, individual basic grade social workers working in local authority social services departments very rarely exercise complete control over the allocation of welfare benefits to their clients. In many social services departments 'benefits' such as residential accommodation, holidays for the handicapped and home helps are allocated centrally. Individual social workers may exert considerable influence over such allocation systems and may attempt to use their professional status in order to gain priority for their own clients, but this form of individual power is not as great as the power exercised by individual doctors over the allocation of medical resources.

Haemodialysis and kidney transplants

One of the most dramatic examples of rationing in the welfare services is the selection of patients for haemodialysis or for kidney transplants. Those selected for treatment are at least given the chance to live, whereas those rejected will most probably die. In Britain, society has left the selection process entirely in the hands of the medical profession. There is very little evidence about the factors which determine consultants' decisions in this particular area. One small study of eight clinicians in one renal dialysis unit in the mid-1970s, asked the doctors to classify the suitability of 100 cases, some real, some simulated, for regular haemodialysis.[29]

Seven categories were used ranging from 'excellent prospect: accept without reservation' to 'unequivocal rejection'. The doctors placed the cases into these categories by using 18 items of information provided for each case including medical factors such as renal lesion, cardiovascular function and other diseases not related to renal functions; medical/social factors, such as age and psychiatric background; and social factors such as employment prospects, number of children and annual income. The study found that only six cases were placed in the same category by all eight clinicians and that was the 'unequivocal rejection' category. The clinicians clearly differed in the extent to which they made effective use of the 18 items of information. Age, psychiatric background, cardiovascular function and other disease were all widely used. Only some of the eight clinicians made regular use of social factors such as employment prospects and number of children. This study was based on a hypothetical situation and cannot be taken as clear evidence of how doctors take such decisions in real life. Nevertheless the researchers concluded that the study suggested real differences in the selection criteria used by different doctors. They advocated that, given such differences, it would be desirable when selecting patients for haemodialysis to collect independent judgements from several doctors and other members of the unit team before deciding the fate of an individual patient. This method of selection would at least ensure some consistency in classification from one occasion to the next.

Taylor *et al.* did not comment on the desirability of including social criteria in the selection process. This issue appears to have attracted far more attention in the United States than in Britain. There, studies have revealed that some renal treatment centres have operated a two-stage selection procedure for life saving treatment. At stage one patients were selected for treatment on purely medical grounds including perhaps their psychological suitability for long term difficult treatment. At stage two remaining patients were selected or rejected primarily on social grounds. In one centre in Seattle, Washington a lay committee comprising a clergyman, a housewife, a banker, a labour leader and two doctors was appointed during the late 1960s to select patients for treatment according to socio–economic criteria.[30] Other factors being equal, this committee chose patients with dependents. It also favoured those who were deemed to be stable and emotionally mature. Finally, it favoured those with a record of public service, such as service as a scout leader, a Sunday school teacher or a Red Cross volunteer.

NHS abortions

In contrast to the severe shortage of kidney transplants, abortions can now be regarded as a form of medical intervention which, in theory at least, can be provided to all who demand it. In practice, women's access to free abortions under the 1967 Abortion Act has been controlled by the decision taken by individual GPs and consultants. In 1970, 12 per cent of 600 GPs replying to a questionnaire on birth control services, reported having a conscientious objection to termination of pregnancy in virtually all cases. Religion was found to be the most important factor influencing the doctors' attitudes towards abortion.[31] According to Oldershaw patients who sought an abortion through their GP in the 1970s ran the risk of finding that the clinical decision required by the Abortion Act had been replaced by a completely negative attitude towards abortion on the part of the doctor.[32] Such a negative attitude would result in their not being referred to a consultant for an NHS abortion. Nor were GPs the only 'hurdle' which NHS patients had to overcome before obtaining an abortion. The GPs surveyed by Cartwright and Waite estimated that one third of their referrals to consultants requesting an abortion under the 1967 Act were refused.[33] One quarter of the GPs reported that they had, on some occasion, been deterred from referring a patient for an NHS abortion by the difficulties of arranging it.

In the early 1970s, figures from different hospital regions on numbers of abortions performed showed wide regional variations. In 1973, a woman with an unwanted pregnancy living in Newcastle had an almost 4 times greater chance of obtaining a NHS abortion than a woman living in Birmingham. These regional differences appeared to be due to the influence of individual consultants whose attitudes to abortion ranged from being totally against on any grounds to being in favour of abortions 'on demand'. The influence which one senior consultant can exercise over the availability of abortions in a particular area of the country is illustrated by the evidence given by Dr McLaren to the select committee on abortion. Dr McLaren, a leading gynaecologist in Birmingham, stated:

If he (a student) has any conscience at all in the matter, he comes to Birmingham [medical school]. There's a market and my Unit is full of Roman Catholics, Irish and conscientious Jews – why not? They are not fools, they are professionals. If they go to a hospital where they have to do abortions they are scarcely worthy of training.[34]

Section 1 payments

Since the passing of the Children and Young Persons Act (1963) social services departments have been empowered to give financial or material aid to families in order to prevent children being taken into care or being brought before a juvenile court. In 1965–6, only £266,600 was allocated under the terms of this section, but by 1976–7 the figure had grown to £4.3 million. Researchers have found that basic grade social workers very rarely have the authority to give a client financial aid without the approval of a superior. In some social services departments senior management staff keep a very close control over the amount of money allocated through 'Section 1' payments. Other managements are much more generous or flexible about such payments with the result that wide variations occur between areas in the number and size of payments made and in the criteria and procedures used to provide a fixed budget each year for such payments. In some areas payments are regularly made to help clients with fuel debts, whereas in other places such grants are very rare.[35] Hill and Laing suggest that the lack of any national guidelines on the criteria for giving financial aid to social work clients leads to 'territorial injustice'. Inconsistencies in the number and size of financial payments given to clients do not occur solely at the area level. Hill and Laing noted from their interviews with social workers that wide variations in the use of Section 1 payments also occurred within area teams.[36] Such variations were due to the freedom which individual social workers exercised over the allocation of financial benefits to their clients. Although social service hierarchies usually closely controlled the allocation of financial payments, this control was essentially negative. Management sometimes prevented social workers making payments which the workers themselves felt were justified. However management did not act to force social workers to make grants which they felt were inappropriate. The decision to refuse an initial request for financial help from a client was usually taken solely by a basic grade social worker. Moreover Hill suggested that:

> In many cases considation of the possibility of a money pay-ment will be upon the social worker's initiative, without a direct request from a client. There are likely to be wide variations in the extent to which social workers translate the presentation of material problems by clients into 'applications' for money payment.[37]

One social worker explained to the researchers:

> I hate having to be faced with the choice of giving money to some-one. Since I came here I haven't given money to anybody, which you know frightens me. Maybe my attitude is affecting what normally social workers would be giving out . . . but I always look at it as a last resort. I feel it's much better if you can find another way round it.[38]

In this instance it appears as though some clients were not getting money they might have otherwise received simply because their social worker disliked handling it.

Buckle claims that individual social workers are often, 'perhaps unwittingly drawn into using such differentiation as "deserving" and "undeserving" in deciding whom to help with financial payments.'[39] She argues that in cases of debt, for example, 'A more "deserving" case is more likely to be viewed favourably and hence financial help is more likely to be forthcoming than where no apparent cause for the debt can be found.' Finally, Buckle claims that the extent to which clients are prepared to go to press their case will also influ-ence the social worker's decision. A family that does not protest when told by their social worker that they cannot have any financial help is less likely to receive help, according to Buckle, than parents who threaten to abandon their children if no help is forthcoming.[40] Other writers have suggested that social workers use their power over the distribution of financial aid as a form of social control. Handler's study of the work of three London children's depart-ments suggested that the chief method employed by social workers to control their client's behaviour was to use their power to dispense financial and material rewards in order to get families to adopt standards which were seen as being more socially acceptable.[41] Jordan has claimed that 'the power to give poor relief becomes quite evidently the most important weapon of authority in the social worker's armoury.'[42] However this claim has since been challenged by Hill and Laing who have pointed out that social workers dealing with families have the power to remove children from their parents and the threat to use this power can be a much greater weapon of coercion.[43]

In brief, the evidence on the allocation of financial aid to social work clients suggests that despite bureaucratic controls, whether a family in financial difficulty receives financial help from a social services department depends primarily, once contact with a social worker has been made, on the decisions made by that social worker. That decision, in turn, appears to be influenced by a variety of factors including whether the social worker thinks the family deserves to be helped; whether she believes that the family's behaviour might be improved by the offer of financial help; whether she feels 'happy' about handling financial payments; and last (and some critics of social worker's professional pretensions would say least) whether the exercise of her professional judgement leads the social worker to decide that her client's needs can best be met through financial assistance.

Concern over professional rationing

Any system of rationing which is based on individual judgements rather than rigid rules and regulations, is bound to result in individual differences in decisions taken and benefits allocated. In theory the long training of professionals is designed to ensure that they base their decision making on the skills and expertise which they have in common with their colleagues. If this ideal worked in practice professionals' decisions on the allocation of welfare benefits would be based primarily on their skilled judgements of clients' needs and we would expect similarly trained professionals to make similar decisions in like cases. We would predict, for example, that two doctors would reach similar conclusions on the treatment needed by a patient suffering from acute appendicitis or any other straightforward medical complaint. In fact, even purely medical decisions are the result of a variety of influences on individual doctors and their professional training and skill play only one part in determining the treatment of a particular patient. Since social workers' skills and knowledge are even less 'scientific' than those acquired by doctors, we would expect even less consensus from social workers about the optimum allocation of benefits in any particular case. Although this lack of professional consensus has caused some concern amongst critics, on the whole it is widely accepted that individual judgements based on professional skill and judgement will not and cannot be completely standardised.

What worries many critics far more than the lack of a completely objective or standard professional assessment of individuals' needs for particular welfare benefits, is evidence that professionals sometimes base their allocative decisions on criteria which are not in any sense 'professional'. The fact that some doctors base their selection of patients for scarce 'life saving' treatment on partly social or economic criteria has aroused considerable concern. Given the severe shortage of certain types of medical treatment in relation to the need for them, very difficult decisions do have to be made. Society may wish to sweep this type of decision making under the carpet and continue to allow the rationing of scarce life saving treatment to take place at an informal, individual and sometimes covert level. It should not be assumed, however, that leaving such decisions to individual doctors somehow removes the serious ethical problems which are involved. Sanders and Dukeminier believe that selection of patients for 'life-saving' treatment by *ad hoc* comparisons of their social worth is objectionable even if such comparisons are made by trained medical personnel. 'Medical men', they argue, 'are no more qualified to play God, to look at two persons and say one is worth more than the other, than ordinary mortals.'[44] A similar argument can be made in relation to individual doctors' control over access by patients to free abortions. It may be convenient for society to leave the very difficult ethical and moral problems involved in abortion to the consciences of individual doctors, but this does not necessarily make it right to do so.

The issue of whether or not professionals should act primarily as agents of social control in allocating welfare benefits is an extremely complex one. In the late 1960s and early 1970s, it became fashionable for left-wing critics of welfare professionals to accuse them of being agents of social control. Social workers in particular were frequently portrayed as agents of a capitalist state which was intent on suppressing rather than helping the poor and powerless. However it can be argued that while some forms of social control appear to be harsh and denying it is in clients' long term interests to conform to the norms of behaviour expected of them by the society in which they live.[45] Moreover social workers and other welfare providers who allocate benefits to those whom they judge to be most deserving may well be allocating benefits according to a principle which many people in society would applaud. On the other hand, it is open to doubt whether welfare professionals are appropriately trained or qualified to judge clients according to their merit rather than their needs. There is certainly a danger that the allocation of benefits by individual professionals according to their judgements of clients' deserts will result in prejudiced or arbitrary decision making and denial of help to clients in need.

The final concern expressed over professional rationing is that clients have so few clear cut rights in relation to professionally provided welfare services. The stark contrast between the rights to benefit enjoyed by social security claimants and the total lack of rights of social work clients has been singled out for criticism by Jordan. He suggests that clients themselves are, 'all too aware of the diminution of their rights under provisions from "the welfare". They experience the need to request help from social workers as like asking for charity. What social workers consider to be flexibility they see as partiality.'[46] Social workers' powers to make payments are totally discretionary. Dissatisfied clients have no right to a second opinion or an appeal and cannot therefore effectively challenge the decision made by a social worker. NHS patients have no right to a specific type of treatment. A woman denied a NHS abortion by a consultant who has a conscientious objection to all abortions has no right of appeal against the decision. Her only option – if she can afford it – is to turn to the private market where abortions 'on demand' are readily available.

Conclusion

Denegrating the professions and professionals is now very fashionable in certain intellectual and radical circles. The leading exponent of the art, Ivan Illich, has revived belief in Shaw's contention that the professions are 'a conspiracy against the laity'. Illich and his followers have propogated the view that professionalism is a threat to society.[47] According to these extreme critics of welfare professionals, all social services including education, health care and social work should be 'de-professionalised'. Despite a growing awareness of the Illichian attack on the professions, most people still hold the view that, as experts in their particular field, professionals should be left free to respond individually to clients' welfare needs. Calls for removing some professional powers have concentrated on professionals' influence over the setting of overall priorities with the social services. There have been far fewer calls to remove individual professionals' power and freedom over the allocation of benefits and services to their own clients.[48]

It clearly makes sense to allow individual experts to respond flexibly to complex and uniquely individual welfare needs. It would be virtually impossible to provide appropriate sensitive services to such groups as the chronically sick, the mentally ill, problem families and slow learners if all welfare resources were to be allocated according to rigid rules and regulations. On the other hand, it would be foolish to assume that tighter controls over professional rationing would inevitably by impractical and/or undesirable. Where individual professionals base their own allocation decisions on personal preferences or values rather than professional expertise, they lay themselves open to the charge of behaving unprofessionally.

If society did impose tighter controls over individual professional rationing, such a change would not necessarily guarantee that a greater emphasis would be placed on the meeting of individuals' welfare needs. First, tighter controls could mean that less rather than more individuals would gain access to certain services or benefits. For example, any tightening up of the statutory regulations governing the grounds on which doctors are allowed to perform abortions might well reduce or even eliminate abortions performed solely for social reasons. Second, formal rule-bound systems of rationing can just as easily be used to impose social control on certain groups of clients as can a rationing system based on individual professional decision making. The rules governing the allocation of social security benefits make a number of distinctions between deserving and undeserving claimants which significantly affect individuals' access to help, and are clearly intended to act as a form of social control.

The main advantage of rationing by rules or regulations is that such systems usually ensure some degree of uniformity of response to similar needs. In other words, rule-based systems are most likely to fulfil the objective of distributing benefits according to principles of proportional justice. However even if the substitution of statutory rules for discretionary decision making could be implemented against the wishes of powerful professional groups, any benefits to clients produced by a more bureaucratic system of welfare rationing might well be outweighed by the loss of the sensitivity and skill exercised by good professionals in response to complex individual needs. On balance, therefore, it would seem unwise and premature to advocate any wholesale move towards the bureaucratisation of professional welfare rationing. What other reforms have been suggested to protect clients from the worst effects of professional power over the allocation of benefits and services?

According to Wilding,[49] professionals and their clients should be persuaded to form a much more equal partnership in relation to the delivery of welfare services. Of course there will always be some situations, particularly where important welfare benefits are in very scarce supply, where rationing must be imposed from above on individual clients. On the other hand it would be feasible for clients to play a much more active role in determining the distribution of a range of welfare benefits. If, for example, patients could be persuaded to take a much more active role in consultations they could begin to exert at least some control over the length and nature of their contacts with doctors. Similarly, social work clients could be more actively involved in determining the nature of their relationship with social workers. There would undoubtedly be considerable practical difficulties in securing a greater say for individual clients in the delivery of social services. In particular, it would be difficult to persuade professionals to give up some of their power in order to create a less unequal relationship with their clients. Nevertheless there are encouraging signs. Some better educated clients are already demanding a more active role as welfare clients, whilst a few radical professionals have voluntarily changed the nature of the relationship with their clients to make it less unequal.

At present, society does very little to sanction those professionals who misuse or abuse their powers. Even fellow professionals rarely attempt to sanction those colleagues whom they know to be providing an inadequate – or worse – service. In recent years the professions themselves have begun to discuss ways of regulating their own standards. In the medical profession, for example, the idea of medical audit is gaining some ground. Given the power of the professions, this may be a move which should receive strong support and encouragement from all those concerned about the abuse of professional powers. Wilding suggests that as well as supporting the expansion of professional self-audit in all the professions, those concerned with the imbalance of power between the professions and their clients should also try to persuade political and managerial bodies to exert more authority over professionals. He argues that, 'Management can and should press the professions to a self consciousness about the implications and impact of the decisions they make. It can confront them with a profile of how they use their time, the decisions they make, the resources they use and comparisons with the work of their colleagues and with national norms.'[50]

A final suggestion for controlling rationing by professionals is that better systems of redress should be established for the dissatisfied or aggrieved client. One way of strengthening the rights of clients in relation to professionals' discretionary decision making would be to make greater use of the legal system to redress wrongs imposed on clients by professional welfare providers. However, the American experience of mounting law suits against doctors and the cost of such litigation to all concerned (except lawyers) suggests that legal remedies against poor professional decision making should be used only as a last resort. Negligence litigation does not ensure that proper professional standards are generally maintained, nor does it discipline bad professionals.[51] Kennedy proposes that, 'A wholly separate method of supervision and sanction must be created, with power of suspension or removal from practice for those found to be incompetent. The impetus will have to come from the consumer, and the consumer will have to be prominently represented on any Board or Committee which is set up.'[52] At present there are few signs of a widespread consumer movement to reduce professional power.

Any attempt to change the degree of professional power within the social services will meet strong resistance. According to Prottas:

In professionalized and semi-professionalized organisations the street-level bureaucrats' response to close supervision may well be so negative and their resentment so strong that the hierarchy is constrained to proceed slowly, if at all, with any attempts to

extend the purview of their oversight . . . considering the importance of the street-level bureaucrat to the organisation and the
range of tools available to them, any action that makes them
resist as a group is likely to be unprofitable unless the specific
issue involved is of great moment.[53]

It remains to be seen whether the disadvantages of uncontrolled
professional decision making within the social services will ever be
seen as an issue momentous enough to warrant action to curb the
power of professionals in the welfare field.

7
The Right to Social Security Benefits

Britain's social security system, whilst still based on the Beveridge blueprint of 1942, has evolved over the years into a highly complex and confusing conglomeration of financial benefits. For purposes of analysis we can identify three distinct types of social security benefits each of which is allocated according to significantly different principles. National insurance benefits such as unemployment benefit, sickness benefit and retirement pensions are given only to those who have made the requisite contributions to the national insurance scheme, Non-contributory benefits, including child benefit and a range of benefits for the uninsured disabled, are allocated to all those deemed to fall into a particular category of need or responsibility, regardless of either their income or their contributions record. Finally, supplementary benefits and a range of other benefits including family income supplement and rent and rate rebates are allocated only to those who are judged both to be in need and to have the requisite low income as measured by a means test. This chapter will examine the processes by which these three types of social security benefits are allocated to individual claimants. The examination will reveal a number of key issues in relation to claimants' access to financial benefits. These issues include the nature of a citizen's right to different types of social security benefits; the extent of the diminution of such rights in practice; the role of individual non-professional social security staff in determining claimants' access to benefits and finally the conflict between the objective of distributing social security benefits in order to secure proportional justice and the aim of meeting the unique needs of highly vulnerable individuals.

The right to national insurance benefits

The national insurance scheme is firmly based on the principle that individuals earn a right to benefit through their own contributions. This right has always been legally protected. The statutory rules governing eligibility for national insurance benefits have always been publicly specified in detail. Dissatisfied claimants have had the right to appeal to a tribunal whose decisions have the force of law and have thus established legal precedents. A contributor's right to national insurance benefits has traditionally been held in high regard. In 1942 Beveridge argued that the British people wanted a national insurance scheme because they desired 'benefit in return for contributions, rather than allowances from the state.'[1] Titmuss made a similar point whilst writing about superannuation. He argued that, 'people do not want to be given rights to pensions, but . . . want to earn them by their contributions.'[2] It has also been believed that contributions form a much stronger claim to benefit than any other criterion such as citizenship. Beveridge, for example, argued that 'payment of a substantial cost of benefit as a contributor' provided a firm basis for a claim to benefit.[3]

Despite a traditional emphasis on the strength of a contributor's right to national insurance benefits, this right is both limited in principle and even more circumscribed in practice. One of the main drawbacks of any insurance system is that certain people can never accumulate rights to benefits. Beveridge himself was fully aware of this problem. He acknowledged that 'However comprehensive an insurance scheme, some, through physical infirmity can never contribute at all and some will fall through the meshes of any insurance.'[4] All insurance schemes, whether private or public, voluntary or compulsory, are based on a principle which inevitably excludes certain categories of people from benefit. As Abel-Smith has pointed out in relation to health care insurance:

> There is a limit to the extent to which the principle of social insurance can be adapted to meet social needs and still remain credible as an insurance scheme, as something different from an earmarked tax to finance a public service. If some categories are not excluded from the rights purchased by paying the insurance contributions it ceases to be insurance in any normal sense of the term.[5]

Those excluded from this country's national insurance scheme because of their poor or non-existent contribution record include some of the poorest, weakest and most vulnerable members of society. The severely disabled and chronically sick, one parent families (other than widows) and school leavers, are usually completely excluded from the national insurance scheme because of their poor or non-existent contribution record. Other claimants, including many unemployed men and women, receive only partial help from the insurance scheme because of the inadequacy of their contributions.

The limitations imposed on the national insurance scheme by its emphasis on individuals' contribution records are not the only factors which restrict rights to benefits. The unemployed in particular do not enjoy an unconditional right to insurance benefit, however adequate their contribution record. In practice, the right to unemployment benefit has always been limited in duration despite Beveridge's view that it should be given as of right for as long as a person was unemployed. After one year's unemployment, claimants must transfer from the insurance scheme to the means-tested supplementary benefits scheme. From the perspective of the individual claimant, such a transfer, involving as it does a detailed means test which is 'widely felt to be intrusive and irksome'[6], may be seen as a punitive denial of the right to receive unstigmatised, adequate support from the state throughout any period of unemployment.

The combined effect of inadequate contribution records and the one year limitation on unemployment benefit meant that by the end of 1980 half of unemployed claimants were not receiving any unemployment benefit, more than a third of the unemployed were totally dependent on supplementary benefit and just over 15 per cent were not receiving any sort of benefit at all. In May 1980 of those unemployed not receiving unemployment benefit, 47.7 per cent were not entitled to benefit because they had exhausted their one year's entitlement and 28.6 per cent had a deficiency in their national insurance contributions record.[7]

A second major condition attached to the claiming of unemployment benefit is that those judged to be responsible for their own unemployment can be disqualified from benefit. Unemployment benefit can be withheld for a period of up to six weeks if a worker is judged to have left his last job voluntarily or to have been sacked for industrial misconduct. Industrial misconduct includes absenteeism or lateness at work as well as dishonesty or negligence. Unemployment benefit is automatically withheld from all strikers but, in addition, a worker who is laid off because of a strike will only receive unemployment benefit if he can prove that he has no direct interest in the trades dispute. Kincaid describes how the National Insurance Commissioner has frequently interpreted these rules in a broad way which disqualifies many borderline cases from benefit. According to Kincaid the national insurance scheme has been 'adjusted to back up the disciplines exercised by the employers and by the labour market.'[8] He argues, 'it is surely wrong to use social security rights as part of the armoury of sanctions and penalties which keeps people at work or prevents them from improving their position. The right to benefit should depend on need and not be greater or lesser depending on the cause of unemployment'.[9] Kincaid claims that the restrictions on the right to unemployment benefit in effect give officials operating the scheme the arbitrary power to disqualify the unemployed from benefit. Leaving aside Kincaid's political arguments, it is difficult to refute his case that the right to unemployment benefit is weakened by the actual process by which an individual's eligibility for benefit is assessed.

A final practical limitation on contributors' rights to national insurance benefits is that unlike privately insured claimants, their contributions do not secure them a right to a particular level of benefit. In 1975 Barbara Castle, then Secretary of State for the Social Services, acknowledged in the House of Commons that the national insurance system had never provided insurance in the commercial sense, but she went on to argue that:

> There has been an enduring feeling in this country, particularly among the trade unions, that there is a kind of guarantee about a contributory system – a guarantee that would not obtain in the same way if the scheme were financed entirely out of taxation. It gives some assurance that Governments will not use the lack of a contributory principle as an excuse to economise in the important matter of pensions.[10]

The phasing out of the earnings-related supplement and a real cut in the value of basic rate unemployment, sickness and maternity benefits in 1980 effectively destroyed the argument that the contributory principle protects the real value of insurance benefits.

In 1980 the severe limitations of the national insurance scheme were summed up by Metcalf:

> Its coverage is poor and getting worse; it is neither particularly redistributive nor does it provide adequate income maintenance, it is forcing people to rely on means-tested supplementary benefits; it does not protect beneficiaries from attacks on their benefits and its existence makes it more difficult to help groups like the disabled and one-parent families who fall outside the insurance net.[11]

Yet despite all these weaknesses of the scheme it remains, in the eyes of most people in Britain, the one part of the social security system in which those eligible to claim benefit have a real right to it. In order to understand this relative popularity of insurance based benefits we must examine the nature of claimants' rights to the other types of social security benefits.

The right to non-contributory benefits

Eligibility for a group of social security benefits known collectively as non-contributory benefits is basically determined by some form of needs test rather than a means test or by reference to an individual's contributions records. Welfare rights campaigners frequently argue that all social security benefits should be distributed as of right solely on the basis of claimants' needs. Non-contributory child benefit is often cited as a good example of the advantages which flow from the allocation of benefits according to needs or responsibilities rather than means or merit. This benefit is available to anyone (usually the mother) responsible for a child under 16 years of age. It is given to rich and poor alike and does not appear to label or stigmatise those poor families who benefit significantly from it. The application process for child benefit is relatively simple and straightfoward, and it has an exceptionally high take-up rate.

Not all non-contributory benefits, however, are as universal, simple or stigma-free as child benefit. Some tests of need for non-contributory benefits for the disabled have proved to be restrictive and in certain cases humiliating. The mid-1970s saw the introduction of a range of non-contributory benefits for the disabled including attendance allowance, mobility allowance and non-contributory invalidity pension. The introduction of these financial benefits was clearly a major advance for most disabled people. Tens of thousands of disabled people were able to enjoy an increased standard of living or to stop claiming means-tested supplementary benefits. Yet the process of claiming these benefits and the complex eligibility rules which surround them have denied assistance to many disabled people who strongly believe that they should be entitled to help, and a great deal of controversy has surrounded the practical application of these new 'rights' for disabled people.

One major complaint against the new benefits is that the tests for eligibility are too stringent. The mobility allowance, for example, is given to those claimants who show that they are unable or virtually unable to walk and the approach taken by officials has been to look at claimants' mechanical ability to walk. As the eligibility test is presently designed the mentally handicapped have had very great difficulty in claiming mobility allowance if they are physically able to walk. Douglas says that despite assurances from the DHSS in 1979 that Downs Syndrome sufferers would henceforth be eligible for the allowance, 'the Downs Syndrome child who walks round in ever decreasing circles and nowhere else without being led or pulled is (still) unlikely to receive the allowance' since, 'the test as it is currently defined allows no room for the person who does not and will not walk to any purpose.'[12] Douglas argues that although one can understand why the DHSS chose a simple test of a person's ability to walk as the criterion for eligibility for mobility allowance, it would be much fairer to take into account a person's total circumstances and to give the allowance to anyone who would otherwise be unable to participate in the life of the community because they would be unable to get out and about.

Whilst the eligibility rules for mobility allowance have caused some controversy, far more heat has been generated by the rules governing eligibility for the housewives' non-contributory invalidity pension (HNCIP). For single men and women who do not have an adequate national insurance contributions record, entitlement to a non-contributory invalidity pension (NCIP) is based solely on their incapacity for work. The major disadvantage of NCIP is that its rate is only 60 per cent that of insurance based invalidity benefit. Since 1977 married women have also been entitled to a non-contributory invalidity pension but in order to qualify for it they have had to undergo an additional test through which they must prove incapacity to perform their 'normal household duties'. Since 1978 disabled housewives have not only had to prove that they cannot perform a substantial range of household tasks but also that the remaining housework which they can do is insubstantial. The severity with which this household duties test has been applied since 1978 has left many severely disabled housewives ineligible for benefit.

The following two cases, taken from an Equal Opportunities Commission research project, give some indication of the extent of disability suffered by unsuccessful claimants. 'Mrs McG. has had multiple sclerosis for five years. She cannot lift light objects, walk short distances or climb stairs. She can only do shopping with help, and cannot do any cooking, washing up, heavy cleaning, ironing household laundry or make the beds'.[13] Mrs McG. had her original claim for HNCIP rejected. Another woman who had her claim turned down by a local insurance officer had described the effort and pain involved when she attempted even very light household tasks:

> I cannot twist my wrist and arm to dust, washing a cup is painful and it is impossible for me to push a vacuum cleaner or carpet sweeper, or wash a floor . . . when I have managed to do the washing (by machine) I am in terrible pain for the following two days and nights . . . Just how bad do you have to be to qualify for this pension . . . unable even to make a cup of tea? Though even this is difficult enough – the electric kettle is too heavy, I use a small saucepan and if I fill the teapot I am unable to lift it.[14]

A second major problem identified in the rationing process of non-contributory benefits is the subjective nature of the assessment of claimants' disabilities. Eligibility for attendance allowance is determined by the judgement of just one doctor. The subjective nature of this assessment has been acknowledged by the Social Security Commissioners, one of whom agreed that, 'different DMPs [delegated medical practitioners] could well take different views on identical facts.'[15]

A third problem experienced by some disabled claimants is the stigma and distress they feel when claiming certain disability benefits. An Equal Opportunities Commission survey revealed in 1981 that a number of disabled housewives found the questions on the HNCIP claim form, which is designed to elicit the extent to which a claimant can perform household duties, 'embarrassing', 'impertinent', 'humiliating' and 'degrading'. Some claimants appeared to have emotional difficulties in filling in a self-assessment form on which they had to openly state how little housework they could do. The daughter of one disabled woman explained that her mother was 'very upset' by the type of questions asked. Before she had become disabled she had 'always kept her house spotless' and the daughter thought 'it was degrading for her to be put through this type of senseless bureaucracy.'[16] One disabled woman summed up her feelings about the process of claiming HNCIP thus: 'It is bad enough to suffer physically but to suffer the degradation of a type of physical means test is beyond belief.'[17]

Evidence is mounting that a significant number of the physically disabled and mentally handicapped fail to claim all the benefits to which they are entitled. According to the *Disability Rights Bulletin* as many as one third of those eligible for attendance allowance were failing to claim it in the early 1980s and the take-up rate was particularly low amongst the elderly. It estimated that up to 30,000 people over 75 may be failing to claim attendance allowance and the probable take-up rate amongst the elderly is under 60 per cent.[18] Lack of take-up of disability benefits may be caused by a number of factors. According to Bennet and McGavin not only are the procedures for claiming benefit difficult and sometimes humiliating for the disabled, but also some benefits are not as well understood as they might be.[19] They interviewed one woman who thought she was ineligible for a mobility allowance 'because I have to take a taxi everywhere'. They suggested that the disabled may be particularly confused about eligibility for the attendance allowance. Many of those interviewed believed that the attendance allowance could only be claimed by those living alone or that it could only be claimed by those actually paying someone to look after them.

As well as the problem of non take-up of benefits, there was some evidence in the early 1980s that increasing numbers of applicants for certain disability benefits were being refused help. By the end of February 1980 a total of 86,512 applications for HNCIP had been received by the DHSS. Slightly less than half of these applications resulted in an initially successful claim. As many as 20 per cent of unsuccessful claimants had appealed to a local tribunal. This rate of appeal is unusually high. The appeal rate for NCIP between 1975 and 1977, for example, was only 0.3 per cent.[20] The high appeal rate for HNCIP suggests that many genuinely disabled women are now being denied help.

Empirical evidence suggests that there is a wide gap between the formal rights of the disabled to a range of financial benefits and their practical chances of receiving help. There are a number of explanations for this gap. It could be that while successive governments have fully intended that all disabled people receive the maximum amount of financial help which is their 'right', practical problems involved in determining exact eligibility for disability benefits have led to a disparity between intentions and results. In other words, the problems associated with disability benefits could be regarded as purely administrative. Certainly it would be virtually impossible to draw up eligibility rules for a benefit such as mobility allowance which would not leave those who fell just outside the criterion for receipt of benefit feeling hard done by. If those who are virtually unable to walk are given mobility allowance, those who are almost virtually unable to walk but who fail to receive mobility allowance may feel that the allocation of this benefit is unjust. Secondly, any lack of take-up of certain benefits for the disabled may be partly explained by the natural reluctance of many people to admit their own disabilities. A disabled housewife may strongly resist having to publicly acknowledge that she is incapable of performing basic household duties. Finally, the severely disabled may experience far more difficulties than the able bodied in claiming what is rightfully theirs. According to Chappell, 'The severely disabled are often the least able to complete the bureaucratic obstacle course presented by the DHSS.'[21]

Some critics of existing benefits for the disabled have suggested that this 'obstacle course' is not simply a matter of the failure to implement the government's good intentions but is part of deliberate policy to keep down the costs of disability benefits. The main problem with disability benefits is thus perceived as lack of political will rather than administrative difficulties. This argument is supported by the history of HNCIP. Despite the difficulties experienced by many of those who tried to claim HNCIP, by September 1978 the number of successful claims had reached 43,000. The government, which had previously estimated that the total number of women who would prove to be eligible for HNCIP was only around 40,000 became worried that the cost of this benefit might significantly exceed official estimates. In order to prevent such an outcome the DHSS tightened the regulations governing eligibility for HNCIP by ruling that a disabled wife henceforth had to prove that any housework which she could still do was insubstantial rather than just proving as heretofore that what she could not do was substantial. Patrick Jenkin criticised the Labour government for this move and summed up what had happened by saying, 'They [the government] underestimated the number of disabled housewives and, as a result, failed to earmark enough money to meet the cost. Having decided to leave to the adjudicating authorities the precise ambit of the "household duties" test they abruptly changed the rules when a decision went against them.'[22]

The difficulties experienced by many of those who attempt to claim HNCIP illustrate the importance of rationing in practice as opposed to formal rights in determining individuals' access to welfare benefits. Although political rhetoric suggests that non-contributory benefits are intended to be allocated as of right to all those citizens who fall into a particular category of need or responsibility, in practice, non-contributory benefits can be deliberately rationed so severely that a claimant's right to benefit is clearly undermined. Nevertheless most welfare rights workers accept that in principle at least non-contributory benefits are preferable to means-tested benefits.

The right to supplementary benefit

Beveridge argued that means-tested national assistance 'must be felt to be something less desirable than insurance benefit; otherwise the insured persons get nothing for their contributions.' Assistance was, therefore, only to be given 'subject to proof of needs and examination of means.' It was also to be subject 'to any condition as to behaviour which may seem likely to hasten restoration of earning capacity.'[23] Such arguments are hardly the basis for a non-stigmatising 'rights' based system of assistance, and it became clear in the 1950s and early 1960s that national assistance was widely regarded as a stigmatising service which doled out charity rather than benefits as of right. In 1966 the Labour government attempted to increase the take-up of means-tested benefits. It did so mainly by changing the name national assistance to supplementary benefits and by stressing that those claiming supplementary benefit had a legal right to it. The 1966 Social Security Act stated, 'Every person in Great Britain of or over the age of sixteen whose resources are insufficient to meet his requirements shall be entitled, subject to the provision of this Act to benefit.'[24]

Essentially the meaning of a right in the context of welfare benefits is related to its legal status. The strongest right to benefit lies where Parliament has given statutory force to certain rights for individuals who fall into particular categories. The 1966 Social Security Act gave statutory force to minimum scale rates of benefit and to certain additions to them. But it also delegated wide discretionary powers to a Supplementary Benefits Commission (SBC). These powers included the discretion to give certain claimants more or, in some cases, less benefit than that laid down in the statutory regulations. The SBC subsequently drew up and then continued to amend and supplement a mass of detailed rules and instructions for use by the front line staff who actually had to implement its discretionary powers.

During the 1970s discretion rapidly grew to play a major role in the allocation or rationing of supplementary benefits. By 1979, 61 per cent of those receiving weekly payments of supplementary benefits were also receiving an Exceptional Circumstances Addition (ECA) and well over 1 million Exceptional Needs Payments (ENPs) were being awarded annually.

Throughout the 1970s critics of the supplementary benefits scheme argued that in practice claimants' rights to supplementary benefit were being undermined in a variety of ways. The fact that so many discretionary decisions were made by reference to a complicated set of 'secret' rules meant that claimants had no way of knowing exactly what extra benefits the SBC had decided they might be eligible for. Moreover claimants and their advocates could not effectively challenge decisions made according to unknown rules, hence the demands in the early 1970s for the publication of the SBC's secret 'A' code on which so many of the decisions made by local officers were based. In later years some welfare rights campaigners came to the conclusion that the 'A' code itself was far too complicated for general consumption. Nevertheless they continued to press for a simplified form of the rules and regulations governing the supplementary benefit system to be published on the grounds that without knowledge claimants were powerless to secure what was rightfully due to them. In order to strengthen claimants' rights to benefits designed to meet exceptional circumstances or needs welfare rights campaigners pressed for these benefits to be defined by statute as well as simplified and published. They argued that the lack of a legal right to certain benefits increased the stigma imposed on supplementary benefits claimants. Administrators of the supplementary benefits scheme – as well as its outside critics – argued that claimants would have much more clear cut rights if discretionary benefits were simplified and/or made the subject of statutory provisions. The Chairman of the SBC himself, commenting on the discretionary system of allocating ENPs wrote:

> I think it is degrading to ask people to come forward and plead with strangers over a counter in a crowded social security office for relatively small sums of money to buy shoes and clothing for themselves and for their children. I think it is degrading for them to have strangers coming into their homes and asking questions about worn underclothing . . . That is no way to treat the public in a country where citizens should have rights, privacy and independence.[25]

In its 1976 report the SBC admitted that there is a basic contradiction between the concept of entitlement to benefit and the widely ranging use of discretionary powers',[26] while in 1978 the Review Team recommended that the responsibility for defining the conditions of eligibility for supplementary benefits should be placed with ministers and Parliament, and that the fact that since 1966 entitlement to benefit was a right by statute should 'be clarified and spelled out in more detail in legislation in a way that is more or less binding on staff and appellate authorities.'[27]

The concept of a right to benefit entails the principle that claimants with identical needs and circumstances will be entitled to identical benefits regardless of such factors as where they live, which social security office they attend or the cause of their dependency on social security. One of the main criticisms of the pre-1980 supplementary benefits scheme was that it failed to treat those with similar needs in a similar way. Much of this criticism was directed at the discretionary elements of the scheme. In 1975 the SBC admitted that it could not be sure that discretion gave help to those in greatest need,[28] while the Review Team argued that ECAs and particularly ENPs could operate unfairly as between claimants 'because some are unaware of them or how to apply for them and because claimants in similar circumstances may be treated differently.'[29] In the 1970s some local DHSS offices gave out eleven times more ENPs than others, a difference that could not be justified by varying levels of deprivation. The Child Poverty Action Group argued that in a system where discretionary payments are 'administered on the basis that the initiative generally lies with the claimant', many claimants would not know that provisions existed to meet their special needs.[30] Consequently a discretionary system was bound to favour the better informed or more articulate claimant or those few fortunate enough to have the support of an advocate. Even some claimants expressed their dislike of the discretionary basis of ENPs. According to the Review Team, claimants were confused about their eligibility for discretionary payments and critical of what they saw as arbitrary and discriminatory benefits which went to other claimants but not to them. The Review Team's report stated: 'There are indications that people prefer benefits which come automatically and are paid regularly, to single payments such as ENPs for which a specific claim has to be made and justified in detail.'[31]

Although the discretionary allocation of social security benefits always attracts the charge of being inequitable, its critics usually accept that it nevertheless plays an important role in responding to the unique needs of individual claimants. A former Chairman of the SBC claimed, 'for the individual, the existence of . . . discretionary powers may be more valuable than a precisely prescribed right because they give the scheme a flexibility of response to varying situations of human need.'[32] Thus the main issue in the 1970s was not 'discretion or no discretion' but rather 'How much discretion?', and it was generally agreed that, 'a last resort system of income maintenance will always have to retain a good deal of discretionary powers.'[33]

Many of those who argued for less discretion in the supplementary benefits system were fighting not just for a procedural strengthening of claimants' rights but also for a real increase in the overall amount of benefits provided. The Child Poverty Action Group's evidence to the Review Team made it quite clear that the question of the adequacy of the scale rates was central to their thinking on discretion. Lister stated that:

[The] widespread reliance on discretion to meet normal everyday needs in ordinary circumstances has undermined the discretionary element of the scheme. The reason is clear . . . it is that the scale rates are too low 'for people to meet all ordinary living expenses in the way that suits them best' as the Supplementary Benefits Handbook tells them they should. The solution is also clear: the scale rates must be raised to a level high enough to ensure that in ordinary circumstances claimants can meet all normal needs without recourse to [discretionary payments].[34]

The Social Security Act 1980 – a welfare rights gain?

The 1980 Social Security Act made fundamental changes to the supplementary benefits scheme. It abolished the SBC, translated most of its discretionary rules and regulations into statutory regulations and laid them open to the scrutiny of Parliament and the general public. The second major change implemented by the 1980 Act was a significant, some would say drastic, reduction in 'officer discretion'. Officers were no longer to have the discretionary power to award lump sum payments for everyday needs such as clothing and footwear which henceforth had to be met from the scale rates. However claimants with truly exceptional needs such as funeral expenses, lack of furniture and bedding or the needs of a new-born baby would henceforth be legally entitled to a lump sum payment to cover those needs. The 1980 Act did leave local officers the discretionary power to give a single payment to any claimant who did not meet the eligibility conditions for exceptional payments laid down by the new regulations, but officers could only make such a payment if it would be 'the only means by which serious damage or serious risk to the health or safety of any member of the assessment unit [i.e. family] could be prevented.'[35]

Did these major changes to the supplementary benefits system meet the demands of those clamouring for reform in the 1970s? At first sight it looked as though significant gains had been made by the welfare rights lobby. Claimants now had a legal right to a whole range of benefits to meet exceptional needs and circumstances provided they fulfilled certain specified eligibility criteria. In theory, therefore, the changes made it much easier for claimants to get help for special needs by proving their legal entitlement to it. Again, in theory, the publication of all statutory regulations relating to entitlement to benefit ensured that all claimants and their advocates could find out exactly to what they were entitled. Finally, the simplification of the scheme was said to make it much more easy to understand. The supposed advantages of the new scheme were summed up by Patrick Jenkin when he told the House of Commons that the new Act was, 'a great advance in fairness . . . In place of complexity there will be simplification. In place of secrecy there will be published rules. In place of discretion there will be clear legal entitlement.'[36]

In practice many of the supposed gains to claimants were far from evident. The scheme was not simplified to the extent that it became easily comprehensible to the general public. By November 1981 there were not only 13 sets of incredibly complex supplementary benefits regulations plus seven sets of amendments, but also a very extensive internal code of instructions for benefit officers. There was even some evidence to suggest that benefit officers themselves did not at first understand some of the complex new regulations.[37] Apart from being extremely complex and written in legal jargon, the new regulations, at over £40 (1982) a set, were hardly readily obtainable to claimants: so much for publicised simplicity. But at least, said the supporters of the changes, the new scheme did give claimants firmer and clearer legal rights to a range of hitherto discretionary benefits. Donnison, welcoming the new Act, argued:

> The scheme on which nearly a tenth of the population depends for its income cannot continue to be run by a commission not directly accountable to anybody, exercising massive discretionary powers without any obligation to make its policies publicly clear. It is a great advance that all the rules and policies of the commission will in future be brought before Parliament.[38]

Yet critics of the new scheme were quick to point out that unless rights can be exercised or enforced they are hardly worth having. If benefit officers had gone out of their way to ensure that all claimants knew about their new legal entitlements the new scheme would certainly have given many claimants stronger 'rights' than the old system. However a survey carried out by Community Care and the Child Poverty Action Group in 1982 found evidence of supplementary benefits officers applying regulations more rigidly and of an increased emphasis on discovering fraud. One respondent commented, 'The emphasis has moved in favour of catching a few frauds rather than ensuring that claimants are paid their entitlement.'[39] Cutbacks in DHSS staff and the rapid rise in the number of claimants has had, according to the survey, a dramatic effect on the speed of administration. Apparently, even 'emergencies' had to wait. One respondent reported, for example, that a claimant had waited five weeks for a visitor after a request for an emergency payment. 'Legal entitlement often means very little . . . in the real world of administrative inefficiency, error and delay . . . In an urgent case the fact that a claimant may have a legal right to payment means nothing at all if the local office simply says "no". An appeal hearing in six weeks will probably be too late.'[40]

Critics of the new supplementary benefits scheme stressed that legal entitlement means virtually nothing to claimants if what they are legally entitled to is actually less than what they used to receive under the old supplementary benefits scheme. Whereas under the old scheme at least some families received discretionary clothing grants, under the new scheme grants to replace clothes lost through normal wear and tear are no longer given to any families. According to Allbeson, 'The new supplementary benefits scheme may have produced a more equitable system but it is the equity of common poverty.'[41]

It has not only been the discretionary elements of the supplementary benefits scheme which have been criticised for distributing benefits inequitably. The basic rules governing the allocation of supplementary benefits have always treated – and continue to treat – some groups of claimants more favourably than others. Unemployed claimants, unlike the sick and one parent families, have never been entitled to draw the long term supplementary benefit scale rate which is over 20 per cent higher than the short term rate of benefit. The 1980 changes to the supplementary benefit scheme did nothing to alter the bias in the rules against unemployed claimants and therefore the SBC's criticism that the social security system treats the unemployed 'as if they were an inferior caste' remained valid.[42]

Those attempting to access the effect of the 1980 Social Security Act on claimants' access to supplementary benefits must examine the context in which the scheme operates. In February 1980 Reg Prentice, then Minister for Social Security, launched a drive against social security fraud and abuse which involved an attempt to save £50 million by employing extra staff devoted mainly to unemployment review and liable relatives' work. Despite the massive rise in unemployment in the early 1980s those without work once again came under attack. According to official spokesmen honest claimants had nothing to fear or to lose from anti-fraud drives. Yet Reg Prentice argued in 1971 (when still a member of the Labour Party) that the 'myth about widespread abuse' does 'awful damage' to individual people in need, because 'these myths help to create among some people – I have met them in my advice bureau, and other hon. members will have the same experience – the sense that there is something shameful about applying for benefits to which they are entitled.'[43]

According to Donnison, the transformation of the legal structure of the supplementary benefits scheme and the provision of written assessments for claimants which showed how these benefits were calculated, seemed important to their advocates but were actually 'small scale tactical matters'. He argues that 'strategic changes' of the sort that would be needed to bring about real benefits to supplementary benefits claimants would call for a large-scale redistribution of resources. 'To achieve such fundamental changes in policy calls for what amounts to a new set of moral values.'[44] Those values were the antithesis of the ideology popularised by the Thatcher government at the very time that the Social Security Act was receiving consent.

Conclusion

It is widely assumed that a legal right to a specific financial benefit is more advantageous to the majority of claimants than a system based on discretionary decision making. Throughout the late 1960s and 1970s welfare rights campaigners fought to increase claimants' statutory rights and to decrease the discretionary element of this country's social security system. Yet a close study of the actual distribution of a range of social security benefits suggests that a statutory right to benefit may be so weakened by the rules and procedures governing the actual allocation of benefits that the claimant gains virtually nothing from it. In theory a benefit as of right should give an individual a stronger claim to help than a discretionary benefit, but in practice the distinction between these two types of benefits may become blurred. How benefits are actually rationed and the extent to which the state either promotes or attempts to restrict a particular benefit may be more significant in terms of claimants so-called 'welfare rights' than the legal basis of that benefit.

Adler and Asquith have pointed out the importance of distinguishing between claimants' procedural rights and their substantive rights to benefits. Procedural rights refer to the process of having a claim dealt with according to legal rules whereas substantive rights refer to outcomes, i.e., what claimants actually receive. According to Adler and Asquith, 'most of those who have wished to limit discretion have wished to strengthen the procedural rights of those who are subject to it. Of course, it does not follow that, by doing so, the substantive rights of those who are subject to these powers will be enhanced in any significant way.'[45] A number of those who campaigned against the discretionary nature of the pre-1980 supplementary benefits scheme were well aware that an increase in procedural rights without a concommitant increase in substantive rights would be a hollow victory. This explains why so many welfare rights campaigners strongly criticised the no-cost enhancement of claimants' procedural rights which took place in 1980. The argument that procedural rights without a commitment of resources are of little practical use to claimants is supported by the history of HNCIP. The many difficulties experienced by severely disabled wives who have attempted to claim this benefit shows that where benefits are deliberately rationed in a highly restrictive way claimants' procedural rights do not always guarantee them access to financial help.

One of the key complaints of critics of the pre-1980 supplementary benefits scheme was that individual social security officers sometimes used their discretionary powers in a biased, arbitrary or unjust way. This criticism was closely linked to the call for more rules and regulations within the supplementary benefits scheme. Yet detailed rules and regulations could never eliminate individual decision making within the British social security system. However many detailed rules were drawn up individual social security officers would still have to use their own judgement to determine a particular claimant's exact eligibility for benefit.[46]

Prottas has suggested why it is so difficult to eliminate low level staff's discretion in public welfare agencies, and why the creation of too many rules and regulations may be counterproductive. Either staff processing client applications will spend all their time trying to learn and then apply ever more complex rules to complicated individual cases, or they will simply use their discretion to ignore some of these rules. According to Prottas street-level bureaucracies (including social security systems):

> proliferate rules so as to direct the behaviour of the street-level bureaucrat in as many areas as possible. As a result the street-level bureaucrat must choose which rules will be applied as their number prohibits their universal application. At the same time, many rules *must* remain general to permit the street-level bureaucrat to apply them to the myriad individual situations that he or she encounters. [Therefore he concludes] No system of rules can completely eliminate street-level discretion in street-level bureaucracies.[47]

Prottas's thesis may help to explain the general disillusionment with the reform of the supplementary benefits system. Critics argue that the administration of the scheme has become even slower since the reform. This may be partly due to low level staff attempting to apply even more complex rules to each individual case – a process which according to Prottas may lead to the whole bureaucracy eventually grinding to a halt. On the other hand, if social security officers attempt to combat this problem by ignoring some of the new rules and withholding information from clients about their new rights, critics will complain that the arbitrary exercise of discretion has not been eliminated by the change to a formally more rule-bound system.[48]

A key justification for the retention of an element of discretionary decision making within the social security system is based on a concern to provide a flexible and humane response to each individual's particular needs. The long debate over the role of discretion in the pre-1980 supplementary benefits scheme was in part a genuine search for the right balance between proportional justice (i.e. a concern to achieve fairness between individuals) and creative justice (i.e. a concern to deal with the uniqueness of an individual's needs). In principle a discretionary allocation system is best equipped to ensure creative justice whereas a rule-bound system is much more likely to result in proportional justice. An ideal mixture of the two would presumably produce an optimal balance between the two types of justice. In practice, however, both types of rationing can be used either positively or negatively. If the emphasis within the social security system were to be firmly placed on ensuring that all genuine needs were met, individual discretionary powers could be used positively to ensure that all those with exceptional needs received extra benefits. But discretion within Britain's social security system has more frequently been used as a negative rationing device. Rather than seeking out those with special needs, social security officers have tended to give extra help only to those who have demanded it, and even then discretionary powers have frequently been used to judge such claims as inappropriate or unnecessary. The large discretionary element in the pre-1980 supplementary benefits scheme contained a strong emphasis on economy. On the other hand, rationing by rules and regulations is by no means inevitably more generous or positive than rationing by discretion. It merely provides the basis for a more equitable distribution of existing resources. Rights, rules and regulations versus discretionary decision making have been singled out as key variables in our social security system. However as far as the individual's access to benefit is concerned, the key issue may well be whether or not rationing of any sort is undertaken in a context of generosity or economy rather than which precise method of rationing is utilised.

Rationing methods *per se* are not the sole determinants of the distribution of welfare benefits. They are certainly not a major factor in determining the overall level or adequacy of benefits provided. Some welfare rights campaigners have acted as though the main problem with the British social security system and particularly the supplementary benefits scheme is basically administrative or technical. They have fought for changes in the methods of rationing or distribution of social security benefits on the grounds that such changes could lead to substantive improvements in the benefits provided to the majority of claimants. Radical critics of the system, on the other hand, maintain that its basic inadequacies lie far deeper than at the level of administrative rationing or distribution. They claim that before social security claimants can make any *significant* gains, much more fundamental changes must be made to the social security system and indeed to society as a whole.

8

Access to Public Housing

Whereas access to either the owner-occupied sector or the privately rented sector is primarily determined by ability to pay, council housing, at least in principle, is allocated according to need. In practice the objective of giving priority to those in greatest need usually conflicts with other objectives such as the protection of council property. Research has demonstrated that the criterion of need is by no means always placed first in the allocation process. In order to understand why local authorities sometimes fail to give priority to those in greatest need, we must attempt to unravel the process or rather processes by which applicants gain access to council accommodation. This chapter will be concerned not only with the question of how those in need gain access to council housing *per se* but also with the type of accommodation they are offered. In an advanced, reasonably affluent, society most people would probably agree that a public sector housing system should provide not just bare shelter but a decent standard of accommodation. Very few people in our society have no roof whatsoever over their heads. Many, on the other hand, live in accommodation which is officially recognised as unfit for habitation. The type of accommodation lived in and its location is crucial in determining a person's overall welfare and living standards. Perhaps more than any other service housing has an influence on many aspects of people's life, including their health, contact with friends, their status in the community and their access to jobs and recreation. The key question today in relation to the allocation of public housing is therefore not just 'who gets housed', but 'who gets housed in what standard of accommodation?'. This chapter will examine both 'primary rationing systems', which determine who is eligible for some sort of council housing, and 'secondary rationing systems', which determine the type and quality of accommodation offered. In looking at both rationing systems, attention will be paid to the mix between rules and regulations and discretionary decision making by individual housing officials. This chapter will also go beyond a study of rationing methods themselves in order to investigate the main constraints imposed upon the allocation process by factors outside the control of the allocators. In particular it will examine the constraints placed on allocation processes by the quantity and quality of housing stock available.

Eligibility for council housing

There is no national system for allocating public housing in Britain. Each local authority is free to determine its own allocation policy and a wide variety of rationing schemes have been devised to determine eligibility for council housing in different areas. The legislative framework for allocating council housing is vague. Local authorities have a statutory duty to provide houses to meet the needs of the district and where necessary to rehouse persons displaced by slum clearance and to relieve overcrowding. The Housing Act (1957) states that, in the selection of their tenants, local authorities 'shall secure that a reasonable preference is given to persons who are occupying insanitary or over-crowded houses have large families or are living under unsatisfactory housing conditions.'[1] Only 'over-crowded' was defined by the Act, the other terms including 'insanitary', 'unsatisfactory housing conditions' and 'reasonable preference' were left open to interpretation and thus gave local authorities a great deal of discretion in determining their own priorities in catering for housing needs. The Housing (Homeless Persons) Act 1977 imposed a statutory duty on local authorities to make housing available to certain persons having a priority need who are without accommodation, namely families with dependent children, persons made homeless as a result of any emergency or disaster and persons who are vulnerable due to age, mental illness or handicap, physical disability or other special reasons.[2] However local authorities do not have to house such persons themselves, as long as they ensure that housing is available from somewhere. Moreover, the Act modified local authorities' new statutory duties to house homeless persons in priority groups in two significant ways. If homeless people have no local connection the authority can under certain circumstances send them back to their own local authority.[3] Second, if a person makes him or herself intentionally homeless, the local authority does not have to provide him or her with permanent accommodation.[4] In practice, many local authorities have used this last loophole to severely restrict the number of homeless people helped under the terms of the Act.[5]

Local authorities have received both statutory guidelines and a great deal of advice from central government on the selection of tenants and on allocation procedures. This advice has been given via circulars and reports by the Central Housing Advisory Committee (CHAC). Various circulars over the years have emphasised the needs of particular groups such as key workers or the elderly, while CHAC reports have given detailed advice to local authorities in an attempt to reform unfair and inefficient rationing methods. However, the principle of local authority discretion in the allocation of housing has remained firm.

In nearly all local authorities demand for council housing far outstrips its supply. Councils therefore have to decide firstly who should be deemed eligible for consideration for a tenancy and secondly who, among the eligible group, should be given priority.

The first step applicants must take if they wish to obtain a council tenancy is to get their name on their local authority's waiting list. Housing waiting lists are sometimes referred to as housing queues, but the term queue over-simplifies a very complex process. Some local authorities operate open waiting lists which allow any family or individual to put their name down for council accommodation. Other authorities restrict access to their waiting list by devising eligibility criteria which exclude certain would-be tenants from taking even this first step in the allocation process. Some local authorities require that an applicant must have lived in their area for up to several years before being accepted onto the waiting list. Other eligibility filters used at this stage include the exclusion of all single people under a certain age and, in a few local authorities, the exclusion of all would-be applicants with an income above a certain level. Thus even to be allowed to apply for council housing in some areas applicants must fulfil certain eligibility qualifications quite unrelated to their need for housing.

The CHAC report on housing allocation procedures, issued in 1969, stressed that, 'no one should be precluded from applying for or being considered for a council tenancy on any ground whatsoever' since 'only if all applications are admitted is it possible to assess needs'.[6] Local authorities who exclude certain groups of people such as the young and single from even applying for council housing, regardless of their housing needs, clearly run the risk of completely excluding certain needy groups from their sphere of vision. Yet in 1981 Sier reported that a number of local authorities were reducing their housing waiting lists by placing additional restrictions on access to them. Some had introduced income limits, others had introduced or increased residential qualifications. According to Sier, 'The imposition of restrictions ignores the important function of the waiting list as an indicator of housing need on which housing programmes can be based.'[7]

Having got his or her name on a waiting list, the second step for a housing applicant is to be deemed eligible for active consideration for a dwelling. There is little advantage for a person in being allowed to put his or her name on a waiting list if he or she stands absolutely no chance of ever reaching the top of it. Many local authorities use stringent residential qualifications to determine eligibility for rehousing. By the late 1960s only 17 per cent of a sample of local authorities required applicants to have resided in the area for a specific period before putting their names on the housing list. However three quarters of these authorities required a residential qualification ranging up to six years or more before actively considering an applicant for rehousing.[8] Lack of a residential qualification is by no means the only eligibility bar to rehousing. Other bars include cohabitation, being an owner-occupier (regardless of the suitability of the accommodation owned) and being under a certain age.

The case for a residential qualification rests mainly on the belief that the principle of allocation according to need should be qualified by a recognition of the prior claim of local residents on a local authority's services. Some local authorities also maintain that an open access policy would lead to an influx of applications for housing from residents of other areas. In 1969 the CHAC report accepted, reluctantly, that in certain areas of severe housing pressure, such as Inner London, a local authority might be compelled to discriminate against non-residents and newcomers to the area. As the Standing Working Party on London Housing explained, 'Where so many families have lived for years in overcrowded and insanitary conditions, it is not an easy decision to allow newcomers to the area (who on arrival have to accept perhaps even worse conditions) to be given priority for the little accommodation which the local authority can make available for families on the waiting list.'[9]

The objective of giving priority to local residents in need of rehousing may be regarded by many as a perfectly legitimate goal for local authorities but it does conflict with the aim of always allocating council accommodation to those in greatest need. The same is true for any eligibility rule which excludes certain groups of people from consideration for rehousing. Universally applied eligibility rules may also inadvertently discriminate against certain groups, such as immigrants who, for example, may more frequently have insufficient residential qualifications than the indigenous population. By themselves, strictly enforced rules and regulations do not guarantee a non-discriminatory allocation system. According to Corina when a local authority in the South of England tried to eliminate bias in allocation by using a computer, the computer allocated poor tenants to poor estates.[10]

Once housing applicants have passed through a variety of eligibility filters designed to remove certain groups from the allocation process, they must then join a queue of eligible applicants waiting to be allocated accommodation. At this stage of the process another rationing exercise takes place which determines the priority given to each application. A small minority of local authorities operate so called 'merit schemes' to place applicants in order of priority. Under a merit scheme each individual application is judged on its merits by a group of councillors or by housing officers.

Merit schemes are in effect totally discretionary. Their main advantage is that they allow for full account to be taken of individual, complex needs which might not be amenable to a less personal, more formalised assessment process. The main disadvantage of merit schemes is that applicants cannot be informed of the rules by which their applications are assessed because they simply do not exist. 'Consistency and impartiality' are, therefore, 'difficult to achieve and virtually impossible to demonstrate.'[11] The two other main types of systems used by local authorities to determine priority for housing are date order schemes and point systems. In theory date order schemes are relatively straightforward. Applicants are housed according to the date on which they joined the housing queue. In practice even this apparently straightforward queuing system is usually complicated by the existence of separate queues for different types of accommodation in different areas. Moreover

local authorities using date order schemes have to devise some procedure for the consideration of special or urgent needs and in most
cases this will involve the exercise of discretion by individual
councillors or housing officers. In practice, therefore, it would be
quite wrong to regard date order schemes as simple queuing systems.

The final system for determining priority, the points system, is
most commonly used where supply of housing is far outstripped by
those deemed eligible for it. Under this system, applicants are
allocated points for a range of items such as overcrowding, medical
need, lack of facilities and time spent on the waiting list. Those with
the greatest number of points have the greatest priority for rehousing. Housing managers themselves generally regard points schemes
as the fairest way of allocating council housing according to need,
although a survey of local authorities in 1980 found that only just
over half of them used a points scheme.[12] Each local authority using
this scheme works out its own points system so that considerable
variations occur in the way points systems work. Murie *et al*.
demonstrated in 1976 how four identical families in different housing circumstances, and in different types of need, were given a
different order of priority by four points schemes then in operation.[13]
Such variations could be taken as evidence that local authority control over public housing leads to territorial inequality. However
Murie points out that although local policy differences do result in
households living in a given housing situation standing a better
chance of early rehousing under one local authority's allocation
system than under another's, 'much of the variation is superficial.
Authorities place emphasis on "housing need" and while they may
not define this in precisely the same way, there is a consensus about
the factors which should be taken into consideration. Lack of a
separate house, overcrowding, ill-health and sub-standard
accommodation appear again and again in eligibility rules and
point systems.'[14]

A major criticism of this approach is that it fails to take into
account social factors relevant to housing need such as applicants'
degree of ability to cope with their housing problems and degree of
ability to improve the situation on their own. According to Niner
most council house allocation schemes inhibit self-help among
applicants. Couples who wish to delay having a family until they are
adequately housed, for example, will almost inevitably be out-
pointed by a similar couple with small children whose accommoda-

tion will be classed as overcrowed. Niner recognises however that 'there are profound technical problems' in devising a rule-based priority system which fully takes into account social as well as housing needs. If every applicant were considered individually more nebulous types of need could be considered but such an approach would be administratively impossible in a large authority. 'The present allocation systems work because applicants are grouped and dealt with according to predetermined rules . . . The more factors that are to be taken into account, the more unwieldy the administrative procedures become.'[15] Niner also points out the impossibility of combining a system which treats all applicants consistently and fairly with an attempt to take individual situations into account and to weigh priorities on a more personal level. The 1980 Housing Act has placed a legal requirement on local authorities to publish their allocation schemes. Presumably the government wishes local authorities to operate schemes based on rules which can be fully understood by those seeking council accommodation. The problem is that a rule-bound allocation system may be seen to be fair and consistent whilst ignoring applicants' complex needs. Yet once discretion is allowed to modify the rules the criteria on which allocations are made inevitably become vaguer and far more difficult to explain adequately to a disappointed applicant.

So far the discussion has focused on the problems associated with determining eligibility for council accommodation in general. In other words, it has been looking at the primary rationing of public housing. Whatever the practical shortfalls of local authorities' primary rationing systems, it is generally accepted that need, however defined, is the main consideration in the determination of eligibility and priority for council accommodation. Attention will now be turned to the fourth, and in some ways most crucial, stage in the rationing of public housing, the allocation of a particular type of accommodation in a specific area to the individual applicant. It is at this key point in the rationing process that a concern about need appears to be replaced by a concern to judge the merits and suitability of prospective tenants for particular types of housing.

Eligibility for desirable council housing

There is now a considerable mass of empirical data which shows that council estates are segregated, with certain types of tenants being clustered on unpopular, low standard estates. In 1973 researchers in Oldham found that an increasing proportion of incoming tenants on a rundown, stigmatised estate, were 'problem' families. These new tenants were either members of a one-parent family and/or without a stable income from work; living on social security benefits; previously 'unsatisfactory' tenants; or known to an agency of social control such as the police.'[16] Many local authorities deny that they operate a deliberate policy of offering varying qualities of accommodation to different types of applicants. Yet researchers and workers in the field have discovered the widespread existence of a grading system of applicants which takes place behind closed doors and which crucially determines the types of housing they are offered. This covert system of rationing is that which Karn calls a 'secondary rationing system'. She writes, 'There is a curious jump from a primary rationing system which stresses overt rules and the definition of need as a means of qualifying for a council house, and a secondary rationing system based on discretion and judgements of "reward" or "merit" when it comes to the really critical decisions about the type of house and estate allocated.'[17]

How does this secondary rationing system operate? Many local authorities employ housing visitors who grade applicants according to their suitability for the different types of accommodation available to let. In the 1970s district housing offices in Liverpool were found to be grading prospective tenants either A, B, C or D.[18] Those graded C or D were excluded from new council housing. One housing inspector explained how he graded tenants. 'For "C" the bedding would have to be dirty and in a "D" your feet stick to the floor. An "A" would be given only for a place with fitted carpets and really clean.'[19] In Hull a sample of comments made by housing investigators in 1972 included 'good type of tenant, every effort made, suitable for any property offered'. 'Fair only – suitable for pre-war property' and, 'A good type of applicant – this is not a long-haired person, suitable for a post-war re-let.'[20] In Oldham, whose housing officials freely admitted that they used certain selection procedures which resulted in 'problem' families being allocated to the very unpopular Abbeyhills estate, housing visitors judged applicants on, amongst many other items, their carpets. 'You can tell whether they are today's crumbs or last week's'. Other factors were decorations and bed linen and the general appearance of their children. 'You can tell whether they are a caring family.'[21]

It is easy to mock the officials who make such judgements and to pour scorn on their values and obvious prejudices. It would also be easy to gain the impression from various accounts of the way in which housing visitors grade prospective tenants that they are all powerful. Jacobs, for example, comments, 'housing visitors seem to have almost absolute discretionary powers to decide a family's future.'[22] The CHAC report commented that grading systems left 'too much scope for personal prejudice and unconscious bias to be acceptable.'[23] Untrained housing visitors and counter staff may sometimes reveal strong personal prejudices against certain types of applicants for housing but this should not be regarded as the fundamental cause of discriminatory grading systems. Housing visitors and counter staff are usually carrying out duties imposed on them by their superiors. The policy of grading tenants according to their merits rather than their needs is usually formulated either by politicians or by senior housing officials. In order to fully understand why the grading of applicants is so widespread and persistent we must first examine the prevailing ideology of housing management and secondly explore the constraints under which housing officials operate.

Constraints on council housing allocators

Housing managers are primarily concerned to keep their housing stock in the best possible order. They often express a concern to be fair, particularly to good tenants and upright citizens. They defend their allocation policies on the grounds that allocating 'problem tenants' to low quality housing minimises the cost of misuse of dwellings and of rent arrears, deters potential trouble makers and protects 'good tenants' from unsuitable neighbours. Most housing managers appear to place the welfare of the community as a whole above the needs of those individuals and families whom they perceive as undeserving or trouble making.

We must not however place too much emphasis on the beliefs and actions of housing officials in any attempt to explain the strong and persistent relationship between individual deprivation and poor council accommodation. According to Ginsburg, it is tempting 'to identify the housing official personally as the oppressor' when, in fact, housing officials operate a system which is fundamentally controlled by local and national government policies, past and present.[24] Certainly some local politicians have played and do play an active role in shaping housing allocation policies and should be held accountable for those policies. Of course local politicians may claim that they themselves are restrained by public opinion. They need to retain public support for their policies and the public may well approve of punitive measures against the 'undeserving poor', including harsh treatment for the intentional homeless and housing 'queue jumpers'.

Housing officials themselves emphasise the severe constraint imposed upon them by the nature of the housing stock they must manage. Many local authorities now own dwellings of very mixed quality and desirability. If politicians and society as a whole expect low standard or unpopular council accommodation to be used, housing managers are left with the unenviable task of finding households to occupy it. In 1971, following an outcry against Glasgow corporation's grading policy, the *Glasgow News* predicted that this policy was unlikely to be abolished since, 'the whole machinery of house allocations depends on it. The fact is that a great deal of corporation housing in Glasgow leaves a lot to be desired, and some of it is just plain lousy – no one wants to live in these houses but – short of knocking them down – someone has to.'[25]

Some local authorities may have a deliberate policy of maintaining some dwellings at a very low standard in order to punish or to deter the 'undeserving' accommodation seekers. Various reports on the operation of the Housing (Homeless Persons) Act 1977 have found that some local councils deliberately place homeless families in sub-standard dwellings in order to discourage deliberate homelessness or 'queue jumping'.[26] Whether or not housing officials either suggest or condone such policies, it is clear that the ultimate responsibility for this version of Poor Law 'less eligibility' lies with local politicians. But local politicians themselves certainly do not have complete control over either the quantity or the quality of the local housing stock. Central government has always exercised some control over local housing expenditure. Since the mid 1970s successive governments have made major cuts in housing expenditure and by the early 1980s house building had reached an all time low. The outlook for improving the standard of council housing in the future is, therefore, particularly gloomy. Faced with the unpopular and in many cases structurally unsound legacy of their 1960s building programmes, most local authorities cannot afford the massive repair and improvement programmes necessary to bring their housing stock up to a uniformly acceptable standard. As whole estates become run down they become generally recognised as undesirable, low status or even slum areas.

The severe constraint imposed on local authority housing allocation policies by the existence of sub-standard houses and low status estates is compounded by the attitude of prospective tenants to such housing. It must be acknowledged that prospective tenants themselves may unwittingly play a part in allocating the most deprived to the worst types of public housing. Applicants with the most power, particularly those whose existing housing conditions are not unbearable, will usually refuse an offer of accommodation on an undesirable estate even though they realise that their refusal will mean a long wait for an alternative offer. Only those who are most desperate for housing, and those with no power to fight the system, will accept the worst of a council's accommodation. A survey of housing applicants in Hull found that 80 per cent of applicants interviewed said there were estates to which they would not want to go while 63 per cent said they would refuse accommodation on an unwanted estate even if they then had to wait a long time for an alternative offer.[27] Corina reports that when Oldham's housing officers were asked why they didn't try 'to leaven the composition of Abbeyhills by putting "good" tenants on the estate', they replied, 'Would you take a house on Abbeyhills?'. The researchers had to admit that they would not. To which the officials responded, 'Do you think that you could find "good" tenants who would go on Abbeyhills?'. Alternatively when the researchers asked why 'problem families' could not be dispersed amongst 'good' tenants, the officials replied, 'Would you like it if we put such and such a family near you?'.[28] Corina continues:

Once again the honest answer, which represents the views of most tenants on the 'good' estates was that one wouldn't like such and such a family living next door and if possible, not even on the same avenue. The constraint is quite clear and it is not just that the existing tenants would complain but that the chain reaction would start (i.e. good tenants would begin to leave the estate) and with it the seeds of deterioration would be sown.[29]

Although housing officials argue cogently that the grading of prospective tenants is inevitable, critics of this policy do not accept this view. The CHAC report stressed that only a few prospective tenants might 'not take care of a new house' and argued that it was 'a far cry from allocating specially selected housing to unsatisfactory tenants to grading all according to their "fitness" for particular types of houses.'[30] Jacobs suggests that a compassionate society, 'would make life as easy as possible for those least able to cope rather than force them to live in the most difficult circumstances.'[31] Nor do critics accept the argument that someone must be forced to live in very low quality housing. One radical alternative to grading tenants to fit existing housing stocks would be to increase public expenditure on housing and attempt to bring all public housing up to an acceptable, even a desirable standard.

The constraints imposed on housing officials by the nature of the housing stock and by the choices made by prospective tenants is not confined to the final stage of the housing allocation process. All aspects of the rationing of housing are ultimately dependent on the nature of the housing which is available. However hard housing officials try to make their selection procedures fair, they can do very little to alter any fundamental mismatch between needs and resources. This is reflected in the fact that restrictions on eligibility for council housing tend to be most severe where supply is at its lowest in relation to demand. Furthermore, the type of property available to let has a strong influence over applicants' chances of being rehoused. Murie *et al.* found that despite significant differences in the priority systems devised by local authorities, small families with young children were housed much more quickly than single people, and the elderly and large families. They discovered that since most local authorities gave priority to clearance rehousing and transfer applicants who asked for one-bedroomed flats, houses and bungalows, for which there was a high demand, waiting list applicants were left with a choice of two or three-bedroom flats or maisonettes. Consequently small families which would 'fit' into these types of dwellings stood the best chance of being offered accommodation.[32] Clearly, if councils had more three-bedroomed houses or one-bedroomed flats to offer the outcome of their selection procedures would be very different. Whom councils select for accommodation and how selectively they must operate may be partly determined by individual prejudice and by managerial or political ideologies but most writers agree that the quantity, quality and type of housing available to let all play an important part in constraining councils' selection policies.

Conclusion

The fact that need is not always the primary consideration in the distribution of public housing has worried many critics of the system. They have made attempts both to locate the cause of this problem and occasionally to apportion blame for the many failings of local authorities' systems. They have found that no allocation system is ideally suited to the goal of giving priority to those in greatest need. Informal systems allow too much scope for arbitrary decision making by biased individuals. Formal systems, including very sophisticated points systems, cannot fully respond to the complexities of individuals' housing needs. As well as pointing out the inadequacies of the methods of allocation used by housing departments, critics have also focused attention on the prejudices of front line housing staff and on the ideology of housing managers. Both these groups have been blamed for the emphasis placed on the protection of housing stock and on the labelling of certain groups of needy applicants as undeserving or unsuitable. A great deal has now been written demonstrating the strong relationship between the labelling of certain applicants as undesirable and the concentration of deprived families in low standard or stigmatised public housing. However researchers who have attempted to formulate solutions to this problem have tended to conclude, albeit reluctantly, that housing officers and local politicians have very little freedom for manoevre when allocating council property.

All the evidence so far available shows that local authorities' allocation schemes and individual decisions made by housing officials do play some part in determining an individual applicant's chances of receiving an offer of reasonable accommodation. On the other hand, housing officials and local policy makers are severely constrained by a variety of factors beyond their control. In the main allocation schemes are drawn up in response to a number of structural pressures. Therefore, 'in no real sense of the word can allocation policy be assumed to be a result of the unfettered discretion and/or the preferences of those responsible for the implementation of that policy'.[33]

Faced with a severe cutback in housing finance, a statutory sales policy allowing good tenants to buy good council stock, and an economic recession which increases those unable to house themselves in the private market, constraints on housing allocation policies in the 1980s are likely to increase considerably. This does not mean that housing officials will have no power whatsoever to influence the outcome of their own selection procedures.[34] But given the constraints on housing allocations discussed in this chapter it seems highly unlikely that local politicians or housing officials could, even by a supreme effort of will, radically change the distribution of council accommodation. Indeed given the increasing constraints on public sector housing, we must conclude that less resources for housing are likely to produce even more restrictive and judgemental rationing systems than those presently in operation.

9

Charges and Means Tests

Universalists, such as Titmuss and Townsend, have consistently condemned the use of charges and means tests in the welfare sector. This may explain why so many students of social policy dismiss out of hand all arguments in favour of selective welfare provision and why little empirical research has been carried out into consumers' reactions to the use of charges and means-testing. The consequences of their use have tended to be assumed rather than proved. Yet taken at face value much of the selectivists' case in favour of charges and means tests makes good sense. It is difficult to deny, for example, the logic of concentrating scarce welfare resources on those otherwise unable to obtain help. Indeed universalists do not deny that the only way to ensure that the social services redistribute welfare to the poor is to positively discriminate in their favour. Supporters of the NHS and compulsory state education now accept that the relatively affluent have tended to get more out of them than the poor and deprived. According to Brian Abel-Smith, 'The main effect of the post war development of the social services has been to provide free social services to the middle classes.'[1] Universalists, however, reject consumer charges combined with means tests as the answer to this problem.

In recent years the universalists have found themselves increasingly on the defensive. From the mid-1970s following the economic crisis and the call for savings in public expenditure, a new interest developed in the use of charges in the welfare field, an interest which was both theoretical and practical. This chapter will examine the political objectives of existing consumer charges in the social services; review the fragmentary evidence on the effects of these charges on consumer demand for services; assess the advantages and disadvantages of using charges as a rationing device in the welfare field and finally review the debate on the use of means tests to modify welfare charges.

The objectives of charges

In the late 1970s providers of welfare services began to take a new, if sometimes reluctant, interest in the potential of welfare charges. Undoubtedly the main reason for this upsurge of interest in charging was that it was seen as a means of reducing the public cost of providing welfare services. Since the mid-1970s, for example, the main objective of increases in charges for home helps has been to raise revenue. Indeed this has been one of the main responses of social services departments to cuts in local government spending.[2] Similarly many local education authorities have attempted to raise revenue by increasing their charges for school meals. Between October 1979 and October 1980 the price of school meals rose from the then statutory 35p to an average of 45p. By the autumn of 1980 some local authorities were charging as much as 60p. Other local authorities attempted to save money by running down or even closing their school meals service. Others, however, having raised their charges attempted to keep consumer demand up with an unprecedented wooing of parents and pupils. Warwickshire County Council actually resorted to an advertising campaign which was the subject of much mirth in the media. Another example of a charging policy primarily designed to raise revenue was the Conservative government's decision in 1980 to raise substantially the fees paid by overseas students at British universities. According to the then Secretary of State for Education, Mark Carlisle, the policy of full fees for overseas students was 'intended to cut the £127m subsidy which had arisen from uneconomic fee levels, not to reduce numbers coming to Britain.'[3]

Some welfare charges have primarily been intended to reduce overall consumer demand. In 1951 the Labour Government hoped and expected that their charge for dentures would reduce demand by up to a quarter.[4] In 1958 the Conservative Minister for Health, speaking about dental charges, explained: 'We must get the supply and demand into balance: with this in mind as much as economy we shall impose a charge of a pound.'[5] Certain charges or increased charges have been proposed in order to deter only those who abuse a 'free' service rather than to affect demand from all users including those in genuine need. In 1979 the Conservative spokesman on health, Patrick Jenkin, announced that his party intended to increase prescription charges mainly as a revenue raising exercise but also in order to curb frivolous demands for prescribed drugs and medicines. Another clear example of a charge primarily intended to control abuse is the board and lodgings charge levied on parents whose children are 'in care'. From the earliest days of children being taken into care by public authorities officials have paid particular attention to the role of parental contributions as a means of controlling abuse rather than raising revenue. The Royal Commission of 1884 on Reformatory and Industrial Schools stated that payments by parents were 'the best check on the abuse' of these schools 'by parents who wish to get rid of their children's maintenance and education.'[5] The primacy of the objective of checking abuse by parents by charging them for state residential care clearly survived well into the 20th century. In 1952 the Home Office stated, 'one method – we think a legitimate method of discouraging people putting their children too lightly into public care is to make them pay a reasonable sum while the children are there.'[7] The fact that it now costs more to collect these charges than they raise in revenue suggests that deterring abuse is still the main objective of this particular welfare charge.

Those on the right of the political spectrum tend to support charges regardless of the revenue they raise or the demand they curb simply because they represent the application of market principles, albeit modified in practice. But even those on the left have occasionally accepted the need to impose a charge in order to remove the stigma of 'receiving something for nothing', a stigma which may be strongly felt by those socialised into a predominantly market orientated society. In 1948 the Labour government legislated for substantial charges to be made for residential accommodation for the elderly in order to free old peoples' homes from the stigma attached to the old workhouse system. Aneurin Bevan argued, in support of this charge, 'There is no reason at all why the public character of these places should not be very much in the background because the whole idea is that the welfare authorities should provide them and charge an economic rent for them, so that any old persons who wish to go may go there in exactly the same way as many well-to-do people have been accustomed to go into residential hotels.'[8] Although charges made for residential accommodation for the elderly are of considerable financial importance to local authorities, the rationale for these charges is still essentially symbolic. According to Parker, 'the charge was undoubtedly seen as signifying an end to pauper status. "Paying your way" symbolised the charge, even though it might entail no more than a transfer payment routed via the old person.'[9]

The effect of charges on overall demand

The actual effects of social policy measures are often markedly different from their intended effects. The small amount of evidence available on the deterrent effects of welfare charges must be interpreted with great care. Charging policies do not take place in a vacuum. It is, therefore, difficult to separate the direct effects of charging from the myriad of other factors which influence demand for, and use of, the statutory social services. In 1951 following the introduction of a substantial charge for dentures' figures from the Ministry of Health's Annual Report suggested that the charge had caused a 50 per cent drop in demand for NHS dentures, but Parker points out that the introduction of this charge probably coincided with a natural decline in demand for dentures quite unrelated to their cost.[10] A second cautionary note sounded by Parker is that the effect of a new or higher charge may be dramatic but short-lived.[11] Consumers of welfare services, like consumers in the private market, appear to grow accustomed to higher prices particularly if they do not rise with inflation. In 1971 an increase in the price of school meals from 9p to 12p was followed immediately by a 14 per cent drop in demand for meals. A few months later demand was approaching its old level and continued to rise.[12] A final caveat concerning the deterrent effect of charges is the problem of pinpointing the real focus of demand for statutory welfare. In the NHS, for example, doctors rather than patients make most direct demands on health care resources. It is doctors who decide what drugs or medicines a patient will be prescribed and whether or not he or she will receive hospital treatment. Despite general practitioners' complaints about patients who insist on 'a pill for every ill', doctors have far more control over the extent and cost of NHS prescribing than do their patients.

There is very little sophisticated evidence on the effects of NHS charges on patients' demand for health care. Bare statistics show that increases in prescription charges have usually been followed by at least a temporary fall in the number of NHS prescriptions dispensed, but such statistics must be treated with caution. As Martin and Williams have pointed out, charges are only one element in a situation which may be affected by numerous influences including seasonal variations in morbidity, the extent of self-medication and exhortations by the DHSS for economy in prescribing.[13] They suggest that the apparent decline in the number of prescriptions dispensed after the introduction of a shilling (5p) charge per prescription form in 1952 was due largely to the inflation of the 1951 figure by the influenza epidemic of that year. In December 1956, the charge was changed to one shilling an item, and the average number of prescriptions per patient dropped from 5.51 in 1956 to 4.93 in 1957, the lowest figure recorded in any full year since the NHS had been established. But this drop was accompanied by a sharp increase in the average cost per prescription. According to Martin and Williams's calculations, about 40 per cent of this increase was due to doctors prescribing larger quantities. It is, therefore, impossible to determine how much of the drop in the number of prescriptions dispensed was due primarily to changes in patients' behaviour and how much due to changes in doctors' prescribing behaviour. In 1971 the prescription charge was increased from 12½p to 20p, but by this time the large percentage of patients exempted from paying any prescription charges made the base statistics on numbers of prescriptions dispensed of little use to those interested in the effect of increased charges on patient demand. Lavers has calculated, however, that the increased charge led to a drop of 11 per cent in the number of *charged* prescriptions dispensed in the year following the rise and he has argued that this drop was due primarily to changes in patient behaviour.[14]

In 1979 the Conservative Government increased prescription charges from 20p to 70p and in December 1980 the charge was increased to £1. Very little evidence on the effects of these increases has yet appeared. A survey of 200 chemists around the country carried out by Taylor Nelson Medical and Social Surveys in 1981[15] found that 58 per cent of chemists surveyed had noticed a decrease in the number of prescriptions patients asked them to dispense following the increased charge. Two-thirds of the chemists said that more people were consulting them for advice on their ailments and a similar proportion reported an increase in their sale of non-prescribed medicines. But half the chemists also noticed a change in GPs' prescribing habits towards increasing the quantity of each item prescribed in order to offset the increased cost to the patient. Again it appears, although the evidence is as yet very thin, that the behaviour of doctors may be playing a part in determining the effects of an increased prescription charge.

There have been very few studies of the effects of NHS dental and opthalmic charges on consumer demand. A small scale study carried out in the late 1970s suggested that the relatively low dental charges then imposed did have some deterrent effects.[16] In 1979–82 dental charges trebled. In 1982 Waind reported that dentists were beginning to express their concern about the deterrent effect of such charges on their poorer patients, but he did not present any statistical evidence on this issue.[17] The question of whether or not NHS charges deter those wishing to use opthalmic services appears to be particularly difficult to answer because of the confusion in many consumers' minds between private and NHS services. The fact that many consumers dislike NHS frames may also affect their use of opthalmic services.[18]

Since 1949 all NHS consultations have been completely free of charge. One British supporter of consultation charges has claimed that they would not only provide a more just financial reward for GPs but would also 'put an end to the misuse of the doctor's services by calling him both too often in a particular case and also for unnecessary purposes.'[19] According to Reisman, 'were at least some welfare to be rationed by price, consumers might come to think of a visit to the doctors (to ask about a hangover) in terms of nine pints of best bitter foregone and might demand less marginal treatment if a genuine sacrifice had to be made in exchange for the benefit.'[20]

The only recent evidence on the relationship between consultation charges and consultation rates comes from countries whose health care systems are very different from Britain's. Maynard has summarised the results of three experiments in North America all of which introduced charges into insurance schemes which had previously provided health care totally free at point of use.[21] The results of all three experiments showed significant drops in patient demand following the introduction of charges. In the Palo Alto experiment at Stanford University, California the average number of visits per patient to the health clinic fell from 4.27 per annum to 2.9 per annum after the introduction of a 25 per cent charge for each clinic service used. In the Saskatchewan experiment the introduction in 1968 of a $1.50 charge for a surgery consultation and a $2.00 charge for home, emergency and outpatient visits reduced the use of physicians' services by the poor ('poor' as defined by the Economic Council of Canada) by an estimated 18 per cent. Beck calculated that of these charges the impact upon the poor was considerably greater than the reduction of service experienced by the entire population, which was estimated at 6 to 7 per cent.[22]

This evidence suggests that consumer charges do result in a drop in demand for physician services but Maynard warns that the results of these experiments have all the problems associated with such social engineering. Some studies on the effects of pricing health care have actually shown that charges *increase* consumption, presumably by legitimising demand. Finally, Maynard emphasises that we do not know enough about the role of doctors as demanders of health care services. He concludes, 'Our knowledge of the effect of prices levied on the behaviour of consumer-demanders and on the behaviour of doctor-demanders is noticeable by its absence.'[23] Under the present system of free consultations in Britain GPs can and do exercise a significant control over their consultation rates. They do so mainly by controlling the extent to which they tell patients to return for follow-up consultations. We do not know how this type of control might be affected by consultation charges, neither do we know to what extent patients might react to consultation charges by using substitute services such as accident and emergency departments, although there is some evidence to suggest that patients already refer themselves directly to these departments for primary care where access to GPs is restricted or delayed.

Turning from NHS charges to charges in the personal social services, we are told that these services 'probably contain more variations, inconsistencies, anomalies and means testing in relation to charges than any other social service.'[24] Yet the impact of this agglomeration of charges on consumer demand for personal social services received virtually no systematic or rigorous investigation until very recently. Some work is now being done in this area, however, and some interesting results have emerged so far.

According to Judge, the clearest evidence of charges within the personal social services having a deterrent effect on demand, comes from the post-war history of the provision of local authority day nurseries.[25] In 1952 the Conservative government authorised local authorities to impose 'suitable' charges on day nursery care. The main aim of this change in policy appeared to be to save public expenditure. Most local authorities subsequently increased charges for day nursery care and this increase had an immediate and continuing effect on consumer demand. In 1952 demand, as measured by attendances at day nurseries, dropped by 20 per cent. Judge concluded from his study, 'the imposition of increased charges for day nursery places in 1952 had a very significant impact on the demand for, and supply of, public day care which has probably persisted to this present day.'[26] Judge also pointed out that the charges for local authority nursery care led to consumers transferring demand from the public sector to private nurseries and baby minders.

In recent years a number of small studies have been carried out to determine the effect home help charges or increased charges have had on consumer demand for this service. Judge and Matthews have distinguished three possible consumer reactions to the imposition of charges for home help services.[27] First, consumers may be deterred from making an initial demand for the service because of the price they expect to have to pay for it. There is little evidence to show whether or not consumers do react in this way but Hunt, in a survey of home help organisers noted, '28 organisers thought that some people were deterred from asking for a home help and that some gave up having one because of the cost. 14 thought some people were deterred from asking but that none gave up.'[28] Second, consumers may stop receiving the service if a charge is either imposed or increased. Studies carried out in one or two local authorities do show a relationship between increased charges and terminations. In Essex, for example, 8 per cent of clients cancelled the service after the imposition of a flat rate charge of £1 per week in April 1977.[29] Third, consumers may respond to charges by choosing not to receive their full allocation of a home help. In Devon, 16.5 per cent of home help consumers paying the standard charge reduced their level of service following a price increase of 45 per cent (from 55p to £1).[30]

In contrast to this evidence that home help charges do deter some clients from making full use of the service, some social services departments have claimed that after abolishing all charges for home helps they experienced no increase in demand. This suggests that if charges were raised there ought to be no decline in demand.[31] But, as Judge explains, the price mechanism does not operate in the welfare sector in the same way as in the private sector. In the welfare sector charges are just one of a number of rationing mechanisms employed by the providers of welfare services to control consumer demand. Home helps, for example, are usually allocated by welfare providers according to their judgements about clients' needs. In many local authorities strict eligibility criteria determine who will qualify for help. In certain local authority areas, an elderly person has to be living alone and suffering from some degree of incapacity before they will even be considered for help. In such cases the supply of home helps is restricted to a level below latent demand at prevailing charges. In other words, if one person is put off using the services because of the charge, there will be someone else willing or eager to take their place. This means that an increased charge will not necessarily lead to a fall in effective demand for a service. What it may do, although more research is needed into this area, is to re-distribute services to those better able or willing to afford them at the new price perhaps at the expense of those deemed to be most in need of help by welfare providers.

Do charges deter those most in need?

The key debate about charges in the social services has not centred on the effect they have on overall levels of demand but on whether the imposition of charges is likely to deter those in greatest need, as opponents of charges claim, or whether, as supporters of charges contend, they simply squeeze out marginal demands from the least needy consumers. What evidence is there to enlighten this debate?

As Maynard has pointed out in relation to attempts to assess the extent to which health care charges deter those in genuine need of health care, the definition of 'need' in such cases is a contentious issue.[32] Welfare providers' definitions of welfare needs may not match consumers' own definitions. Yet the evidence on the extent to which welfare charges deter those in genuine need is based almost exclusively on providers' judgements.

Some studies of utilisation rates of health care services have suggested, as one might expect, that poor patients are more likely to be deterred by health care charges than others. A small study of the extent to which patients do not present their prescriptions to pharmacists found in 1981 that patients in social class IV had the highest rate of 'non-compliance' and that nearly 40 per cent of patients in this class did not get their prescriptions dispensed.[33] This study did not prove that poorer patients were deterred from presenting their prescriptions because of the cost but it did suggest that those in lower socio-economic groups who pay prescription charges may find a prescription of several items expensive. One pharmacist commented that many patients asked for only the most important item on the prescription. But the study also listed a number of other factors which may have accounted for the class variation in the presentation of prescriptions. Included in these was the lack of need for the prescriptions given to them on the part of some of the patients who went to their GPs for sickness certificates. A retrospective study of the abolition of charges to patients for use of a deputising service in Denmark found that increase in demand was greatest, almost double the average, in areas which had a low average income amongst employed people and a high proportion of old people.[34] Given the relatively high levels of morbidity amongst the poor and the elderly such findings do suggest that health care charges may deter those very groups who are most in need of health care services.

There is not enough firm evidence to show conclusively whether health charges deter those who would otherwise misuse or abuse the service or whether they deter a significant number of patients with genuine health care needs, but according to Judge and Matthews the weight of existing evidence does support the NHS Royal Commission's conclusion that charges 'could well discourage patients from seeking help when they really needed it.'[35]

Little evidence exists about the relative needs of those deterred by consumer charges in the personal social services. Judge and Matthews reporting a drop of 20 per cent in demand for meals on wheels following a significant price increase in one London Borough, suggested that the subsequent elimination of the waiting list for this service may have meant that clients receiving the meals who gave them up because of the cost were replaced by clients who had been assessed as of a lower priority by the service providers. They concluded, 'In this instance the effect of the price increase may have been not only to mute demand but also to redistribute the benefit of a meal from a "needy" to a less "needy" client.'[36]

Several studies of the users of home help services have attempted to assess the relative needs of those who ceased using the service following a charge increase. In 1980 Bradford home help organisers felt that the largest category amongst the 150 clients who had discontinued the service after the imposition of a flat rate charge could be described as 'marginal cases' who did not highly value the service they received.[37] However there were also smaller groups who were assessed as being in high need who either could not pay or who refused to do so on principle.

A study of 366 cancellations of home help service in the London Borough of Redbridge found that those clients who cancelled the service following the imposition of a flat rate charge tended to be less needy in terms of health and handicap, social isolation and need for emotional support. On the other hand, these clients had been receiving less home help time and tended to receive help with heavy housework which could not be provided from any other source. Finally, the Redbridge study found that very poor 'needy' users of the home help service had absorbed home help charges by cutting down on other essentials such as food and heating.[38] This finding suggests that in services where clients may have no other source of help researchers should seriously consider the possibility that imposing or increasing charges may lower the living standards of the poorest welfare clients.

Advantages and disadvantages of charges

Supporters of charges argue that their extension would significantly increase allocative efficiency in the welfare sector. An increased use of charges, they claim, would make both consumers and producers much more aware of the true costs of providing and using welfare services. For example Seldon says, 'the absence of prices [in the welfare sector] as landmarks, benchmarks, bearings and signposts causes confusion, distortion and waste, and their restoration wherever possible is essential in making the best use of resources.'[39] This argument will not be pursued here.[40]

An attractive argument used by supporters of charges is that they promote consumer choice and participation in the allocation of welfare resources. They do so by enabling consumers to signal their preferences directly to those providing the services. Judge and Matthews, for example, suggest that a system of charging combined with welfare vouchers might enable even the poorest clients of social service departments to choose for themselves which particular mix of services they wish to receive.[41] An elderly client receiving both social work assistance and a home help, for example, might decide that the social worker was relatively useless and would therefore 'spend' his or her welfare voucher to increase consumption of the home help service. Those on the left reject the concept of consumer sovereignty within a capitalist society on the grounds that the system of production manipulates consumers and does not allow them the choice to obtain the goods and services which they would naturally desire in a less manipulative system. They have tended to support consumer participation within the social services rather than the concept of consumer choice which, they argue, can mean choice for the few at the expense of the many. The argument that an increased use of charges could promote consumer choice within the social service must also be evaluated in the light of the existing powers of welfare providers. In many instances society has deliberately chosen to override consumer freedom of choice in order to place decision making about the allocation of welfare services in the hands of expert welfare providers. Unless the power of these providers is reduced, welfare charges *per se* will not create anything approaching sovereignty for the welfare client. Patients are not given a much greater choice over their consumption of prescribed drugs and medicines by the imposition of higher prescription charges if GPs still totally control the prescribing process. Thus, 'the more the locus of decision making about the consumption of a service is removed from the actual consumer (for whatever reasons) the more the case for using consumer charges is correspondingly weakened.'[42]

Opponents of welfare charges raise a number of objections to their use. Some universalists object to all forms of charging on principle as an outright attack on the welfare state. Opponents of charges also argue that they may prevent adequate individual consumption of socially beneficial welfare goods and services. This argument is part of the debate about whether or not most of the services provided by the welfare sector are primarily private or collective goods, an argument which will not be pursued here. Finally, opponents of charges are particularly concerned with the deterrent effect which they have on welfare demands from poor clients. This concern is enhanced by their belief that the poorer groups in society tend to have the greater welfare needs.

If some potential welfare clients are too poor to be willing or able to pay flat rate charges for welfare services, one solution is to provide social services free of charge to rich and poor alike. An alternative solution is to charge the rich but subsidise the poor. Subsidies could take a number of forms. Those deemed too poor to pay charges could be given welfare vouchers which would cover the cost of the service or services they required. One method of sub- sidising poor welfare charges is by a system of means-testing. Since much of the debate against the use of means-testing in the welfare sector has centred around the use of means-tested social security benefits rather than the use of means-tested charges, some of the evidence used in the following evaluation of the use of means-tests to modify welfare charges will be taken from the debate over means- tested financial benefits.

Means-testing

Selectivists argue that the widespread use of charges combined with means-testing would ensure that welfare resources were concen- trated on those in greatest need. Selectivists tend to use the word 'need' to mean 'unable to afford' or 'poor'. Seldon and Gray, for example, refer to public support for the view that 'free health prescriptions should be reserved for people in need.'[43] By this they do not mean that free prescriptions should go only to the sick but that they should go only to those who are both sick and poor. Selectivists are misleading when they imply that universal services go to everybody whereas selective services go only to those in real need. In fact so-called universal services go only to those who fall into a particular category of need or into a particular eligibility group. Thus free health care, in theory at least, goes only to the sick whilst child benefit goes only to parents with dependent children. Selective services on the other hand, go only to those who not only belong to a particular category of need but who also have incomes below a certain prescribed level.

Selectivists argue persuasively that universal services cannot possibly give adequate help to the poor and deprived. According to Seldon and Gray, 'it is the "poor and the poorest" who lose by universalism.'[44] 'Universal services supplied without charge or test of need [i.e. a means test] make it difficult or impossible for best intentioned politicians to find the money to give more generous assistance to victims of special hardship or handicaps.'[45] Certainly many of those who wish to see a more egalitarian distribution of welfare benefits accept that *in principle* means-tested charges appear to be an effective device for channelling resources to poorer welfare consumers. Why then do most universalists object so strongly to means-testing? They put forward a number of key objections not all of which are controversial. The arguments that means-testing is costly in administrative terms and that means-tested benefits are a disincentive for the poor to work, or to work harder, would probably be accepted by most supporters of means-testing and will not be examined further. The other main objections made by universalists to means tests are more contentious. First, they claim that means-tested benefits will inevitably fail to reach all those entitled to them and are, therefore, an inherently unfair and inefficient form of subsidy. Second, they argue that means tests are socially divisive. Means tests identify and separate the poor from the rest of society. They impose a stigma on those who submit themselves to be means-tested whilst the threat of being stigmatised deters many more from taking up their rights. Finally, universalists argue that means-tested benefits and services which are given only to the poor will be poor benefits and services.

No one denies that existing means-testing fails to ensure that all those entitled to subsidies or special financial benefits actually receive them. In 1979 the percentage of those entitled to free prescriptions on the grounds of low income alone who actually got them was estimated at only 2 per cent.[46] Similarly in 1977 less than 2 per cent of those eligible for free welfare milk and vitamins on the grounds of low income (excluding those already receiving supplementary benefits) received any help.[47] Much of the evidence on low take-up of means-tested benefits is related to social security benefits rather than means-tested charges for services. The overall take-up rate for supplementary benefits was officially estimated in 1978 to be around 74 per cent.[48] This meant that approximately £400m of benefits was left unclaimed in one year. Selectivists argue that the problem of take-up is over stated since many of those officially eligible for a means-tested benefit would receive such a small amount of cash that it may simply not be worth the bother of claiming it. However the main thrust of the selectivists' case is not that the problem of take-up has been exaggerated but that it would not be difficult to solve. Seldon and Gray answering the argument 'the means tests we have already do not work', state simply 'then let us devise workable ones.'[49]

Opponents of means-testing are well aware that low take-up rates are partly due to the administrative weaknesses of existing schemes, weaknesses which could be eliminated. They fully acknowledge and protest against the fact that lack of advertising and a proliferation of complicated claim forms cause a considerable loss of take-up of means-tested benefits. They do not accept, however, that administrative improvements and better advertising could ever produce acceptably high levels of take-up. Their main objection to means-tests is not that they are badly administered but that they are inherently stigmatic:

> Central to the universalist argument is that the stigma induced by the means test deters the eligible from claiming their entitlement. However vertically efficient the incidence of the subsidy of a means-tested service might look it is inevitably inefficient in that the potential for stigma of the means test deters many in need from applying.[50]

The belief that stigma is the key factor in low take-up of means-tested benefits has influenced both academics and social policy makers. Is this belief supported by empirical evidence? Davies's work on the causal factors of low take-up of free school meals led him to suggest that the importance of stigma may have been over-estimated. In 1967 Alf Morris stated in a debate in the House of Commons on free school meals, 'it is estimated that last year 660,000 children were entitled to receive free meals but well over 300,000 of these children refused to take free meals. They refused ... because their parents were sensitive to taking charity.'[51] Yet when Davies carried out a survey of non-take-up of free school meals he found that 'less than one family in ten who had considered applying did not do so because they were unwilling to reveal personal income or felt that applying would have injured their pride or risked the embarrassment of their children.'[52] Davies concluded that ignorance of the free meal scheme appeared to be considerably more important than stigma as a factor causing low take-up of this benefit. Davies's tentative conclusion from data collected in the late 1960s that stigma as a cause of low take-up of means-tested benefits may have been overemphasised, is supported by other evidence. Meacher's study in 1973 of the take-up of rate rebates found that ignorance of the benefit, of the income limits and of the claiming procedure, appeared to account for 72 per cent of non-take-up by those eligible for help.[53]

The success of advertisement campaigns for certain means-tested benefits, at least in the short term, also suggests that ignorance may be a more important cause of non-take-up than stigma. A government campaign to improve take-up of free welfare milk, prescriptions and remission of dental and optical charges in 1971 led to a substantial increase in the number of applications for these benefits. For example whereas only 15,000 free prescriptions were granted on the grounds of low income in 1970, in 1972 following the advertisement campaign the figure was 69,000.[54]

Not all who write on welfare matters accept that the problem of stigma in relation to means-tested charges has been exaggerated. A report in *New Society* in January 1982 claimed that cut backs in the school meals service in general and a reduction in the number eligible for free meals had significantly intensified the stigma attached to taking free meals, and that this in turn was affecting take-up rates. The report noted that between 1979 and 1980 there was a 79 per cent drop in the number of primary school children taking free meals in Dorset. According to this report not all of this drop could be explained away by loss of entitlement and the fall in numbers on the school rolls.[61] It concluded that many parents who were still entitled to free school meals must have decided that they would rather provide meals themselves and thus suffer a fall in living standards rather than 'subject their children to embarrassment and humiliation at school.'[55]

Opponents of means tests are not solely concerned with the effects of stigma on the take-up of means-tested benefits. They also strongly object to those means-tested benefits which impose stigma on those who do claim them. The Lancashire School Meals Campaign, for example, objected to the increased stigma which it claimed was being imposed on those children still taking free school meals. 'As the UK sinks into recession school meal-times see poorer pupils being systematically humiliated. Different tickets or discs are given to free recipients. In some schools now they eat separated from other pupils.'[56] The Child Poverty Action Group also collected evidence of this increased stigma. A single mother wrote, 'The meal system didn't start out as a means of discrimination, but my daughter feels it very much as so many children have dropped out . . . although she is unhappy about it she needs that meal regularly so I "enforce" the taking of it.'[57]

Much of the concern expressed in the early 1980s over the stigma associated with free school meals focused on the danger of the school meals service becoming a residual welfare service for poor children only. The Child Poverty Action Group claimed, 'As "paying" children withdraw, we are faced with the prospect of school meals being *only* for non-payers. If we worry about the stigma now associated with *not paying,* it falls into insignificance with the potential stigma attached to eating school meals.'[58] According to Titmuss, any selective service used only by the poor will become a stigmatising second rate service. Titmuss also strongly objected to means-testing on the grounds that it forced the poor to stand up and define themselves as poor and involved a 'humiliating loss of status, dignity or self-respect.'[59]

Much of the evidence on the stigma attached to means-tested benefits is related to social security benefits. There is less evidence of stigma attached to the use of means-tests to subsidise the poor who use services such as home helps and meals on wheels. There is no doubt that claimants of means-tested social security benefits have been stigmatised or have at least felt stigmatised but the causes of this problem need to be carefully examined before the assumption is made that all means tests are equally stigmatic.

According to the Schlackman report on public attitudes towards the supplementary benefit system, 'degrading' was the epithet most commonly used to describe the process of claiming by both claimants and non-claimants alike.[60] Interviews with claimants have shown that while some claimants feel stigmatised simply by having to ask for help at all, others feel that stigma is imposed upon them either by the process of claiming or by the attitudes of non-claimants towards them. One woman who felt it was wrong to be claiming said, 'I feel guilty about claiming supplementary benefit or asking for any extras. I don't like relying on DHSS.' Another claimant felt stigmatised because, 'people look down on us as scroungers.'[61] A number of claimants appear to blame social security offices and staff for the shame they felt when applying for help. One woman commented, for example, 'They make you feel terrible. They treat you like dirt.'[62]

The stigma which is undoubtedly still associated with claiming means-tested social security benefits can be explained in a number of ways. It may not be the means test itself which imposes stigma but other factors associated with those who claim means-tested benefits. As Reisman has pointed out, 'means testing is not the unique source of stigma and may not even be an important source of spoiled identity to the poor. Social values are a hard task master and are themselves a much greater threat to personal dignity than the need to submit to any means test.'[63] Reisman suggests that the greatest source of stigma in a competitive society may well be failure in the market place. A society which places great store by material success may well stigmatise the poor whether or not they apply for means-tested benefits. One claimant of supplementary benefits, explaining the stigma attached to the system said, 'by having supplementary benefits it means you're a loser. It's as simple as that.'[64] A second source of stigma in our society is that attached to those who receive without reciprocating. According to Forder our strongly held belief that 'income for which a return is or has been made is more acceptable than that provided without return' partly explains why, 'means-tested benefits have a lower legitimacy than almost any other kind of income that is not specifically criminal.'[65] He does not discuss the possibility that users of universal services may also feel some shame at receiving 'free' benefits. Little research has been done on this issue and we do not know whether the poor in particular feel any stigma in using 'free' social services. However Pinker suggests that 'most applicants for social services remain paupers at heart' and that this applies as much to universal as to selective services.[66] A final explanation of the stigma attached to means-tested poor relief is based on society's attitude towards dependency. In our society an adult who is dependent, particularly for any length of time, will suffer stigma. Dependents are receivers of help and the extent to which they will be stigmatised is determined by their potential to become 'givers' at some future date. The long term unemployed thus suffer far more stigma than those who have only been unemployed for a very short period. The chronically sick are more stigmatised than the acutely ill. Students and their parents do not appear to feel stigmatised by applying for means-tested university maintenance grants. This can be explained by a number of the factors discussed above. Students who gain entrance to university are clearly seen as successes rather than failures in our competitive society. They are regarded as potential givers to society in that their education is expected to enhance their value as skilled workers. Finally, students are seen as only temporarily dependent on state support. The derogatory term 'perpetual student' suggests that even students can suffer a mild form of stigmatisation if they continue to be dependent on the state for too long.

If stigma is primarily attached to states of dependency rather than whether or not a particular service is means-tested, stigma may not inevitably be attached to means-tests used to alleviate the deterrent effect of charges for such services as home helps or meals on wheels. Stigma may be attached to the need for these services *per se* but if means-tests are administered sensitively there may be little extra stigma involved in receiving these services free of charge. The fact that some home help clients appear to have terminated the service following the imposition of a flat rate charge on the grounds that they objected to the charge on principle suggests that some social service clients may be coming to regard certain free services as a right rather than as stigmatised charity.

Conclusion

For many years most writers on social policy and the welfare state simply ignored the existence of a whole range of consumer charges within the statutory social services. Similarly providers of welfare services made little attempt to rationalise the use of charges either within one particular service or across a range of services. Since the mid-1970s the change in the economic and political climate has led to a far greater interest in charges from both welfare practitioners and researchers. Empirical evidence is now beginning to enlighten the debate over the advantages and disadvantages of charging welfare consumers. Some research suggests that charges may sometimes deter those in genuine need of help and that in certain cases they may cause hardship to poor welfare consumers who continue to use services for which charges are made. Before we can reach any stronger conclusions on the effects of charges on welfare consumers, however, we need to find out far more about the characteristics of those who are deterred by charges and about the circumstances of those who continue to use services which incur charges. In particular researchers should undertake the difficult task of attempting to measure the relative needs of these two groups.

The assumption that means tests are inherently stigmatic and cannot therefore be used effectively to mitigate the adverse effects of consumer charges on the poor, is not conclusively confirmed by the available evidence. On the other hand, the selectivists' claim that means-testing could be used to concentrate welfare resources effectively on the most deprived can be challenged without assuming that means tests are inherently stigmatising. In order to understand the apparently deterrent effect of some means tests we must study closely the values and overall welfare objectives of the society in which such means-testing takes place. Means-testing *per se* can be used both positively and negatively. In theory it can be used to ensure that resources are concentrated on those in most need, but in practice it can be used to reduce social expenditure and as a means of social control. According to Townsend existing means tests are 'essentially devices which ration and control' and in a society which upholds the virtues of self-help, work and thrift, there will inevitably be a general discouragement to use means-tested services, a discouragement which manifests itself in the operating rules and administration of means tests.[67] Moreover means tests are often used in a way which denies help to the 'undeserving poor'. Townsend claims that people who behave unconventionally by, for example, disrespecting marriage or voluntarily choosing not to work 'will tend to be deprived of the benefits of means-tested service.'[68] He does not provide a great deal of evidence to support this claim but his argument that there is an inherent conflict in means-tested services between relieving poverty and implementing social control merits careful consideration.

It now seems likely that high flat rate charges for welfare services do have an adverse effect, in one way or another, on the poorest welfare consumers. Moreover selectivists have yet to demonstrate that the use of means-tested remission of charges could fully exempt the poor from the deterrent effects of charges without imposing other disadvantages upon them. However those who vehemently oppose the use of all charges and means tests within the social services cannot simply assume that the effects of these rationing devices are wholly negative. Only when both sides in this debate base their arguments on hard data rather than on ideological and emotional grounds, will the real advantages and disadvantages of rationing by charges and means-tests become fully apparent.

10
Strategies for Reform

Previous chapters examined the ways in which welfare providers control clients' access to the social services. It is now time to take an overview of the existing system of welfare rationing. This will begin by identifying the key failures attributed to current rationing methods. It will then examine critically three distinct approaches to the reform of welfare rationing which will be labelled 'administrative reformism', 'the market solution' and 'the Marxist alternative'.

Key failures of welfare rationing

Four main failures of the existing forms of welfare rationing can be identified. First, they fail to ensure that all those in need of help actually receive it. Means-tested benefits, for example, are strongly attacked on the grounds that many of those with a 'right' to such benefits fail to claim them. Other forms of eligibility criteria are criticised on similar lines. For example, certain non-contributory cash benefits for the disabled are allocated according to such stringent definitions or measurements of disability that some severely disabled individuals are not helped by their provision. In addition, consumer charges, particularly in the health and personal social services, are criticised for deterring individuals in genuine need of help from seeking it. In fact, a careful search through the disadvantages attributed to all the various rationing methods which we have studied in this book, would reveal that virtually all of them have, at some time or another, attracted the criticism that they exclude some individuals with real welfare needs from gaining access to the service they require.

Many critics of welfare rationing accept that demand for 'free' welfare will always exceed its supply and therefore that no rationing method could ever ensure that all those 'in need' received adequate help. This does not mean, however, that existing patterns of welfare distribution are also accepted as inevitable. Most writers on welfare issues insist that the primary, if not the sole objective, of all forms of welfare rationing ought to be to give priority to those in greatest need. In practice, critics of the social services claim, many types of rationing frequently fail to give priority to the most needy. This second main criticism of welfare rationing is prominent in the debate over the role of discretionary benefits in the social security system. The Chairman of the SBC himself admitted in 1976 that discretionary payments were not always given to those in greatest need of them. He also accepted that discretionary benefits sometimes went to those who were deemed to be most deserving rather than to 'undeserving' claimants in greater need. Other rationing devices attract similar criticism. Critics claim that rules governing eligibility for council housing, such as residential qualifications, ensure that urgency of need is not the primary consideration in the allocation of much public housing.

All forms of rationing which rely heavily on the judgement and discretion of individual welfare professionals are criticised for leading to a somewhat arbitrary distribution of welfare services which inevitably fails to secure equal treatment for those in equal need. Thus it appears that, either deliberately or inadvertently, the welfare state has failed to ensure a fair distribution of benefits based solely on an assessment of individuals' relative welfare needs.

The many disadvantages of existing methods of welfare rationing are not confined to the problems of those who, for one reason or another, fail to gain access to the service they require. A third major failing of administrative rationing is that welfare clients and potential clients rarely have a significant degree of choice regarding the quantity or nature of the services and benefits they receive. According to Reisman, 'the client in the welfare state has had inadequate opportunity to choose . . . where welfare professionals do not compete for sovereign consumers the individual has no alternative to the posture of the taker rather than the chooser'.[1] Many examples of the restrictions on consumer choice and power have been discussed during the course of this book, such as the lack of choice given to applicants for public housing and the imbalance of power between welfare professionals and their clients.

The fourth failure attributed – at least in part – to welfare rationing is the continuing inequalities between the social classes in their use of welfare services. The informal rationing devices employed by some GPs, for example, may exacerbate initial class differences in demand for, and use of, primary health care services. Similarly, the way in which pupils are allocated to individual comprehensive schools; the way in which teachers allocate their own time and attention to individual pupils in their classes and the emphasis placed on 'A' level results by university selectors, are all forms of welfare rationing which may tend to exacerbate social class inequalities in the field of education.

Administrative reformism

A group of writers on welfare rationing are optimistic that reforms to the present system of statutory welfare provision could substantially reduce the problems created by existing rationing devices.[2] This group explains the failure of rationing mainly in terms of lack of planning and control. Parker concluded his seminal article on rationing thus:

> The existence of 'universal provision' has unfortunately seduced many into believing that the problem of rationing no longer arises. As a result, its political and administrative implications tend to have been side-stepped, and the problem all too often allowed to resolve itself without conscious planning or public debate – often to the detriment of the weakest and most needy.[3]

The implication of Parker's conclusion is that more conscious planning, more open rationing, would benefit the weakest and most needy. Hall puts forward the similar view that 'frequently . . . services are received not by those in greatest need (by any definition)' and that this is primarily due to a lack of 'rational decision making about how resources should be allocated between the range of demands being made.'[4]

These writers argue that in order to ensure that their primary objective of distributing welfare according to individuals' needs is met, social policy makers and planners must openly discuss the problems of rationing and take explicit decisions on how resources should best be allocated. Thus Hall proposes that rationing methods should be 'rational and systematic and based on conscious decisions by service providers about high and low priority needs',[5] while Cooper calls for more information on resources, needs and demands to be made available to all those involved in the provision of health care so that 'unavoidable rationing' can take place 'more rationally, consistently and efficiently to the mutual benefit of tax payers and patients.'[6]

How would this reformist approach solve the four main failures of existing rationing methods that have been identified? First, reformists do not pretend that a better planned system would meet all welfare needs. They accept that there will always be a mis-match between resources and needs because 'needs are potentially infinite: resources always limited and therefore scarce.'[7] The second problem of rationing that was identified, the failure to give priority to the most needy, is dealt with by their claim that if rationing were planned in a more efficient and coherent way cases of urgent need would be less likely to slip through the welfare net unintentionally. Moreover, they say, less wastage of resources would enable more to be spent on those in genuine need. Reformists believe in a rational model of social policy. They do not look for hidden motives lying behind the provision of statutory welfare services. They accept as genuine the stated objectives of the social services which emphasise the meeting of individuals' welfare needs. They believe, therefore, that rationing which is arbitrary or which discriminates against those in greatest need cannot accord with the intentions of social policy makers. What is required is for welfare planners and providers to pay far more attention to the needs of the less articulate and the most deprived. Parker quotes with approval Enoch Powell's claim that the 'worst kind of rationing is that which is unacknowledged'[8] and goes on to argue that unless rationing is 'conscious and explicit some form of rationing will emerge (by default) through the manner in which the service is provided. Where this happens, those who are most easily deterred, least articulate, worst acquainted with the service, least able to wait, or who fall outside the conventional categories of eligibility will tend to be penalised.'[9] The corollary of this argument is that if welfare rationing becomes more conscious and explicit those least able to cope with the present system will receive all the help and attention they so clearly need. Indeed

Parker specifically recommends policy makers to implement planned programmes of positive discrimination in order to ensure that those in greatest need receive their fair share of help. He suggests, 'a share of any service needs to be specifically earmarked for those least likely to consume it if left to press their own claims in a rationing situation.'[10] Parker fails to address the possibility that many of those in urgent need of state support may deliberately be denied help by official rationing rules and regulations.

The issue of consumer choice and power is ignored by Parker but it has been addressed by other writers who are reformist in their suggestions for change. Wilding, for example, recognises that the present relationship between professionals and their clients is unsatisfactory. He argues that what is needed is a new form of 'professional-client relationship in which discussion and dialogue can take place with mutual respect for what both parties can contribute.'[11] How is this new relationship to be brought about? Wilding accepts that the various attempts which have already been made to represent consumer views to welfare professionals and planners – such as Community Health Councils and parent governors in schools 'can hardly be called encouraging.'[12] But he does not believe that previous failures should lead us to abandon attempts to incorporate consumers' views within the existing social services. He therefore suggests a range of reforms which taken together might lead to a less unequal relationship between professional welfare providers and their clients. If a less unequal relationship could be secured, he argues, welfare clients would be free to exercise more self-determination and choice in the welfare field.

Some writers on welfare issues, whilst accepting that welfare services are far from perfect, have argued that they have at least secured equal access to welfare for all social classes (cf. Cochrane, 1972). Other reformists have clearly recognised the failure of both the NHS and the education services to ensure either equal access or, more significantly, equal use by all social classes. Suggestions for reforms which would alleviate this problem have been legion – particularly in the field of education. Once it was recognised that equality of provision alone would not solve the problem of social class educational inequalities, reformers suggested that various forms of positive discrimination should be devised in order to ensure that children from disadvantaged backgrounds received extra educational resources. However after the optimism of the

Plowden era the late 1970s saw the onset of the pessimistic attitude that schools made no difference, and many educational reformers became temporarily disillusioned with the view that tinkering with the allocation of educational resources could solve educational inequalities.

Despite many setbacks in their search for successful administrative reforms within the statutory social services, most reformers appear to remain optimistic that changes to the existing welfare system could improve the distribution of welfare benefits in our society. Their optimism is based on their belief that the social services are primarily intended to help those in need rather than to control or manipulate them. They also believe that we live in a pluralist society in which pressure groups and popular movements can effectively fight for reforms and influence the political process. This optimism and belief in the welfare state is not shared by either the pro-marketeers or the radical left.

The market solution

The main response of the anti-collectivists or pro-marketeers to the problem of welfare rationing is to advocate a return to rationing by price. The pro-marketeers' main concern is with the freedom of the individual and their key argument is that consumer power and choice can only be adequately secured in a market system. Anti-collectivists pour scorn on all attempts to give more power to consumers within the existing social services. According to Harris and Seldon, 'the recent efforts to introduce the voice of the parent-earner in *ad hoc* machinery like Parent–Teacher Associations, or Area Health Authorities remains defective because they ... rest on "representation" that cannot speak effectively for all the earners whose earnings the representatives, or even worse, permanent officials, are spending.'[13] Pro-marketeers argue that not only must the price mechanism be restored, but also state monopolies over services such as health and education must be broken up if consumers are to have real choice over the consumption of welfare. In 1967 a study group of the Institute of Economic Affairs stated, 'We believe that if people are to develop their talents they must be able to exercise their preferences freely . . . Hence, wherever administratively feasible, welfare should be provided through markets comprising suppliers competing to supply consumers able and willing to buy by choosing between them.'[14]

Pro-marketeers accept that under a totally competitive market system, some people might lack the resources to buy the welfare goods and services they and their families needed. Their solution to this problem is to provide these people with the sufficient purchasing power either in cash – which would permit and encourage maximum consumer choice – or in the form of vouchers earmarked for specific service. The earmarked voucher would, according to the Institute of Economic Affairs study group, 'enable market prices to be restored as the means of registering preferences . . . it would attract new suppliers, encourage innovation and for the first time, create the vehicle for freedom of choice in welfare for wage-earners as well as people with higher incomes.'[15] According to Rhodes Boyson the educational voucher would fully arm all parents with the power of consumers who could take their custom elsewhere. 'This could improve most schools, force the improvement, closure or take-over of bad schools, strengthen the family and strike a blow for the free society by giving parents real choice in such an important area of their lives.'[16]

Those in favour of the restoration of a market system for welfare claim that apart from restoring consumer power and choice it would actually meet more needs than the present system does because supply would no longer be artificially restricted. They claim that individuals would be willing to pay more for services if they could be assured that their payments directly benefited themselves and their families. Harris and Seldon quote with approval Douglas Houghton's comment that, 'while people would be willing to pay for better services for themselves, they may not be willing to pay more in taxes as a kind of insurance premium which may bear no relation to the services actually received.'[17] According to Harris and Seldon, 'the dependence of welfare on finance extracted from citizens as taxpayers may not increase, but reduce the resources devoted to education and medical care by frustrating individual and family choice.'[18]

A similar argument was used by the authors of the Jones Report on the financing of health services.[19] They claimed that if private consumption expenditure on health care were to be encouraged there could be a considerable increase in revenue for health care services and a guarantee that supply would automatically reflect demand for health care.

Pro-marketeers do not only argue that more welfare needs could be met under a market based welfare system. They also suggest that if most consumers bought their own welfare through the private market the state could provide much more efficient and effective help for the poor and deprived. According to Harris and Seldon,

> The best that can be said for the universalist policy of free services is that it operates like a blunderbuss, by scattering benefits widely it aims to miss no-one who may be in need of them. Yet, despite the mischievous and wilful obfuscation about dislike of 'means tests' a more efficient method of raising minimum standards is available through a 'selective' policy of topping up low incomes.[20]

In a similar vein the Jones Report claimed that if most people were privately insured for health care, groups such as geriatrics, the chronically sick and the long term mentally ill, who would remain dependent on state provided services, could 'expect to benefit from increased public expenditure made possible by the transference of other sectors of the health service to a separate insurance system.'[21]

Pro-marketeers have little to say about social class inequalities in the welfare sector. Indeed Milton Friedman argues strongly against any attempts by governments to bring about equality of outcome between individuals or social groups in areas such as income distribution or educational qualifications. According to Friedman, 'A society that puts equality – in the sense of equality of outcome – ahead of freedom will end up with neither equality nor freedom.'[22]

Despite their libertarian principles, some pro-marketeers have suggested that rationing under a market system may actually be more egalitarian than various forms of administrative rationing. According to the Institute of Economic Affairs Study Group,

> Rationing by price in the market is more egalitarian than rationing by officials controlling queues waiting for insufficient supplies. Patients waiting for doctors, parents waiting for headmasters, hopeful tenants waiting for council officials and pensioners waiting for pensions officials make a better case for themselves or their children if they are literate, physically fit, well-connected or politically alert. The wage-earner does not do

as well as the salary earner. But cash, or its equivalent, speaks the same language in the market whatever the social class of its owner.[23]

The Marxist alternative

In recent years Marxists have produced a strong critique of the welfare state. Although they differ amongst themselves over the exact emphasis to be placed on the variety of factors which have produced the failures of the present welfare system, they unite in their emphasis on the severe limitations placed on attempts to meet individuals' welfare needs under capitalism.

Marxists argue that existing rationing methods used within the social services fail always to give priority to those in greatest need not because these methods are badly planned or controlled, but because of the inherent contradictions of the capitalist welfare state. According to Gough the welfare state 'simultaneously embodies tendencies to enhance social welfare, to develop the powers of individuals to exert social control over the blind play of market forces; and tendencies to repress and control people to adapt them to the requirements of the capitalist economy.'[24] The failure of welfare rationing to give priority to the most needy is not seen, therefore, as simply a technical or administrative problem nor is it seen as the problem of individual welfare providers exercising too much discretion over the allocation of welfare benefits. Dale, for example criticises non-Marxist discussions of welfare rationing for focusing attention on the role of social service staff 'without sufficient analysis of the constraints within which they operate and how such constraints should be explained.'[25] According to Marxists individual social service staff can play only a minor role in determining which groups of clients will receive priority in the distribution of welfare resources. Rather in a capitalist society the social services will inevitably tend to give priority to those clients deemed to be 'deserving' by a capitalist based ideology.[26]

The problem of lack of choice for the consumer is not a major concern of Marxist critics of the welfare state. In the past few years, however, a number of them have discussed the wider issue of the imbalance of power between welfare providers and welfare consumers. The power exercised by welfare professionals and other social service staff over welfare clients is explained by these writers primarily in terms of the function welfare providers perform for the capitalist state, rather than in terms of either the status of professionals or the dynamics of bureaucracies *per se*. According to Ginsburg:

> Obvious negative aspects of welfare state management, as experienced by its employees and consumers, are bureaucratism, remoteness and lack of effective democratic control through Parliament, trade unions and local councils . . . these are not incidental or accidental features of the welfare state that can be eliminated by further administrative reform. On the contrary, they play a central role in fulfilling some of the essential functions of capitalist welfare, rationing benefits and services according to ideological criteria of deservingness and containing individual and collective pressure for change.[27]

Marxists stress that social class inequalities within the welfare sector are neither inadvertent nor accidental. They accept that the existence of free or subsidised welfare services does benefit the working class, but argue that it is quite wrong to suggest that the welfare state is 'an oasis of socialism' or that social services are primarily designed to promote the interests of the working class. The constraints of capitalism mean that reforms within the welfare sector alone can do little to alter the subordinate position of the working class in capitalist societies. Ginsburg states,

> The possibility of securing a fundamental shift in the structure of class inequality in favour of the working class through administrative and policy reform or working class struggle within the state apparatus is severely constrained by the essential form and function of the state as a capitalist state which boils down to the reproduction of the relationship between capital and labour.[28]

If explanations by Marxists of the failures of welfare rationing and the welfare state in general lead them to dismiss reforms of the social services as marginal and incapable of securing any significant changes, what alternative solution do they propose? Deacon has pointed out that although Marxist critiques of social policy under capitalism have been instructive, Marxists have not, with very few exceptions, described what social policies might be like in socialist society.[29] Deacon himself has attempted to fill this gap and most of the following description of socialist social services is taken from his writing.

The first major change under socialism would be that economic policy would be directed towards the goal of meeting people's needs rather than producing surplus value for profit. Resources would then be much more readily available to meet needs since wasteful production and consumption would be eliminated. Moreover, demand for statutory welfare services would concomitantly decrease, partly because the process of production would no longer create problems such as occupational diseases and pollution but also because the nature of human needs would change under socialism. According to Heller, for example, human beings under socialism would place less emphasis on material needs and more emphasis on non-material needs, such as that for free time to develop the personality and human relationships.[30]

Under socialism, there would no longer be a conflict between meeting the needs of the economic system and meeting individual needs since the former would, in any case, be subordinate to the latter. The contradictory nature of welfare provision under capitalism would therefore be replaced by a welfare system which would be solely concerned with meeting individuals' needs. Such a system would at least be intended always to give priority to those with most need and any arguments about whose needs were greatest would be amicably settled by democratic discussions between all those concerned.

According to Deacon the orthodox left in this country has given little thought to the issue of freedom of choice and self-determination for welfare consumers but he suggests that under a truly socialist system, professionalism, with all its negative and controlling functions, would disappear. Technically expert providers of services such as health and education would be imbued with a new 'ideological orientation' and would regard their far better educated clients as 'equals'. In some areas of social welfare provision (e.g. social work) the tasks previously allotted to the technical expert or professional will largely have been taken over by neighbours, friends, locality based committee members and party activists.[31] Meanwhile, welfare bureaucracies would be kept in check by a system of democratic control by a combination of worker participation, consumer participation and local community control.

Welfare rationing under socialism would be based on consumers' own perceptions of their needs. Consumer definitions of need would 'determine resource allocation between individuals' but 'felt-perception' of need would be shaped by a process of informed discussion with equal others in the community. Individual consumers would thus be given power to determine their own lives but they would exercise this power not in an individualistic way, but in association with others in the local community. It would be these local communities which would collectively decide on the exact mix of welfare services and benefits to be provided in their areas.

The issue of social class inequalities would not arise in a classless socialist society. According to Deacon, 'fundamental conflict over resources and service allocation between antagonistic social classes will be replaced by reasoned and comradely disagreement as to the specific details of how and what resources are required to cater for particular need groups.'[32] Deacon concludes that in a socialist society, 'Problems of rationing would be placed in a totally new context. Both prices and bureaucrats and hence the techniques associated with both may be replaced as rationing agents by a self-consciously regulated consumption based on collective appreciation of the self-imposed limits of the supply side.'[33]

Assessment of alternative strategies

This chapter has described three very different approaches to the reform of welfare rationing. Although proponents of these approaches would no doubt vehemently oppose either of their rivals' solutions, an uncommitted adjudicator may see both strengths and weaknesses in all three approaches.

Administrative reform is by its very nature slow and piecemeal. Nevertheless those who argue that piecemeal change is the least painful and most feasible approach can claim that past events support their view. The history of the welfare state cannot be interpreted as one of uninterrupted progress in the meeting of human needs, but equally we cannot ignore the genuine advances which have been made even though they have been made slowly. Despite its many faults the present supplementary benefit scheme, for example, is less stigmatic and less deterrent than its predecessor, national assistance, which in its turn was welcomed as being less stigmatic than locally administered poor relief. While it is true that administrative reform cannot create more welfare resources, better planning of allocation procedures can help to ensure that the resources which are available go to those groups and individuals whom social policy makers *intend* to benefit from them. Parker and Hall are right to emphasise the dangers of uncontrolled informal and covert forms of rationing.

However it would be extremely difficult to eliminate or even to significantly reduce informal welfare rationing. Prottas has pointed out the many problems faced by those who attempt to reform public welfare agencies.[34] First, welfare agencies have unclear and sometimes contradictory goals. It is therefore virtually impossible to devise unambiguous and unconflicting regulations to govern the actions of those who work in them. Second, since the behaviour of welfare clients is totally unbureaucratic in form, too specific rules governing every possible interaction between clients and welfare workers would be unworkable. Third, the costs of monitoring welfare workers' behaviour very closely would probably be unacceptably high. Finally, welfare workers are likely to resist strongly any attempt to tighten supervision of their actions and if welfare workers become too alienated by the conditions under which they work this could actually lead to a decreased compliance with the agency's goals.

The second main weakness of a reformist approach is its inability to tackle the many failures of rationing which are *not* the result of lack of planning or the actions of uncontrolled front line social staff. As Dale has pointed out:

> It is too easily assumed that there are rational, technical answers to apparently arbitrary decisions. Whilst the search for more efficient and equitable procedures is a valid one, it all too easily ignores the underlying contradictory functions of the social services which are inevitably reproduced to some degree or other in the actions of the social service bureaucracies.[35]

All those who suggest change by piecemeal reform are by no means naively optimistic about the chances of eventually achieving a radical transformation of the existing welfare system. Wilding for example has very clearly articulated his doubts about the chances of small-scale reform leading to significant change. He admits, 'There are severe limits to what can be achieved through sneaky social change – the philosophy of Fabian reformism. Things can be changed – history proves that – but not drastically and the more incisive and radical the proposals, the more likely they are to be strongly resisted.'[36]

The pro-marketeers' appeal to free choice and the rights of the individual cannot be ignored by supporters of the welfare state. Nor is consumer choice the only advantage of a market system of welfare distribution which deserves careful consideration. Anyone put off the pro-market solution to welfare rationing by the fervent tones of certain anti-collectivists should study Reisman's cool and cogent arguments in favour of a greater use of the price mechanism in the welfare sector.[37] His claim that the price mechanism fulfils the three vital functions of deterring excessive demand, collecting information on consumer preferences and comparing the relative value of alternative goods and services, cannot be lightly dismissed as heartless or extreme. Nevertheless two major flaws in the pro-market solution to the failures of welfare rationing can be identified, at least as it is proposed by writers associated with the Institute of Economic Affairs.[38]

First, the price mechanism can only give *all* consumers significantly more choice than they have within 'free' state services if poor consumers are subsidised to such an extent by the state that they no longer have significantly less spending power than the rest of society. Yet certain anti-collectivists are firmly against anything other than a bare minimum amount of redistribution in favour of the poor. The Institute of Economic Affairs group argued in 1967 that state aid in Britain should be designed to abolish absolute or subsistence poverty which they defined as 'the deprivation of the materials required for tolerable existence'.[39] The group clearly distinguished this type of poverty from relative poverty which they saw as simply a measure of the distribution of income and not the rightful concern of the state. This lack of interest in relative inequality can be seen clearly in certain pro-market suggestions for privatising education and health care. Rhodes Boyson's educational voucher proposal, for example, would allow those parents who wished to do so to add their own money to the voucher in order to purchase more expensive forms of education. Such proposals have led the left in this country to argue that the voucher system would simply subsidise private education for the middle classes at the expense of those who could not afford to top up the value of the basic voucher.

The second major weakness in the case put forward by certain pro-marketeers is their failure to openly acknowledge that rationing by price is nevertheless rationing and that even under private market systems resources to meet welfare needs are not infinite. The impression gained from reading authors such as Seldon and Harris is that they suggest that everyone could have their needs met under a market system.[40] Everyone would be able to exercise maximum choice if only the state would remove its artificial restrictions on both suppliers and consumers of welfare services. Evidence of existing private markets in welfare should warn against such an optimistic picture. Opponents of voucher schemes have pointed out that vouchers would not eliminate problems of scarcity. If all parents were given education vouchers of equal worth and some schools attracted more pupils than they could cater for – a highly likely possibility – how would pupils be selected for these scarce places? The possession of an educational voucher would clearly not allow all parents to choose a highly popular school.

Neither rationing by price nor administrative rationing can meet everyone's welfare needs. Both systems in this sense can be criticised as less than ideal but we do not live in an ideal world. We have to make a choice between two flawed systems. We can allow the majority of consumers to buy welfare in the private market at the expense of those who either will not be able to afford welfare at all or will have to rely on a second rate, and probably stigmatising, selective service provided by the state, or we can restrict the 'freedom' of the majority either by significantly redistributing original incomes or by providing welfare benefits and services in kind on a universal basis.

A growing number of writers on welfare argue that given the inherent weaknesses of all forms of administrative rationing and the failure of the social services to secure a more equitable distribution of welfare in our society, reformers should now attempt to redistribute original incomes rather than to help the poor by providing universal welfare services and benefits in kind. Le Grand, for example, concludes that, 'public expenditure on the social services has not achieved equality in any of its interpretations' and that there does not seem to be much prospect of retrieving this situation 'through any piecemeal reform'. He claims that, 'the forces which create inequalities in the first place and which perpetuate them, seem to be too strong to be resisted through indirect methods such as public expenditure on the social services.'[41] He therefore proposes that a more promising way to achieve equality than by reforming the social services would be through equalising incomes although he recognises the great difficulties in achieving such a goal in a society which is strongly influenced by the ideology of inequality. Le Grand does not propose the privatisation of all universal social services but he does point out that public expenditure on certain services – such as higher education – benefits those in the middle classes far more than those in lower socio-economic groups. He therefore argues that overall 'there is a strong case on egalitarian grounds for reducing the subsidies to education beyond the school-leaving age.'[42] The fact that a growing number of writers who support egalitarianism have become disillusioned with the potential of the social services to redistribute welfare in favour of the poor suggests that perhaps some of the traditional arguments used by the Institute of Economic Affairs should no longer be contemptuously dismissed by those who do not share their libertarian values.

Solutions to the failures of existing welfare rationing which rely upon the creation of an ideal socialist state are open to the criticism that they are unrealistic. Deacon's socialist welfare system does not appear to be based on any firm evidence about real societies, real situations or real people. His view that all the problems of existing welfare rationing would be solved in a "truly" socialist society is partly based on the belief that, given a changed environment and social structure, human beings would no longer compete for scarce resources but would freely agree to reach collective decisions on both the production and distribution of goods and services to meet their needs. This view of the nature of human beings is certainly not universally held. Those who believe that human beings are innately competitive are unlikely to accept the socialist belief that human beings have a co-operative nature that will flourish in the right environment.

Non-socialists frequently claim that the failure of existing 'socialist' countries such as Russia to distribute resources solely according to need, coupled with the repressive nature of the political regimes in these societies, demonstrates that the socialist ideal is unworkable. Many socialists reply that such countries are not examples of socialism at all and that British socialism would be quite different – and better. Here the debate reaches an impasse.

If we cannot test the feasibility of the all-out socialist solution to the problems of welfare rationing we can ask how far radical alternatives to the existing pattern of welfare distribution are feasible within a capitalist society. Certainly many socialists do fight for radical changes in the welfare state without waiting for the revolution even though most of them insist that only very small gains can be made without a radical transformation of society as a whole. There have been successful radical campaigns on specific welfare issues, albeit on a small scale, within capitalist societies. Community action groups and tenants' associations have forced certain local councils to change their practices in areas such as housing management. Radical groups, most notably women's groups, have begun to set up alternative forms of welfare provision which have demonstrated that welfare workers and clients can enjoy a less unequal relationship than that normally seen within the statutory social services. Well Women's Clinics, for example, have challenged the traditional roles of doctors and women patients by giving women as much information as possible about their health problems.

Unfortunately radical attempts to change the nature of the welfare services from below, whether by individual social service staff or by welfare consumers, are open to the same criticism as attempts to reform the services from above. The more radical and significant is the demand for reform the more likely it is to be vehemently and effectively resisted by those entrenched in powerful positions both within and without the welfare sector.

Conclusion

During the 1950s and 1960s welfare rationing was virtually ignored by all those who studied the social services. But by the 1970s it was becoming widely recognised that however much the welfare state expanded, resources would never be sufficient to fully meet everyone's welfare needs. Academics, social policy makers and welfare providers then began to turn some of their attention to the problems involved in allocating existing benefits and services to individual consumers. However just as the study of the theory and practice of service rationing was beginning to develop and to suggest tentative solutions to existing problems, the context in which service rationing was taking place changed. From the mid-1970s onwards the planned expansion of social services was cut back and welfare providers had to face a future where there might be less rather than more resources to meet welfare needs. In 1979 the newly elected Conservative government began to cut not only planned expansion of services but also existing budgets.

Those advocating administrative reform are right to point out that at a time of cut backs and restraints it becomes even more important for welfare providers to be fully aware of their own rationing procedures. At a time of severe resource constraint those working in the social services must strive to protect those in greatest need from the worst effects of cut backs. It will however be very difficult to reduce, let alone eliminate, unplanned, covert welfare rationing. Individual welfare providers whilst professing a genuine concern to help clients in need are highly unlikely to give up any of their discretionary powers without a fight. All the problems associated with the discretionary individual allocation of welfare services and benefits are therefore likely to continue. In any case most welfare providers are faced with severe constraints which are beyond their control. It would therefore be naive to expect welfare providers to protect their clients simply by implementing administrative reforms. However well social service staff ration those benefits under their control, for example, they can not fully protect all welfare consumers from the consequences of cuts.

The Conservatives' attack on the welfare state in the early 1980s was not simply a quantitative one. They attempted not only to cut the overall size of social expenditure but also to restructure welfare services.[43] In the field of social security, for example, they not only cut the real value of a number of benefits, they also placed more emphasis on the social control element of the system. They employed extra fraud officers in the supplementary benefits system at a time when staff were having to cope with far greater numbers of claimants. In the context of cut backs and a new emphasis on social control any attempts to reform particular types of welfare rationing are likely to fail or backfire. The supplementary benefit system, for example, appears to be less accessible to claimants, less fair and less efficient in 1982 than it was before a major reform intended to give claimants a fairer deal.

This book has paid a great deal of attention to the disadvantages of specific types of welfare rationing and ways of reforming these particular faults have been reviewed. It has emphasised, however, that administrative reforms alone will not solve all the problems of welfare rationing. What matters most to those in need is not the exact type of administrative rationing used, but whether or not they gain access to the service or benefit they seek. Welfare rationing inevitably leads to some demands for help being rejected. To what extent various rationing methods will be used to ensure that as far as possible all welfare applicants are treated fairly and with respect depends far less on the mechanics of the devices used than on the objectives of those who use them and the contexts in which they operate. Doctors' appointment systems can work to the advantage of both doctors and patients if they are used positively to facilitate smooth patient access to health care rather than negatively to protect doctors from genuine demand. Means tests are not inevitably stigmatic. The context in which they are used and the spirit with which they are operated can be as important as the tests themselves.

All the evidence which we have reviewed suggests that limited reforms could be achieved if policy makers and welfare providers paid more attention to the practice of rationing within statutory social services. We must conclude pessimistically, however, that without major changes in the ideological, political and economic contexts in which welfare rationing takes place reformers are highly unlikely to secure a significantly more equitable or more egalitarian distribution of welfare through the existing statutory welfare system.

References

Chapter 1

1. See P. Donaldson, *Economics of the Real World* (Harmondsworth: Penguin Books, 1973).
2. D. Reisman, *Richard Titmuss: Welfare and Society* (London: Heinemann, 1977) p. 156.
3. K. Judge, 'Resource Allocation in the Welfare State: Bureaucrats or Prices?', *Journal of Social Policy*, vol. 8, pt 3, p. 365.
4. See A. Weale, *Equality and Social Policy* (London: Routledge & Kegan Paul, 1978) p. 86.
5. See Radical Statistics Health Group, *In Defence of the NHS* (London: Radical Statistics Health Group, 1977) p. 7.
6. M. Brown, *Introduction to Social Administration in Britain* (London: Hutchinson, 1971) p. 11.
7. D. Marsh, *The Future of the Welfare State* (Harmondsworth: Penguin, 1964) p. 15.
8. M. Cooper, *Rationing Health Care* (London: Croom Helm, 1975) p. 50.
9. J. Sleeman, *Resources for the Welfare State* (London: Longman, 1979) p. 4.
10. Dr John Rae, 'Red Lights in the Tinsel', *The Times Educational Supplement*, no. 3209, p. 4.
11. J. Higgins, 'Social Control Theories of Social Policy', *Journal of Social Policy*, vol. 9, pt 1 (1980) pp. 1–24.
12. P. Berger and B. Berger, *Sociology: A Biographical Approach* (Harmondsworth: Penguin, 1976) p. 201.
13. S. Bowles and H. Gintis, *Schooling in Capitalist America* (London: Routledge & Kegan Paul, 1976).
14. N. Ginsburg, *Class, Capital and Social Policy* (London: Macmillan, 1979) p. 107.
15. British Association of Social Workers, *The Social Work Task: a BASW Working Party Report* (Birmingham: BASW Publications, 1977) p. 22.
16. Case Con Manifesto in R. Bailey and M. Brake, *Radical Social Work* (London: Edward Arnold, 1975).
17. K. Judge, *Rationing Social Services* (London: Heinemann, 1978) p. 5.
18. For a discussion of financial rationing see: H. Glennerster, *Social Service Budgets and Social Policy* (London: Allen & Unwin, 1975); T. A. Booth, *Planning for Welfare* (Oxford: Blackwell, 1979);

K. Judge, *Rationing Social Services*; and A. Walker (ed.), *Public Expenditure and Social Policy* (London: Heinemann, 1982).
19. Supplementary Benefits Commission, *Annual Report, 1975* (London: HMSO, 1976).
20. M. Hill, *The State, the Administration and the Individual* (London: Fontana, 1976) p. 94.
21. M. Cooper, *Rationing Health Care*, p. 59.
22. R. Parker, 'The Problem of Rationing', *Social Work*, vol. 24, no. 2 (1967) pp. 9–14 reprinted in E. Butterworth and R. Holman (eds), *Social Welfare in Modern Britain* (London: Fontana, 1975) pp. 204–12.
23. A. Rees, 'Access to the Personal Health and Welfare Services', *Social and Economic Administration*, vol. 6 (1972) pp. 34–43.

Chapter 2

1. V. George and P. Wilding, *Ideology and Social Welfare* (London: Routledge & Kegan Paul, 1976) p. 135.
2. R. Plant, H. Lesser and P. Taylor Gooby, *Political Philosophy and Social Welfare* (London: Routledge & Kegan Paul, 1980) p. 25.
3. David Miller, *Social Justice* (Oxford: Clarendon Press, 1976) p. 129.
4. H. W. Fowler, *A Dictionary of Modern English Usage*, 2nd edition (Oxford: Oxford University Press, 1965) p. 383.
5. A. J. Culyer, *Need and the National Health Service* (London: Martin Robertson, 1976) p. 16.
6. R. Plant, 'Needs and Welfare' in N. Timms (ed.), *Social Welfare: Why and How?* (London: Routledge & Kegan Paul, 1980) p. 112.
7. D. Miller, *Social Justice* (Oxford: Clarendon Press, 1976) p. 134.
8. R. Plant, 'Needs and Welfare', p. 115.
9. Ibid, p. 117.
10. J. Dale and P. Taylor Gooby, *Social Theory and Social Welfare* (London: Edward Arnold, 1981) p. 212.
11. Adam Smith, *The Wealth of Nations*, vol. 2 (London: Dent, 1910) p. 351.
12. I. Gough, 'Human Needs and Social Welfare' unpublished paper (University of Manchester, 1981) p. 3.
13. M. Cooper, *Rationing Health Care* (London: Croom Helm, 1975) p. 20.
14. G. Smith, *Social Need* (London: Routledge & Kegan Paul, 1980) p. 183.
15. Radical Statistics Health Group, *In Defence of the NHS* (London: Radical Statistics Health Group, 1977) p. 25.
16. J. Bradshaw, 'The Concept of Social Need', *New Society*, vol. 20, no. 496 (1972) pp. 640–3.
17. F. Piven and R. Cloward, *Regulating the Poor* (London: Tavistock, 1972) p. 154.
18. I. Gough, 'Human Needs and Social Welfare', p. 16.
19. See M. Carley, *Social Measurement and Social Indicators* (London: Allen & Unwin, 1981).
20. Department of Health and Social Security, *Sharing Resources for*

Health in England (London: HMSO, 1976); P. Townsend, *Poverty in the United Kingdom* (Harmondsworth: Penguin, 1979).

21. Department of Health and Social Security, *Sharing Resources for Health in England*, para. 1.3.
22. Ibid, para. 1.3.
23. Ibid, para. 6.30.
24. Radical Statistics Health Group, *RAWP Deals: A Critique of 'Sharing Resources for Health in England'* (London: Radical Statistics Health Group, 1977) p. 18.
25. Ibid, p. 4.
26. N. Bosanquet, 'Health' in N. Bosanquet and P. Townsend (eds), *Labour and Equality* (London: Heinemann, 1980) p. 214.
27. P. Townsend, *Poverty in the United Kingdom*, p. 54.
28. Ibid, p. 250.
29. Ibid, p. 57.
30. D. Piachaud, 'Peter Townsend and The Holy Grail', *New Society*, vol. 57, no. 982 (1981) pp. 419–21, p. 420.
31. Ibid, p. 421.
32. C. Hakim, 'Social Indicators from the Census', unpublished, quoted in A.C. Bebbington and B. Davies, 'Territorial Need Indicators: A New Approach, Part I', *Journal of Social Policy*, vol. 9, pt 2 (1980) p. 146.
33. A. C. Bebbington and B. Davies, 'Territorial Need Indicators: A New Approach, Part II', *Journal of Social Policy*, vol. 9, pt 4 (1980) pp. 433–62.
34. Gilbert Smith, *Social Need* (London: Routledge & Kegan Paul, 1980) p. 65.
35. Ibid, p. 69.
36. Ibid, p. 73.
37. Ibid, p. 191.
38. Ibid, p. 1.
39. Ibid, p. 197.
40. See A. J. Culyer, *Need and the National Health Service*.
41. D. Nevitt, 'Demand and Need', in H. Heisler (ed.), *Foundations of Social Administration* (London: Macmillan, 1977) p. 122.
42. Ibid, p. 125.
43. See J. Dale and P. Taylor Gooby, *Social Theory and Social Welfare*, pt 2.
44. P. Taylor Gooby, 'The New Right and Social Policy', *Critical Social Policy*, vol. 1, no. 1 (1981) p. 16.
45. See A. Heller, *The Theory of Need in Marx* (London: Allison & Busby, 1976).
46. See J. Dale and P. Taylor Gooby, *Social Theory and Social Welfare*, pt 2.
47. I. Gough, *The Political Economy of the Welfare State* (London: Macmillan, 1979) p. 92.
48. See J. Dale and P. Taylor Gooby, *Social Theory and Social Welfare*, pt 2.

Chapter 3

1. See B. Showler, 'Political Economy and Unemployment' in B. Showler and A. Sinfield (eds), *The Workless State* (London: Martin Robertson, 1981).
2. A. Cartwright and R. Anderson, *Patients and Their Doctors*, Occasional Paper 8 (London: Journal of the Royal College of General Practitioners, 1979) p. 7.
3. Ibid, p. 11.
4. J. Fry, 'The Content of Practice' in J. Fry (ed.), *Trends in General Practice* (London: British Medical Journal, 1977) p. 37.
5. G. Stimson and B. Webb, *Going to See the Doctor* (London: Routledge & Kegan Paul, 1975) p.21.
6. M. Foster, 'The Rationing of Primary Medical Care: A Case Study of Supply and Demand in General Practice', unpublished MA thesis (Manchester University, 1978).
7. Ibid, p. 57.
8. D. Mechanic, 'Correlates of Frustration Among British General Practitioners', *Journal of Health and Social Behaviour*, vol. 11, no. 2 (1970) pp. 87–104.
9. J. Buckle, *Intake Teams* (London: Tavistock, 1981) p. 27.
10. J. Mayer, 'The Social Factors in Surgery Attendance', *Pulse*, 28 May 1977, p. 8.
11. M. Cooper, *Rationing Health Care* (London: Croom Helm, 1975) p. 13.
12. Ibid, p. 14.
13. S. Rees, *Social Work Face to Face* (London: Edward Arnold, 1978) p. 36.
14. Ibid, p. 37.
15. J. Mayer and N. Timms, *The Client Speaks* (London: Routledge & Kegan Paul, 1970) p. 53.
16. Ibid, p. 105.
17. Ibid, p. 53.
18. R. M. Moroney, *The Family and the State* (London: Longman, 1976) p. 45.
19. T. Cresswell and P. Parker, 'The Frail who Lead the Frail', *New Society*, vol. 20, no. 504 (1972) p. 410.
20. Child Poverty Action Group, *So Who's 'Better Off on the Dole*, Poverty Fact Sheet (London: Child Poverty Action Group, 1980) p. 12.
21. A. Laurence, unpublished report summarised in P. Moore, 'Counter-Culture in a Social Security Office', *New Society*, vol. 53, no. 921 (1980) p. 69.
22. Child Poverty Action Group, *So Who's 'Better Off on the Dole*, p. 13.
23. Department of Health and Social Security, *National Health Service: Twentieth Anniversary Conference* (London: HMSO, 1968).
24. R. Titmuss, 'Goals of Today's Welfare State', in P. Anderson and R. Blackburn (eds), *Towards Socialism* (London: Fontana, 1965) p. 360.

25. J. Le Grand, *The Strategy for Equality* (London: Allen & Unwin, 1982) p. 4.
26. A. Cochrane, *Effectiveness and Efficiency: Random Reflections on Health Services* (London: Nuffield Provincial Hospitals Trust, 1972).
27. P. Townsend and N. Davidson, *Inequalities in Health – The Black Report* (Harmondsworth: Penguin, 1982) p. 88.
28. Ibid, p. 81.
29. Ibid, p. 82.
30. Ibid, p. 88.
31. R. Titmuss, *Commitment to Welfare* (London: Allen & Unwin, 1968) p. 67.
32. K. MacDonald, 'Time and the Working Class', unpublished paper presented at the 1976 Conference of the British Sociological Association.
33. A. Cartwright and M. O'Brien, 'Social Class Variations in Health' in M. Stacey (ed.), *The Sociology of the NHS*, Sociological Review Monograph 22 (Keele: University of Keele, 1976); I. C. Buchan and I. M. Richardson, *Time Study of Consultation in General Practice* (Edinburgh: Scottish Home and Health Dept, 1973).
34. Royal Commission on the National Health Service, *Report*, Cmnd 7615 (London: HMSO, 1979) p. 89.
35. P. Townsend and N. Davidson, *Inequalities in Health – The Black Report*, p. 89.
36. J. Le Grand, *The Strategy for Equality*, p. 33.
37. See M. Backett, 'Health Services' in F. Williams (ed.), *Why the Poor Pay More* London: Macmillan, 1977).
38. J. Le Grand, *The Strategy for Equality*, p. 35.
39. *Where*, 'Parental Choice – For How Many?', *Where*, no. 136 (1978) pp. 71–2.
40. Ibid, p. 71.
41. House of Commons Debates 1978–9, col. 185.
42. Ibid, col. 366.
43. R. Boudon, *Education, Opportunity and Social Inequality* (London: Wiley, 1974).
44. J. Le Grand, *The Strategy for Equality*, p. 64.
45. D. Black, *Inequalities in Health* (London: DHSS, 1980).
46. J. Le Grand, *The Strategy for Equality*, pp. 134–7.
47. Ibid, ch. 8.

Chapter 4

1. K. Lewin, 'Frontiers in Group Dynamics: II. Channels in Group Social Planning and Action Research', *Human Relations*, vol. 1 (1947) pp. 143–53.
2. I. Deutscher, 'The Gatekeeper in Public Housing' in I. Deutscher and E. J. Thompson (eds), *Among the People: Encounters with the Poor*

(New York: Basic Books, 1968) p. 39.
3. D. Sweet, 'From a Hole in the Wall ...', *Social Work Today*, vol. 12, no. 45 (1981) pp. 16–17.
4. J. M. Prottas, *People Processing* (Lexington, Mass.: Lexington Books, 1979) pp. 126–7.
5. D. Sweet, 'From a Hole in the Wall ...', p. 16.
6. J. Buckle, *Intake Teams* (London: Tavistock, 1981) p. 71.
7. R. Bessell, *Interviewing and Counselling* (London: Batsford, 1971) p. 70.
8. P. Burgess, 'In Benefit', *Community Care*, no. 346 (1981) p. 9.
9. P. M. Blau, *The Dynamics of Bureaucracy: A Study of Interpersonal Relations in Two Government Agencies*, 2nd edn (Chicago: Chicago University Press, 1963) p. 29.
10. J. M. Prottas, *People Processing*.
11. As Hall, *The Point of Entry* (London: Allen & Unwin, 1974) p. 66.
12. Ibid, p. 66.
13. Ibid, p. 125.
14. J. Buckle, *Intake Teams*, p. 71.
15. M. Foster, 'The Rationing of Primary Medical Care: A Case Study of Supply and Demand in General Practice', unpublished M.A. thesis (Manchester University, 1978) p. 73. A summary of this can be found in P. Foster, 'The Informal Rationing of Primary Medical Care', *Journal of Social Policy*, vol. 8, pt 4 (1979) pp. 489–508.
16. Ibid, p. 497.
17. P. R. Kaim-Caudle and G. N. Marsh, ' "Patient Satisfaction": A Survey in General Practice', *British Medical Journal*, 1, 5952 (1975) pp. 262–4.
18. A. Cartwright and R. Anderson, *General Practice Revisited* (London: Tavistock, 1981) p. 82.
19. Ibid, p. 83.
20. Ibid, p. 83.
21. R. Klein, *Complaints About Doctors: A Study in Professional Accountability* (London: Charles Knight, 1973) p. 45.
22. A. S. Hall, *The Point of Entry*.
23. E. Younghusband, *Social Work in Britain 1950–75: A Follow Up Study*, vol. 1 (London: Allen & Unwin, 1978).
24. J. Buckle, *Intake Teams*, p. 65.
25. M. Drury, *The Medical Secretary's Handbook* (London: Baillere-Tindall, 1975) p. 186.
26. Ibid, p. 188.
27. Ibid, p. 186.
28. D. C. Morrell, *An Introduction to Primary Medical Care* (Edinburgh: Churchill Livingstone, 1976) p. 131.
29. *The Times*, 5 May 1973.
30. M. Foster, 'The Informal Rationing of Primary Medical Care: A Case Study of Supply and Demand in General Practice', p. 80.
31. D. Sweet, 'From a Hole in the Wall ...'.
32. A. S. Hall, *The Point of Entry*, p. 68.
33. Ibid, p. 69.

34. J. Buckle, *Intake Teams*, p. 72.
35. G. Stimson and B. Webb, *Going to See the Doctor* (London: Routledge & Kegan Paul, 1975) p. 116.
36. Ibid, p. 116.
37. M. Foster, 'The Rationing of Primary Medical Care: A Case Study of Supply and Demand in General Practice'.
38. H. Hodgson, 'Patients and Appointment Systems', *Update* (March 1974) pp. 704–8.
39. A. Cartwright and R. Anderson, *Patients and Their Doctors 1977*, Occasional Paper 8 (London: Journal of the Royal College of General Practitioners, 1979) p. 17.
40. A. Cartwright and R. Anderson, *General Practice Revisited*, p. 72.
41. A. Cartwright and R. Anderson, *Patients and Their Doctors 1977*, p. 17.
42. A. S. Hall, *The Point of Entry*, p. 120.
43. P. Foster, 'The Informal Rationing of Primary Medical Care', p. 496.
44. M. Foster, 'The Rationing of Primary Medical Care: A Case Study of Supply and Demand in General Practice', p. 148.
45. G. Stimson and B. Webb, *Going to See the Doctor*, p. 118.

Chapter 5

1. See M. P. Hall, *The Social Services of Modern Britain*, 6th edn (London: Routledge & Kegan Paul, 1963).
2. R. Pinker, *Social Theory and Social Policy* (London: Heinemann) p. 152.
3. London Edinburgh Weekend Return Group, *In and Against the State* (London: Pluto Press, 1979) p. 9.
4. E. Freidson, *The Professions and Their Prospects* (London: Sage Publications, 1973); T. Johnson, *Professions and Power* (London: Macmillan, 1972).
5. A. Etzioni (ed.), *The Semi-Professions and Their Organisation* (New York: The Free Press) p. v.
6. London Edinburgh Weekend Return Group, *In and Against the State*, p. 29.
7. J. M. Prottas, *People Processing* (Lexington, Mass: Lexington Books, 1979).
8. C. Taylor 'Primary Care in Liverpool', *Medicine in Society*, vol. 7 (1982).
9. Patients' Association, *Patient Voice*, 4 (1976).
10. A. Cartwright and R. Anderson, *Patients and Their Doctors 1977*, Occasional Paper 8 (London: Journal of the Royal College of General Practitioners, 1979) p. 3.
11. Ibid, p. 7.
12. Ibid, p. 18.
13. H. Hodgson, 'Patients and Appointment Systems', *Update* (March 1974) pp. 704–8.
14. M. Foster, 'The Rationing of Primary Medical Care: A Case Study of

Supply and Demand in General Practice', unpublished M.A. thesis (Manchester University, 1978).

15. Royal College of General Practitioners, 'Evidence to the Royal Commission on the NHS', *Journal of the Royal College of General Practitioners*, vol. 27, no. 177 (1977) p. 200.

16. M. Foster, 'The Rationing of Primary Medical Care: A Case Study of Supply and Demand in General Practice'.

17. J. Howie, 'Prescribing' in J. Fry (ed.), *Trends in General Practice* (London: British Medical Journal, 1977) pp. 148–58.

18. J. Buckle, *Intake Teams* (London: Tavistock, 1981) p. 99.

19. *Report of the Committee on Local Authority and Allied Personal Social Services*, Cmnd 3703 (London: HMSO, 1968) p. 46.

20. H. H. Perlman, 'Some Notes on the Waiting List' in H. J. Parad (ed.), *Crisis Intervention: Selected Readings* (New York: Family Service Association of America, 1965) p. 200.

21. C. Gostick, 'The Intake Phenomenon', *Social Work Today*, vol. 8, no. 10 (1976) pp. 7–9.

22. J. Jones, 'Intake Structure in Local Authorities', *Social Work Today*, vol. 6, no. 23 (1976) pp. 710–12.

23. C. Loewenstein, 'An Intake Team in Action in a Social Services Department', *British Journal of Social Work*, vol. 4, no. 2 (1974) pp. 115–41.

24. J. Jones, 'Intake Structure in Local Authorities'.

25. J. Buckle, *Intake Teams*, p. 40.

26. O. Stevenson and P. Parsloe, *Social Service Teams: The Practitioner's View* (London: HMSO, 1978) p. 41.

27. Ibid, p. 43.

28. E. M. Goldberg and R. W. Warburton, *Ends and Means in Social Work* (London: Allen & Unwin, 1979).

29. J. Jones, 'Intake Structure in Local Authorities'.

30. C. Loewenstein, 'An Intake Team in Action in a Social Services Department', p. 118.

31. J. Buckle, *Intake Teams*, p. 39.

32. J. Jones, 'Intake Structure in Local Authorities', p. 712.

33. *Higher Education*, Cmnd 2154 (London: HMSO, 1963) p. 231.

34. P. Foster, 'The Ivory Tower Gatekeepers: A Study of the Role of the Admissions Tutor in a Sample of Departments at X University', unpublished paper (Bristol University, 1975).

35. Ibid.

36. W. A. Reid, *The Universities and the Sixth Form Curriculum* (London: Schools Council, 1972) p. 24.

37. P. Foster, 'The Ivory Tower Gatekeepers: A Study of the Role of the Admissions Tutor in a Sample of Departments at X University'.

38. Ibid.

39. Ibid.

40. W. A. Reid, *The Universities and the Sixth Form Curriculum*, p. 42.

41. P. Foster, 'The Ivory Tower Gatekeepers: A Study of the Role of the Admissions Tutor in a Sample of Departments at X University'.

42. Ibid.

43. W. A. Reid, *The Universities and the Sixth Form Curriculum*, p. 77.
44. D. F. Horrobin, *Medical Hubris* (Edinburgh: Churchill Livingstone, 1978) p. 104.
45. Ibid, p. 104.
46. H. J. Perkin, *New Universities in the United Kingdom* (Paris: Organization for Economic Co-operation and Development, 1969) p. 103.
47. P. Foster, 'The Ivory Tower Gatekeepers: A Study of the Role of the Admissions Tutor in a Sample of Departments at X University'.
48. Ibid.
49. Ibid.
50. H. J. Perkin, *New Universities in the United Kingdom*, p. 105.
51. J. M. Prottas, *People Processing*, p. 114.

Chapter 6

1. R. Titmuss, *Commitment to Welfare* (London: Allen & Unwin, 1968) p. 196.
2. See A. Cartwright and R. Anderson, *Patients and Their Doctors 1977*, Occasional Paper 8 (London: Journal of the Royal College of General Practitioners, 1979); and E. M. Goldberg and R. W. Warburton, *Ends and Means in Social Work* (London: Allen & Unwin).
3. See P. Wilding, *Professional Power and Social Welfare* (London: Routledge & Kegan Paul, 1982).
4. S. Rees. *Social Work Face to Face* (London: Edward Arnold, 1978) p. 94.
5. D. Cargill, 'In Breadth or Depth?', *World Medicine* (28 June 1978) p. 39.
6. D. C. Morrell, 'Expressions of Morbidity in General Practice', *British Medical Journal*, vol. 2, no. 5759 (1971) pp. 454–8.
7. M. Foster, 'The Rationing of Primary Medical Care: A Case Study of Supply and Demand in General Practice', unpublished M.A. thesis, (Manchester University, 1978).
8. P. Byrne and B. Long, *Doctors Talking to Patients* (London: HMSO, 1976).
9. G. Stimson and B. Webb, *Going to See the Doctor* (London: Routledge & Kegan Paul, 1975) p. 69.
10. I. C. Buchan and I. M. Richardson, *Time Study of Consultation in General Practice* (Edinburgh: Scottish Home and Health Department, 1973).
11. See B. Glastonbury, 'Are Social Services Departments Bureaucracies?' in B. Glastonbury (ed.), *Social Work in Conflict* (London: Croom Helm, 1980).
12. O. Stevenson and P. Parsloe, *Social Service Teams: The Practitioner's View* (London: HMSO, 1978).
13. Ibid, p. 83.
14. Ibid, p. 83.
15. Ibid, p. 82.

16. R. C. Rist, 'Student Social Class and Teachers' Expectations: The Self-Fulfilling Prophecy in Ghetto Education', *Harvard Educational Review*, vol. 40, no. 3 (1970) pp. 411–51.
17. T. L. Good, 'Which Pupils Do Teachers Call On?', *Elementary School Journal*, vol. 70, pt 4 (1970) pp. 190–8.
18. H. M. Holden, 'The Needs and Expectations of Doctors and Patients', *Journal of the Royal College of General Practitioners*, vol. 27, no. 178 (1977) pp. 277–9.
19. M. Foster, 'The Rationing of Primary Medical Care: A Case Study of Supply and Demand in General Practice'.
20. A. Cartwright and R. Anderson, *Patients and Their Doctors 1977*.
21. S. G. Jeffs, 'Being a Good Doctor', *Journal of the Royal College of General Practitioners*, vol. 23, no. 135 (1973) pp. 683–90 .
22. M. Foster, 'The Rationing of Primary Medical Care: A Case Study of Supply and Demand in General Practice'.
23. See A. Cartwright and M. O'Brien, 'Social Class Variations in Health' in M. Stacey (ed.), *The Sociology of the NHS*, Sociological Review Monograph 22 (Keele: University of Keele, 1976).
24. O. Stevenson and P. Parsloe, *Social Service Teams: The Practitioner's View*, p. 97.
25. B. Glastonbury and D. Cooper, 'Case Studies of Bureaucratisation: Intake and Non-Accidental Injury' in B. Glastonbury (ed.), *Social Work in Conflict* (London: Croom Helm, 1980).
26. C. Brewer and J. Lait, *Can Social Work Survive?* (London: Temple Smith, 1980) p. 183.
27. T. L. Good, 'Which Pupils Do Teachers Call On?', p. 197.
28. J. M. Prottas, *People Processing* Lexington, Mass: Lexington Books, 1979) p. 118.
29. T. R. Taylor *et al.*, 'Individual Differences in Selecting Patients for Regular Haemodialysis', *British Medical Journal*, pt 2, no. 5967 (1975) pp. 351–402.
30. D. Sanders and J. Dukeminier, 'Medical Advance and Legal Lag: Haemodialysis and Kidney Transplantations' in S. Reiser (ed.), *Ethics in Medicine* (London: MIT Press, 1977).
31. A. Cartwright and M. Waite, 'Evidence to the Committee on the Working of the Abortion Act', *Journal of the Royal College of General Practitioners*, 22, Supplement 1 (1972).
32. K. L. Oldershaw, *Contraception, Abortion and Sterilization in General Practice* (London: Henry Kimpton, 1975).
33. A. Cartwright and M. Waite, 'Evidence to the Committee on the Working of the Abortion Act', p. 1.
34. Tribunal on Abortion Rights, *Abortion – The Evidence* (London: National Council for Civil Liberties, 1977) p. 20.
35. See M. Hill and P. Laing, *Social Work and Money* (London: Allen & Unwin, 1979).
36. Ibid, pp. 25–41.
37. M. Hill, 'Resources' in O. Stevenson and P. Parsloe (eds), *Social Service Teams: The Practitioner's View* (London: HMSO, 1978) p. 233.

38. Ibid, p. 237.
39. J. Buckle, *Intake Teams* (London: Tavistock, 1981) p. 98.
40. Ibid, p. 99.
41. J. Handler, 'The Coercive Children's Officer', *New Society*, vol. 12, no. 314 (1968) pp. 485–7.
42. B. Jordan, *Poor Parents* (London: Routledge & Kegan Paul, 1974) p. 104.
43. M. Hill and P. Laing, *Social Work and Money*, pp. 79–80.
44. D. Sanders and J. Dukeminier, 'Medical Advance and Legal Lag: Haemodialysis and Kidney Transplantations', p. 610.
45. See J. Higgins, 'Social Control Theories of Social Policy', *Journal of Social Policy*, vol. 9, pt 1 (1980) pp. 1–24.
46. B. Jordan, *Poor Parents*, p. 118.
47. See I. Illich *et al.*, *Disabling Professions* (London: Marion Boyars, 1977).
48. See P. Wilding, *Professional Power and Social Welfare*.
49. Ibid.
50. Ibid, p. 147.
51. I. Kennedy, 'Consumerism in the Doctor—Patient Relationship', The Reith Lectures: Unmasking Medicine, *The Listener*, vol. 104, no. 2691 (1980) pp. 777–80.
52. Ibid, p. 780.
53. J. M. Prottas, *People Processing*, p. 155.

Chapter 7

1. Inter Departmental Committee, *Social Insurance and Allied Services* (London: HMSO, 1942) p. 11.
2. R. Titmuss, 'Superannuation for All: A Broader View', *New Society*, vol. 13, no. 335 (1969) p. 315.
3. Inter Departmental Committee, *Social Insurance and Allied Services*, Cmnd 6404, 1942, p. 12.
4. Ibid.
5. B. Abel-Smith, *Value for Money in Health Services: A Comparative Study* (London: Heinemann, 1976) p. 43.
6. Supplementary Benefits Commission, *Response of the Supplementary Benefits Commission to Social Assistance: A Review of the Supplementary Benefits Scheme in Great Britain* (London: HMSO, 1979) p. 7.
7. L. Burghes, 'Unemployment and Poverty' in L. Burghes and R. Lister (eds), *Unemployment: Who Pays the Price?*, Poverty Pamphlet 53 (London: Child Poverty Action Group, 1981) p. 83.
8. J. Kincaid, *Poverty and Equality in Britain*, 2nd edn (Harmondsworth: Penguin, 1975) p. 215.
9. Ibid, p. 229.
10. House of Commons Debates, 1975, col. 186.
11. D. Metcalf, 'Goodbye to National Insurance', *New Society*, vol. 52, no. 919 (1980) p. 349.

12. J. Douglas, 'The Struggle for Mobility', *Poverty*, no. 48 (1981) p. 7.
13. C. Glendinning, *After Working All These Years* (London: Disability Alliance, 1980) p. 36.
14. Ibid, p. 37.
15. R. Smith, 'Attendance Allowance', *Poverty* no. 48 (April 1981) p. 11.
16. Equal Opportunities Commission, *Behind Closed Doors* (Manchester: Equal Opportunities Commission, 1981) p. 9.
17. Ibid, p. 9.
18. Disability Alliance, *Disability Rights Bulletin* (London: Disability Alliance, 1981).
19. J. Bennet and P. McGavin, 'Why Do the Disabled Fail to Claim?', *Poverty*, no. 48 (April 1981) p. 21.
20. C. Glendinning, *After Working All These Years*, p. 31.
21. H. Chappell, 'Obstacle Course', *New Society* vol. 56, no. 970 (1981) p. 432.
22. Patrick Jenkin quoted in C. Glendinning, *After Working All These Years*, p. 6.
23. Inter Departmental Committee, *Social Insurance and Allied Services*, p. 141.
24. The Social Security Act 1966, Section 4(1).
25. D. Donnison, 'For Whose Benefit?', *Community Care*, no. 332 (1980) p. 19.
26. Supplementary Benefits Commission, *Annual Report, 1976* (London: HMSO, 1977) p. 115.
27. Department of Health and Social Security, *Social Assistance: A Review of the Supplementary Benefits Scheme in Great Britain* (London: Department of Health and Social Security, 1978) p. 25.
28. Supplementary Benefits Commission, *Annual Report, 1975* (London: HMSO, 1976) p. 12.
29. Department of Health and Social Security, *Social Assistance: A Review of the Supplementary Benefits Scheme in Great Britain*, p. 73.
30. R. Lister, *Patching Up the Safety Net*, Poverty Pamphlet 31 (London: Child Poverty Action Group, 1977) p. 6.
31. Department of Health and Social Security, *Social Assistance: A Review of the Supplementary Benefits Scheme in Great Britain*, p. 72.
32. Lord Collison, *Supplementary Benefits Handbook*, November 1972 edn (London: HMSO, 1972).
33. D. Donnison, 'Against Discretion', *New Society*, vol. 41, no. 780 (1977) p. 534.
34. R. Lister, *Patching Up the Safety Net*, p. 10.
35. Regulatioin 30 of the Single Payment Regulations (1980) quoted in 'The New SB Scheme', *New Society*, vol. 54, no. 940 (1980).
36. P. Jenkin, quoted in C. Glendinning, *After Working All These Years*, p. 20.
37. J. Allbeson, 'Not So Much of a Birthday', *Community Care*, no. 388 (26 November 1981) pp. 20–1.
38. D. Donnison, 'For Whose Benefit?', p. 18.

39. D. Hepinstall, 'Benefits: Simply More Confusion', *Community Care*, no. 407 (1982) pp. 14–16, p. 15.
40. J. Allbeson, 'Not So Much of a Birthday', p. 21.
41. Ibid.
42. Supplementary Benefits Commission, *Annual Report, 1976*, p. 143.
43. House of Commons Debates, 1971, col. 89.
44. D. Donnison, *The Politics of Poverty* (Oxford: Martin Robertson, 1982) p. 225.
45. M. Adler and S. Asquith, 'Discretion and Power' in M. Adler and S. Asquith (eds), *Discretion and Welfare* (London: Heinemann, 1981) p. 17.
46. See M. Hill, 'Some Implications of Legal Approaches to Welfare Rights', *British Journal of Social Work*, vol. 4, no. 2 (1974) pp. 187–99.
47. J. M. Prottas, *People Processing* (Lexington, Mass: Lexington Books, 1979) p. 95.
48. See ibid, ch. 5.

Chapter 8

1. The Housing Act 1957, Subsection 113:25(2).
2. The Housing (Homeless Persons) Act 1977, Subsection 2(1).
3. Ibid, subsection 5(1).
4. Ibid, subsection 5(6).
5. Shelter, *Where Homelessness Means Hopelessness* (London: Shelter, 1978).
6. Central Housing Advisory Committee, *Council Housing Purposes, Procedures and Priorities* (London: HMSO, 1969) p. 54.
7. I. Sier, 'Waiting Restrictions', *Roof*, vol. 6, no. 2 (March–April 1981) p. 3.
8. Central Housing Advisory Committee, *Council Housing Purposes, Procedures and Priorities*, p. 45.
9. Ibid, p. 50.
10. L. Corina, *Housing Allocation Policy and Its Effects: A Case Study from Oldham CDP* (York: CDP Central Research Unit, University of York, 1976).
11. Central Housing Advisory Committee, *Council Housing Purposes, Procedures and Priorities*, p. 43.
12. J. Morton, 'Housing: Home for Headaches', *New Society*, vol. 52, no. 917 (12 June 1980) pp. 221–2.
13. A. Murie *et al.*, *Housing Policy and The Housing System* (London: Allen & Unwin, 1976) p. 121.
14. Ibid, p. 126.
15. P. Niner, 'Local Authority Housing Policy and Practice – A Case Study Approach' (University of Birmingham, 1979).
16. L. Corina, *Housing Allocation Policy and Its Effects: A Case Study from Oldham CDP*, p. 24.

17. V. Karn, 'To HM Government: Warning – Public Sector Demolition Can Seriously Damage Your Wealth', *Roof*, vol. 6, no. 1 (1981) p. 15.
18. J. English *et al.*, *Slum Clearance* (London: Croom Helm, 1976) p. 110.
19. Ibid, p. 110.
20. F. Gray, 'The Management of Local Authority Housing' in Conference of Social Economists, *Housing and Class in Britain* (London: Conference of Social Economists, 1976) p. 80.
21. L. Corina, *Housing Allocation Policy and Its Effects: A Case Study from Oldham CDP*, p. 13.
22. S. Jacobs, *The Right to a Decent House* (London: Routledge & Kegan Paul, 1976) p. 79.
23. Central Housing Advisory Committee, *Council Housing Purposes, Procedures and Priorities*, p. 33.
24. N. Ginsburg, *Class, Capital and Social Policy* (London: Macmillan, 1979) p. 167.
25. S. Jacobs, *The Right to a Decent House*, p. 80.
26. See Shelter, *Where Homelessness Means Hopelessness*.
27. P. Gregory, 'Waiting Lists and Demand for Public Housing', *Policy and Politics*, vol. 3, no. 4 (1975) pp. 71–87.
28. L. Corina, *Housing Allocation Policy and Its Effects: A Case Study from Oldham CDP*, p. 37.
29. Ibid.
30. Central Housing Advisory Committee, *Council Housing Purposes, Procedures and Priorities*, p. 31.
31. S. Jacobs, *The Right to a Decent House*, p. 78.
32. A. Murie *et al.*, *Housing Policy and the Housing System*, p. 131.
33. L. Corina, *Housing Allocation Policy and Its Effects: A Case Study from Oldham CDP*, p. 18.
34. See V. Karn, 'To HM Government: Warning – Public Sector Demolition Can Seriously Damage Your Wealth'.

Chapter 9

1. B. Abel-Smith, 'Whose Welfare State?', in N. McKenzie (ed.), *Conviction* (London: MacGibbon & Kee, 1958) p. 57.
2. See E. Ferlie and K. Judge, 'Retrenchment and Rationality in the Personal Social Services', *Policy and Politics*, vol. 9, no. 3 (1981) pp. 311–30.
3. M. Carlisle, reported in *The Times Higher Educational Supplement*, no. 388 (1980) p. 32.
4. R. Parker, 'Policies, Presumptions and Prospects in Charging for the Social Services', in K. Judge (ed.), *Pricing the Social Services* (London: Macmillan, 1980) p. 28.
5. Ibid.
6. Quoted by K. Judge and J. Matthews, *Charging for Social Care* (London: Allen & Unwin, 1980) p. 54.
7. Select Committee on Estimates, *Child Care: Sixth Report from the*

Select Committee on Estimates, Session 1951–52 (London: HMSO, 1952) p. 74.

8. House of Commons Debates, 1947, col. 1609.
9. R. Parker, 'Policies, Presumptions and Prospects in Charging for the Social Services', p. 36.
10. Ibid, p. 28.
11. Ibid, p. 29.
12. Ibid, p. 29.
13. J. P. Martin and S. Williams, 'The Effects of Imposing Prescriptions Charges', *Lancet*, vol. 1, no. 7062 (1959) pp. 36–9.
14. T. Lavers, 'A Demand Model for Prescriptions', unpublished paper (Institute of Social and Economic Research, University of York, 1977).
15. H. Chappell, 'Deterrent Charges?' *New Society*, vol. 56, no. 970 (1981) p. 484.
16. See R. Simpson, *Access to Primary Care*, Royal Commission on the National Health Service Research Paper No. 6 (London: HMSO, 1979).
17. A. Waind, 'Plaque Jack Wins Through', *New Society*, vol. 60, no. 1018 (1982) pp. 289–90.
18. See R. Simpson, *Access to Primary Care*.
19. W. Davies, *Health or Health Service?* (London: Charles Knight, 1972) p. 17.
20. D. Reisman, *Richard Titmuss: Welfare and Society* (London: Heinemann, 1977) p. 155.
21. A. Maynard, 'Medical Care and the Price Mechanism', in K. Judge (ed.), *Pricing the Social Services* (London: Macmillan, 1980) pp. 86–106.
22. R. G. Beck, 'The Effects of Co-payment on the Poor', *Journal of Human Resources*, vol. 9, no. 1 (1974) pp. 129–42.
23. A. Maynard, 'Medical Care and the Price Mechanism', p. 101.
24. K. Judge and J. Matthews, *Charging for Social Care*, p. 2.
25. K. Judge, *Rationing Social Services* (London: Heinemann, 1978) p. 147.
26. Ibid, p. 152.
27. K. Judge and J. Matthews, *Charging for Social Care*, p. 103.
28. A. Hunt, *The Home Help Service in England and Wales* (London: HMSO, 1970) p. 343.
29. K. Judge et al., *Home Help Charges* (Canterbury: Social Services Research Unit, University of Kent, 1981) p. 15.
30. Ibid, p. 14.
31. K. Judge, 'An Introduction to the Economic Theory of Pricing' in K. Judge (ed.), *Pricing the Social Services* (London: Macmillan, 1980).
32. A. Maynard, 'Medical Care and the Price Mechanism'.
33. A. Rashid, 'Do Patients Cash Prescriptions?', *British Medical Journal*, vol. 284, no. 6308 (1982) pp. 24–6.
34. I. Russell and N. Bentzen, 'Deputising Services in Denmark: The Effect of Abolishing the Charge to Patients', Interim Report presented to SSRC Health Economist Study Group at Bath, cited by K. Judge and J. Matthews, *Charging for Social Care*, p. 98.

35. K. Judge and J. Matthews, *Charging for Social Care*, p. 98.
36. K. Judge and J. Matthews, 'Pricing Personal Social Services' in K. Judge (ed.), *Pricing the Social Services*, p. 120.
37. K. Judge *et al.*, *Home Help Charges* p. 15.
38. M. Hyman, *The Home Help Service: A Case Study in the London Borough of Redbridge* (Redbridge: Social Services Department, 1980).
39. A. Seldon, *Charge* (London: Temple Smith, 1977) p. 30.
40. This argument is considered in K. Judge, 'An Introduction to the Economic Theory of Pricing'.
41. K. Judge and J. Matthews, *Charging for Social Care*, p. 138.
42. Ibid, p. 82.
43. A. Seldon and H. Gray, *Universal or Selective Social Benefits?*, Institute of Economic Affairs Monograph No. 8 (London: Institute of Economic Affairs, 1967) p. 26.
44. Ibid, p. 29.
45. Ibid, p. 3.
46. J. Lorant, 'The Problem of Take Up' in *Dear SSAC*, Poverty Pamphlet 49 (London: Child Poverty Action Group, 1980) p. 55.
47. Ibid, p. 54.
48. Ibid, p. 54.
49. A. Seldon and H. Gray, *Universal or Selective Social Benefits?*, p. 29.
50. B. Davies, *Universality, Selectivity and Effectiveness in Social Policy* (London: Heinemann, 1978) p. 12.
51. House of Commons Debates, 1967–8, vol. 759, col. 606.
52. B. Davies, *Universality, Selectivity and Effectiveness in Social Policy*, p. 68.
53. M. Meacher, *Rate Rebates: A Study of the Effectiveness of Means Test* (London: Child Poverty Action Group, 1973).
54. J. Lorant, 'The Problem of Take Up', p. 55.
55. S. Weir, 'Stigma with Chips', *New Society*, vol. 59, no. 1002 (1982) pp. 142–4.
56. Lancashire School Meals Campaign, *Now You See Them, Now You Don't* (Accrington, Lancashire: Lancashire School Meals Campaign) p. 3.
57. S. Weir, 'Stigma with Chips', p. 144.
58. R. Simpson, 'Education Cuts', *Poverty*, no. 47 (December 1980) p. 14.
59. R. Titmuss, *Commitment to Welfare* (London: Allen & Unwin, 1968) p. 129.
60. The Schlackman Research Organization, 'Report on Research on Public Attitudes Towards the Supplementary Benefit System', unpublished report submitted to Central Office of Information (London, 1978).
61. L. Burghes, *Living From Hand to Mouth*, Poverty Pamphlet 50 (London: Child Poverty Action Group, 1980) p. 15.
62. The Schlackman Research Organization, 'Report on Research on Public Attitudes Towards the Supplementary Benefit System', pp. 40–1.
63. D. Reisman, *Richard Titmuss: Welfare and Society*, p. 51.

64. The Schlackman Research Organization, 'Report on Research on Public Attitudes Towards the Supplementary Benefit System', p. 51.
65. A. Forder, *Concepts in Social Administration* (London: Routledge & Kegan Paul, 1974) p. 37.
66. R. Pinker, *Social Theory and Social Policy* (London: Heinemann, 1971) p. 142.
67. P. Townsend, *Poverty in the United Kingdom* (Harmondsworth: Penguin, 1979) p. 880.
68. Ibid, p. 880.

Chapter 10

1. D. Reisman, *Richard Titmuss: Welfare and Society* (London: Heinemann, 1977) p. 159.
2. See R. Parker, 'The Problem of Rationing', *Social Work*, vol. 24, no. 2 (1967) pp. 9–14, reprinted in E. Butterworth and R. Holman (eds), *Social Welfare in Modern Britain* (London: Fontana, 1975) pp. 204–12; A. S. Hall, *The Point of Entry* (London: Allen & Unwin, 1974); M. Cooper, *Rationing Health Care* (London: Croom Helm, 1975).
3. R. Parker, 'The Problem of Rationing', p. 212.
4. A. S. Hall, *The Point of Entry*, p. 18.
5. Ibid.
6. M. Cooper, *Rationing Health Care*, p. 109.
7. R. Parker, 'The Problem of Rationing', p. 205.
8. J. E. Powell, *Medicine and Politics* (Tunbridge Wells: Pitman Medical, 1966).
9. R. Parker, 'The Problem of Rationing', p. 209.
10. Ibid, p. 210.
11. P. Wilding, *Professional Power and Social Welfare* (London: Routledge & Kegan Paul, 1982) p. 132.
12. Ibid, p. 140.
13. R. Harris and A. Seldon, *Over-Ruled on Welfare* (London: Institute of Economic Affairs, 1979) p. xiv.
14. Institute of Economic Affairs Study Group, *Towards a Welfare Society* (London: Institute of Economic Affairs, 1967) p. 10.
15. Ibid, p. 17.
16. R. Boyson, *Parental Choice* (London: Conservative Political Centre, 1975) p. 13.
17. R. Harris and A. Seldon, *Over-Ruled on Welfare*, p. 75.
18. Ibid, p. 76.
19. British Medical Association, *Health Service Financing*, The Jones Report (London: British Medical Association, 1970).
20. R. Harris and A. Seldon, *Over-Ruled on Welfare*, p. 73.
21. British Medical Association, *Health Service Financing*, p. 152.
22. M. Friedman and R. Friedman, *Free To Choose* (Harmondsworth: Penguin, 1980) p. 181.

23. Institute of Economic Affairs Study Group, *Towards a Welfare Society*, p. 10.
24. I. Gough, *The Political Economy of the Welfare State* (London: Macmillan, 1979) p. 12.
25. J. Dale and P. Taylor Gooby, *Social Theory and Social Welfare* (London: Edward Arnold, 1981) p. 240.
26. See N. Ginsburg, *Class, Capital and Social Policy* (London: Macmillan, 1979) p. 5.
27. Ibid, p. 5.
28. Ibid, p. 2.
29. B. Deacon, 'Social Policy and Socialism', *Critical Social Policy*, vol. 1, no. 1 (1981).
30. A. Heller, *The Theory of Need in Marx* (London: Allison & Busby, 1976).
31. B. Deacon, 'Social Policy and Socialism', *Critical Social Policy*, p. 63.
32. Ibid, p. 64.
33. Ibid, p. 52.
34. J. M. Prottas, *People Processing* (Lexington, Mass.: Lexington Books, 1979) ch. 10.
35. J. Dale and P. Taylor Gooby, *Social Theory and Social Welfare*, p. 240.
36. P. Wilding, *Professional Power and Social Welfare*, p. 148.
37. D. Reisman, *Richard Titmuss: Welfare and Society*, pp. 156–63.
38. Institute of Economic Affairs Study Group, *Towards a Welfare Society* (London: Institute of Economic Affairs, 1967).
39. Ibid, pp. 13–14.
40. R. Harris and A. Seldon, *Over-Ruled on Welfare*.
41. J. Le Grand, *The Strategy for Equality* (London: Allen & Unwin, 1982) p. 137.
42. Ibid, p. 78.
43. I. Gough, 'Thatcherism and the Welfare State', *Marxism Today* (July 1980) pp. 7–12.

Index